Robots and their Impact on Hospitality Leadership

This book analyzes how human resource experts perceive that robots and evolving technologies will impact leadership behaviors and human resource management in the hospitality industry.

As with any new technological innovation, organizations must balance the opportunities afforded by robots with the pressures that are placed on existing organizational processes and strategies. They need to consider not only economic and technical perspectives, but also the user and organizational perspectives when determining the appropriate use and implementation of robots and other technology. Chapters in this collection explore service robots, automation, the Green Collar Revolution, social media, and more in multiple hospitality contexts, including all-inclusive resorts and the industry in Türkiye.

Robots and their Impact on Hospitality Leadership is ideal for professionals and leaders in the hospitality industry, as well as students within tourism and hospitality courses.

Marco Valeri is Associate Professor of Organizational Behavior at Niccolò Cusano University, Italy. He is Honorary Associate Professor at the University of Pannonia, Hungary.

He is a member of several editorial boards of international tourism journals, and reviewer and editor of several handbooks on entrepreneurship, tourism, and hospitality management.

Robots and their Impact on Hospitality Leadership

Edited by
Marco Valeri

CRC Press
Taylor & Francis Group
Boca Raton London New York

CRC Press is an imprint of the
Taylor & Francis Group, an **informa** business

Designed cover image: Shutterstock

First edition published 2026
by CRC Press
2385 NW Executive Center Drive, Suite 320, Boca Raton FL 33431

and by CRC Press
4 Park Square, Milton Park, Abingdon, Oxon, OX14 4RN

CRC Press is an imprint of Taylor & Francis Group, LLC

Library of Congress Cataloging-in-Publication Data
Names: Valeri, Marco editor
Title: Robots and their impact on hospitality leadership / edited by Marco Valeri.
Description: First edition. | Boca Raton FL : CRC Press, 2026. | Includes bibliographical references and index.
Identifiers: LCCN 2025055053 (print) | LCCN 2025055054 (ebook) | ISBN 9781041246244 hardback | ISBN 9781041246251 paperback | ISBN 9781003742791 ebook
Subjects: LCSH: Hospitality industry--Management | Robots
Classification: LCC TX911.3.M27 R624 2026 (print) | LCC TX911.3.M27 (ebook)
LC record available at https://lccn.loc.gov/2025055053
LC ebook record available at https://lccn.loc.gov/2025055054

ISBN: 978-1-041-24624-4 (hbk)
ISBN: 978-1-041-24625-1 (pbk)
ISBN: 978-1-003-74279-1 (ebk)

DOI: 10.1201/9781003742791

Typeset in Palatino
by codeMantra

Contents

Contributors

Bapon Chandra Kuri, Assistant Professor, Tourism and Hospitality Management, Gopalganj Science and Technology University, Bangladesh.

Md. Nahiduzzaman, Lecturer, Department of Finance and Banking, Gopalganj Science and Technology University, Bangladesh.

Shadia Sharmin, Research Assistant, Tourism and Hospitality Management, Gopalganj Science and Technology University, Bangladesh.

Marco Valeri, Associate Professor of Organizational Behavior, Niccolò Cusano University, Italy

Carimo Rassal, Assistant Professor, University of Algarve | University of Évora – CIDEHUS, Portugal

Luana Beckmann, Master's Graduate in Hospitality Management and Administration, University of Algarve, Portugal

Miguel Pinheiro, MBA Graduate, Universidad Camilo José Cela, Spain

Jeetesh Kumar, Faculty of Social Sciences and Leisure Management, Centre for Asian Modernisation, Sustainable Tourism Impact Lab, Taylor's University, Malaysia

Praveena Nair Sivasankaran, School of Engineering, Faculty of Innovation and Technology, Clean Technology Impact Lab, Taylor's University, Malaysia

Manisha Paliwal, Professor and Deputy Head, Research and Development Cell, Sri Balaji University, Pune, India

Chandra Prakash, Assistant Professor, R&D Cell, Sri Balaji University, Pune, India

Omkar Jagdish Bapat, Assistant Professor, BIMHRD, Sri Balaji University, Pune, India

Santosh Kumar Bisoi, Assistant Professor, Faculty of Hospitality & Tourism Management, Siksha 'O' Anusandhan Deemed to be University, Odisha, India

Dimitrios Belias, Assistant Professor, Department of Business Administration, University of Thessaly, Larisa, Geopolis, Greece

Angelos Ntalakos, PhD Candidate, Department of Business Administration, University of Thessaly, Larisa, Geopolis, Greece

Ioannis Rossidis, Assistant Professor, Department of Public Administration, Panteion University, Athens, Greece

Vasilios Kefis, Professor, Department of Public Administration, Panteion University, Greece

Klaas Koerten, Hotelschool The Hague and Delft University of Technology, Netherlands

João Farinha, ISLA Santarém, CINTURS – University of Algarve, GOVCOPP – University of Aveiro, Portugal

Maria de Fátima Pina, ISLA Santarém, ISR – UC Institute of Systems and Robotics, University of Coimbra, Portugal

Buse Kekeç, Department of Tourism Management, Institute of Social Sciences, Sinop University, Türkiye

Gül Erkol Bayram, Associate Professor, Faculty of Tourism, Sinop University, Türkiye

Introduction

Robots have been utilized in industrial settings since the early 1960s, when dedicated machines were introduced on assembly lines to lower labor costs and improve reliability. Over time, robotic technologies have progressed beyond factory automation and are now increasingly employed in service roles outside controlled industrial environments. Service robots are therefore specifically designed to function within human-centered settings. As a result, organizations now anticipate substantially greater returns and strategic value from their investments in robotics.

With ongoing technological progress and the commercial availability of robots that offer autonomy, flexibility, and efficiency, interest is expanding in innovative applications of service robots across all sectors of the economy, including hospitality. Today, robots perform a growing range of "back-of-house" tasks, such as preparing food and cleaning floors, as well as "front-of-house" activities, including serving drinks, managing hotel check-ins, and delivering items to guest rooms. Hospitality businesses worldwide are actively examining how service robots can help them gain a competitive edge in increasingly challenging markets. According to resource advantage theory, firms achieve sustainable competitive advantage by effectively managing internal resources to attain superior financial performance in dynamic and innovation-driven industries, where innovation is central to maintaining competitiveness.

To fully realize the transformative potential of robotics, business leaders must reconsider the interactions among guests, employees, and service robots. Rather than simply replacing human labor with automated systems, robotic technology calls for a new mindset that promotes creativity, technological collaboration, and data-driven competencies within teams. This perspective aligns with organizational change theory, which holds that organizations are constantly evolving and must develop the capacity for fundamental transformation in order to survive and thrive.

As robotic technologies become more widely adopted in hospitality, customer experiences are likely to evolve rapidly. Service robots may enhance transactions by introducing engaging, hedonic elements while also delivering more consistent and predictable services. Nevertheless, public resistance to robots performing traditionally human-centered services may arise. Concerns could stem from the absence of human interaction and from ethical issues related to potential job displacement. When positioned as substitutes for human employees, service robots may challenge traditional perceptions of service, requiring leaders to acknowledge and address these psychological and social implications.

Like any emerging technology, robotics presents both opportunities and pressures for organizations. Companies must carefully balance the benefits of innovation with the impact on existing strategies, structures, and processes. Decisions about adopting service robots should consider not only economic and technical factors but also user and organizational dimensions, including implications for organizational culture, structure, decision-making systems, and the service environment. Although service robots are an emerging focus in hospitality and tourism research, limited attention has been given to their influence on leadership behaviors, particularly from a human resource management standpoint.

How will robots impact leadership in the hospitality industry explores how human resource professionals anticipate that robotics will shape leadership practices and human resource management within the hospitality sector.

Structure of This Book

The book collects 9 chapters written by 22 authors located in 9 different countries (Bangladesh, Greece, India, Italy, Malaysia, Netherlands, Portugal, Türkiye, and Spain) and affiliated with 12 different international universities.

Chapter 1 titled "Nexus between AI Robots and Conventional Leadership Strategy in the Hospitality Industry" is written by Bapon Chandra Kuri, Md. Nahiduzzaman, Shadia Sharmin, and Marco Valeri. This chapter aims to explore the intricate interplay between the application of robots within the hospitality sector and its influence on the leadership aptitude of HR professionals. Many research articles highlighted numerous implications of AI robots, which enhanced service efficiency, allowing HR leaders to concentrate more on strategic pursuits. On the other hand, several hospitality industries encountered negative consequences while adopting AI robots in guest service. Others argue that excessive use of technology in the hospitality industry can provide a good outcome in the short term but bring devastating consequences in the long run. In the pursuit of this study, the author will utilize a qualitative approach and a systematic literature review, chosen for their efficacy in providing a thorough and nuanced comprehension of the subject matter. The result suggested that a controlled, holistic approach can provide logistic support to define future leadership strategy in this technological domain. Furthermore, this chapter illustrates a case study covering the problem and prospects of robots in the hospitality industry.

Chapter 2 titled "Robotics at Play: Leadership Transformations in All-Inclusive Resorts" is written by Carimo Rassal, Luana Beckmann, and Miguel Pinheiro. This chapter examines robotics' transformative impact on leadership and management practices in all-inclusive resorts. It explores how robotics can enhance operational efficiency and guest satisfaction while reshaping leadership roles and responsibilities. Emphasis is placed on adopting integrative leadership to balance technological advancements with the industry's human-centric ethos, ensuring the preservation of personalized guest experiences. A qualitative research methodology involved semi-structured interviews with 41 management-level professionals from 3-star, 4-star, and 5-star all-inclusive resorts in Portugal. The data collection focused on robotics integration, leadership adaptation, and the interplay between technological innovation and traditional hospitality values.

Chapter 3 titled "Redefining Service: Robotics, Leadership, and the Green-Collar Revolution in the Hospitality Industry" is written by *Jeetesh Kumar and Praveena Nair Sivasankaran*. This study explores the transformative impact of robotics and sustainability practices on the hospitality industry. Examining how advanced technologies enhance operational efficiency and customer experiences and how green-collar jobs promote environmental responsibility, aims to provide a comprehensive understanding of these trends. The study highlights leadership strategies that drive innovation and sustainability through case studies and expert insights. Ultimately, it aims to inspire industry leaders to embrace these changes, fostering a more sustainable and technologically advanced future for the hospitality sector. Secondary data and an extensive literature review will be explored to achieve the purpose of the study.

Chapter 4 titled "An Empirical Study on the Impact of Social Media on Customer Decisions: In the Perspective of Hotel Guest" is written by Santosh Kumar Bisoi. This chapter examines the impact of social media on client recognition. In this study of marketing data was investigated. Online sources that consolidated buyer blogs are compared to traditional web promotional material. Blogging is an important tool for social networking, and the hotel industries have recognised that poorly maintained blogs can have both positive and negative effects. One hundred forty-seven numbers of data are collected from secondary sources and 150 numbers of data are collected by framing appropriate questionnaire and collected from the respondents and analysed by different tools of SPSS. In recent years, the internet and social media have become an important aspect of business operations.

Chapter 5 titled "The Human Factor in Automation: Investigating the Role of Leadership and Service Quality in Hotel Employees' Intentions to Use Robots" is written by Dimitrios Belias, Angelos Ntalakos, Ioannis Rossidis, and Vasilios Kefis. This study aims to investigate the impact of using robots in the hotel industry. In other words, this research focuses on examining the effect of leadership styles on the expectations of hotel employees by using robot technology. For this purpose, a quantitative survey was conducted among 195 hotel employees located in the Greece region. The instruments/tools that were used to measure the variables of the research were the following: A) Multifactor Leadership Questionnaire (MLQ-5X) by Avolio and Bass (2004). This instrument measures the three types of leadership (transformational leadership, transactional leadership, and passive leadership), along with their sub-variables: idealized influence (attributed), idealized influence (behaviour), inspirational motivation, intellectual stimulation, individual consideration, contingent reward, management-by-exception (active), management-by-exception (passive), and laissez-faire leadership.

Chapter 6 titled "Effect of Service Robots on Service Jobs: A Meta-Analysis" is written by Klaas Koerten. The purpose of this chapter is to shed light on service robots' potential influence on hospitality jobs, which will inform hotel decision makers seeking to deploy them. Several studies have been conducted on the pros and cons of service robots and the results differ substantially. This study will research why such differences occur, thereby giving a realistic overview of the current possibilities and opportunities of deploying service robots as well as the current range of expectations from service robots. This study is a meta-analysis of research on service robots' influence on service provider jobs. We will perform a systematic literature review to find all sources that researched this relationship, thereby looking at the effect of different factors on the studies' outcomes. Among others, these factors will be whether participants have worked with service robots and how they were informed about service robots by the researchers.

Chapter 7 titled "Navigating the Nexus: Leadership Strategies in the Era of Service Robots" is written by João Farinha and Maria de Fátima Pina. This chapter delves into the pivotal role of leadership in navigating this technological shift, emphasizing the importance of adaptive leadership approaches. Leaders must not only embrace technological advancements but also foster a culture of innovation and collaboration to effectively integrate service robots into existing operations. By upskilling employees and facilitating seamless collaboration between human workers and robots, leaders can leverage the strengths of both resources to deliver exceptional guest experiences. However, this dynamic requires leaders to possess a blend of technical knowledge, emotional intelligence, and strategic vision to navigate the evolving landscape of human-robot interaction. Practical implications for hospitality managers include leveraging service robots to enhance service quality dimensions such as cleanliness, health, and safety, particularly in response to health crises like the COVID-19 pandemic.

Chapter 8 titled "Embracing Robotics: Exploration of the Transformative Impact of Robots on the Practices of Leadership in the Hospitality Industry" is written by Manisha Paliwal, Chandra Prakash, and Omkar Jagdish Bapat. This chapter seeks to explore the transformative impact of robots and robotization technology on leadership practices within the hospitality industry. The research will investigate how robotization technology is changing the traditional leadership roles and the HR/HRM strategies in the hospitality organizations such as top hotels, restaurants, and resorts, leading to the provision of insights which can catalyse transformative changes in the styles of leadership/leadership practices in the hospitality industry along with identification of a few key considerations for navigating through this transition smoothly. The researchers have selected the qualitative approach towards the acquisition of the necessary data through the means of in-depth interviews with the samples, comprising the leaders and experts in the hospitality industry, for gaining insights into their perceptions and experiences regarding the incorporation of robots and robotization technologies into their workplaces.

Chapter 9 titled "Smart Technology and Robotics Applications in the Hospitality Industry in Türkiye: Potential Advantages and Challenges" is written by Manisha Paliwal, Chandra Prakash, and Omkar Jagdish Bapat. This chapter aims to determine the use of smart technologies and robotic applications in Turkey's hospitality sector. A literature review was conducted on the effects of smart applications, robotic systems, and the Internet of Things on guest satisfaction, operational efficiency, and quality management. A conceptual framework was presented for the classification of robots based on service, logistics, and maintenance functions, addressing their benefits and challenges. The research population consists of accommodation facilities in Turkey. Considering the transformative effect of implementing training and awareness-raising programs, the importance of preparing digital training and awareness-raising programs that will support industry stakeholders in the adaptation process during the digital transformation process is emphasized.

1

Nexus between AI Robots and Conventional Leadership Strategy in the Hospitality Industry

Bapon Chandra Kuri, Md. Nahiduzzaman, Shadia Sharmin, and Marco Valeri

1.1 Introduction

The hospitality industry is considered a cornerstone for the travel and tourism sector to capitalize on the country's GDP (Nam et al., 2021). The success of this industry depends upon its functional efficiency, customer satisfaction, brand loyalty, and enhanced service quality (Jin, 2025). However, the innovation of robotics and artificial intelligence (AI) has become a turning point for this industry (Khaliq et al., 2022). These developments have transformed the overall service provision of the hotel industry and optimized the operational processes, reduced the number of stages of service production and delivery (Mingotto et al., 2021). Therefore, many sectors, including the hospitality industry, have incorporated AI and robots in their business operations, significantly reducing operational costs and efforts (Leung et al., 2025).

Additionally, incorporating technologies within the hotel sector empowers human resources with enhanced service quality and operational efficiency (Xu et al., 2020). Moreover, digital transformation creates opportunities for accurate data analysis, resulting in personalized service and proper market segmentation, which facilitates the customer to enjoy the service more efficiently (Liu et al., 2025). In this context, a fundamental revolution of conventional leadership strategies is crucial for incorporating AI and robotics into the hospitality sector. Since, conventional leadership strategies encourage a human-centred approach that prioritizes interpersonal skills and emotional intelligence to build a loyal customer base in the organization (Gupta et al., 2022). These characteristics have been instrumental in encouraging teams, extending a gracious

DOI: 10.1201/9781003742791-1

welcome, and optimizing performance. Nevertheless, as AI robots evolve inherent to service provision, therefore leaders need to embrace a new paradigm that integrates humans with AI (Drexler & Lapre, 2019).

Even though the advantages of AI robots within the hospitality industry are unambiguous, their convergence presents several hurdles. For instance, one critical obstacle is the workforce reshuffling of human labour, which raises concerns about job loss, thus demotivating the employees to remain in the organization for the long run (Ruel & Njoku, 2021). Further, ethical considerations concerning security and confidentiality appear, since AI systems often rely on personal information to function effectively (Yang et al., 2019; Wang et al., 2022; Choi & Wan, 2021). Previously, numerous studies on the application of AI and robotics in the hotel industry have been examined to understand the prospects and challenges in commercial and noncommercial sectors (Kang et al., 2024; Seraj et al., 2025). For example, Bakir (2025) conducted a study on how AI transforms hotel gastronomy in menu design, preparing food, and communication with customers. The result depicted that guests are satisfied with the food preparation and overall service style of the hotel, which increases the revenue and customer loyalty. Moreover, previous studies also wanted to examine how well service robots redefine leadership in hotel management. The result suggested that the hospitality industry gained numerous privileges such as cost-reduction, operational efficiency, and quick service delivery (Koo et al., 2021; Ruel & Njoku, 2021; Mingotto et al., 2021). On the contrary, it also faced a lot of challenges like safety and security issues, ethical considerations, and a lack of emotional feelings (Koo et al., 2021; Skubis et al., 2024). Therefore, restructuring and redesigning the hospitality industry using AI are now indispensable to embrace an AI and human-based leadership strategy.

However, there is insufficient research on the nexus between AI robots and conventional leadership strategy in the hospitality industry. Therefore, this study seeks to thoroughly assess the interplay between AI robots and the conventional approach of leadership in the hotel industry through a systematic literature review of 22 articles and one case study.

1.2 Literature Review

The concept of robots is derived from the mythology of human-related mechanical instruments. In 1920, Czech writer Karel Capek first publicized the term "Robot" in his play "Rossum's Universal Robots". In the 20th century, the emergence of early-automated machines and industrial robots marked the starting point of the arena of robotics institutionalization (Shi et al., 2026). Scientists developed more updated machines capable of performing complicated tasks by integrating AI into robotics, in the 1950s and 1960s.

Therefore, the connotation of "AI robot" involves functions like machine learning, natural language processing, and more efficient tasks in everyday life thus reducing the human effort. In this context, a substantial part of computer science (engineering of intelligent agents) is formed by the development of AI (Tuomi et al., 2025). Similarly, the advancement of AI robots is closely influenced by the changes in robotics, synergistic technologies, and AI (Gonzalez et al., 2024). Moreover, it integrates decision-making with physical abilities, resulting in machines that autonomously perform tasks, interact with humans, and adjust to their surroundings (Cain et al., 2019). The key components of AI are sensors, robotics, and natural language processing (NLP) between humans and robots (Wang et al., 2023). Automated learning techniques, particularly deep learning, are vital for NLP and productivity growth. Similarly, AI analyses data from the previous sources to predict future trends and prospects, which aids the hospitality industry in making significant decisions on product planning, pricing and promotion (Skubis, 2025). In addition, these are also used for computer science proposals and power systems to regulate their behaviour, and sensors make it possible to understand their surroundings by speeding up robots' interactions (Jabeen et al., 2022). Furthermore, a vast array of applications is utilized through AI robots across several industries such as healthcare, manufacturing, agriculture, education and research, and security (Kumar et al., 2021; McCartney & McCartney, 2020; Jin, 2025). Additionally, AI robots are used in planting, harvesting, checking crops, inspecting soil conditions, recognizing pests, and improving irrigation to eventually raise agricultural productivity (Shum et al., 2024). Similarly, AI robots play a significant role in bomb disposal, surveillance, and search-and-rescue missions (Ivanov & Webster, 2019). The previous studies analysed AI from economic, political, and social perspectives. However, the implication of AI in the hospitality industry requires a lot of attention to demonstrate how AI can maximize customer satisfaction and reduce operational costs. While AI and robotics have performed tremendously in the field of physics, chemistry, and engineering sectors, therefore tourism industry is gradually adopting AI to improve its service excellence. In this sense, many studies have been conducted in the field of tourism and the hospitality industry, which are highlighted in Table 1.1. However, studies on the nexus between AI robots and conventional leadership strategy in the hospitality industry have not been examined properly, which leaves a clear gap in the previous literature.

Though the digital transformation of the leadership provides a lot of privileges, ethical considerations related to issues such as vulnerability, accountability, security, privacy, bias, and employment displacement need to be examined in the hospitality sector (Leung et al., 2025). For instance, job displacement might be the consequence of the automation of tasks through AI (Buhalis et al., 2024), causing the rise of unemployment across the world. Furthermore, enormous amounts of data are often gathered by AI robots, resulting in strict compliance with privacy laws and strong security

TABLE 1.1

Literature Review

No.	Authors and publication year	Context	Independent variable	Dependent variable	Findings
1.	Nam et al. (2020)	Prospects and challenges of AI in the hotel industry	AI, Robotics	Hotel, Smart tourism	AI, Robotics→ Hotel, Smart tourism (+)
2.	Khaliq et al. (2022)	Application of AI and robotics in the hospitality sector	AI, Robotics Awareness, Mutual Trust (MT) between employees and management, Competitive Psychological Climate (CPC)	Turnover Intention of Hospitality Employees	Application of AI and Robotics in the hospitality sector: Turnover Intention (+& sig) of hospitality employees Mutual Trust (MT) moderated the relationship between AI and robotics awareness with TI CPC did not moderate the link of AI and robotics awareness with TI
3.	Mingotto et al. (2021)	Challenges and opportunities of AI and robots	Service robots, AI	Customer experience, service management, employee roles	Service robots, AI → Customer experience, service management, employee roles (+)
4.	Xu et al. (2020)	Leadership in hotel operation	Service robots, robotic innovations	Leadership, hotel management, customer experience, and employee roles	Effect of Service Robots on Efficiency and Productivity of Hotel Operations (+ & sig) Service robots in hotels will have significant challenges like high costs, skill gaps, and cultural shifts
5.	Tuomi et al. (2021)	Uses of robots in service sector	Service robots	Service encounter, hospitality management	Application of Service robots: support employees, differentiation, operational efficiency (+ & sig) Implications of Service robots: job displacement, customer expectations (in sig)
6.	Rasheed et al. (2023)	Customer and robot interaction in hospitality	AI, Robotics	Hospitality sector, customer acceptance	AI, Robotics → Hospitality sector, customer acceptance (+, sig)
7.	Wang et al. (2022)	AI and creativity	AI, Robotics awareness	Hotel industry, employee creativity	The use of AI and robotics in the hotel industry: fosters employee creativity through active learning and task crafting (+& sig)

(Continued)

TABLE 1.1 *(Continued)*

Literature Review

No.	Authors and publication year	Context	Independent variable	Dependent variable	Findings
8.	Al-Shami et al. (2022)	AI and its advantages	AI	Hotel performance, competitive advantage	Application of AI: tour planning, reservation services, and room service (+& sig) Additionally, hotel performance is driven by strategic alignment, flexible AI infrastructure, skilled personnel, and proper management
9.	Pillai and Sivathanu (2020)	AI chatbots in service sector	AI-based chatbots	Hospitality and tourism, travel agents, and travel planning services	Adoption of chatbots: ease of use, usefulness, trust, perceived intelligence, and anthropomorphism (+& sig)
10.	Abulsaoud Ahmed Younis & Adel (2020)	AI and human resource management	AI strategy, AI-powered business functions, creativity-oriented HRM	Organizational effective performance, work behaviour, operations management, strategic management, Knowledge-Sharing Quality (KSQ)	AI service directly impacts knowledge-sharing quality and customer-centric HR practices
11.	Abdelmoaty and Soliman (2020)	Digital transformation of tourism	Smart technology applications	Smart services, customer experiences	Smart technology applications → Smart services, customer experiences (sig, +)
12.	Hwang et al. (2020)	Robots in restaurant business	Perceived innovativeness, perceived risk	Attitude towards robotic restaurants, desire to use robotic restaurants, intention to use robotic restaurants, and willingness to pay more for robotic restaurants	Perceived innovativeness positively influences the customers' attitude, which in turn positively affects their desire (+& sig) Desire positively influences intentions to use and willingness to pay more (+& sig) Perceived risk played a moderating role in the relationships between desire and intentions to use and desire and willingness to pay more
13.	Hui et al. (2025)	AI leadership	AI-based virtual assistant, transformational leadership	Absorptive capacity, team innovation	AI-based virtual assistants influenced how transformational leadership impacted knowledge sharing (+& sig)

(Continued)

TABLE 1.1 *(Continued)*

Literature Review

No.	Authors and publication year	Context	Independent variable	Dependent variable	Findings
14.	Chuang (2024)	Human skill and AI	Age of robots, AI	Human skills	The Age of Robots and AI may influence the importance of human skills in the workplace (+& sig)
15.	Cha (2020)	Customer and robot service in restaurant	Service robot	Customer attitude	People open to new experiences are more likely to embrace robots in restaurants, especially if the robots are attractive, useful, and original (+& sig)
16.	Suder et al. (2024)	Smart entrepreneurship	Digitalization	Hotel performance	Digitalization strengthens a hotel's performance and impacts entrepreneurial behaviours (proactiveness and innovativeness) on hotel growth and market performance (+& sig)
17.	Mir et al. (2020)	AI and robotics	AI	Sustainable ecosystem	AI → Sustainable ecosystem (+)
18.	Rampersad (2020)	Robot and job	Problem-solving, critical thinking, communication, teamwork	Innovation	Problem-solving, critical thinking, communication, teamwork → AI innovation (+& sig)
19.	Bag et al. (2022)	AI and its engagement in hospitality sector	AI, industry 4.0, satisfying user experience	Repurchase intention, user engagement	Application of AI: User engagement and conversion, and repurchase intention (+& sig)
20.	Dirican (2015)	AI and robots in business	Robots, Robotics, AI	Unemployment rate, performance, management, CRM analytics	Advancements in robotics, mechatronics, and AI: impact businesses, economics, and the workforce (+& sig)
21.	Khan (2024)	AI in traditional business	AI	Traditional Indonesian business	AI integration, efficiency and innovation (+& sig), but challenges like cost and talent hinder adoption (- sig)
22.	Jabeen et al. (2021)	Automation and AI	AI, automation	Tourism and hospitality industry	AI implementation in hospitality and tourism → human knowledge, service focus (+& sig)

measures in the tourism and hospitality sectors (Guan et al., 2025). Therefore, this chapter covers all aspects of the digital transformation of the hospitality industry and its influences on overall organizational performance. The following questions have been analysed in this study: (1) Will AI robots bring positive outcomes for the hospitality industry? (2) What if robots are vested with full autonomous power to run the hospitality industry? (3) Will human-operated conventional leadership be feasible for industry?

1.3 Evolution and Integration of AI and Robotics in the Hospitality Industry

Henn na Hotel in Japan, launched in 2015 by travel tycoon Hideo Sawade, was the earliest hotel with working robots, gaining a Guinness World Record. Developing sophisticated AI algorithms and machine learning models has significantly augmented the competence of hospitality robots (Gajic et al., 2024). Additionally, AI's potential in concurrent data processing and evaluation has assisted in more tailored and effective guest services. For instance, NPL allows AI systems to perceive and respond to guest inquiries, fostering communication efficacy (Buhalis et al., 2019). Moreover, improved computer vision and smart sensors have upgraded robots' self-governing navigation and interaction with their surroundings (Licardo et al., 2024).

The amalgamation of AI and robotics, big data analytics, and the Internet of Things (IoT) has significantly expanded their potential applications in the hospitality industry (Go et al., 2020). IoT devices in hotel rooms, including lighting systems, smart thermostats, and voice-activated assistants are associated with and administered via AI-based platforms (Chi et al., 2023). These functions gather and comprehend data on guest desires and behaviours, enabling hotels to offer highly customized experiences.

The above-mentioned figure (Figure 1.1) shows how different departments in the hotel industry adopt AI to accomplish their overall service strategy. For instance, the front office department is one of the most remarkable uses of AI and robotics in the hospitality industry (Goel et al., 2022). Similarly, AI-based robots are being significantly deployed in roles such as concierges, receptionists, and bellhops (Wang et al., 2024). Besides providing extensive details about the hotel and other native attractions, this advanced device can validate guests' check-in and check-out (Seo & Lee, 2021). Additionally, AI-powered robots are shifting housekeeping operations within the accommodation sector (Rasheed et al., 2023). For example, floor scrubbers and robotic vacuum cleaners are now ubiquitous across multiple hotels. Moreover, the collaboration of AI and robotics in the food and beverage service department is reforming food production and delivery (Abdelhakim et al., 2023). The implication

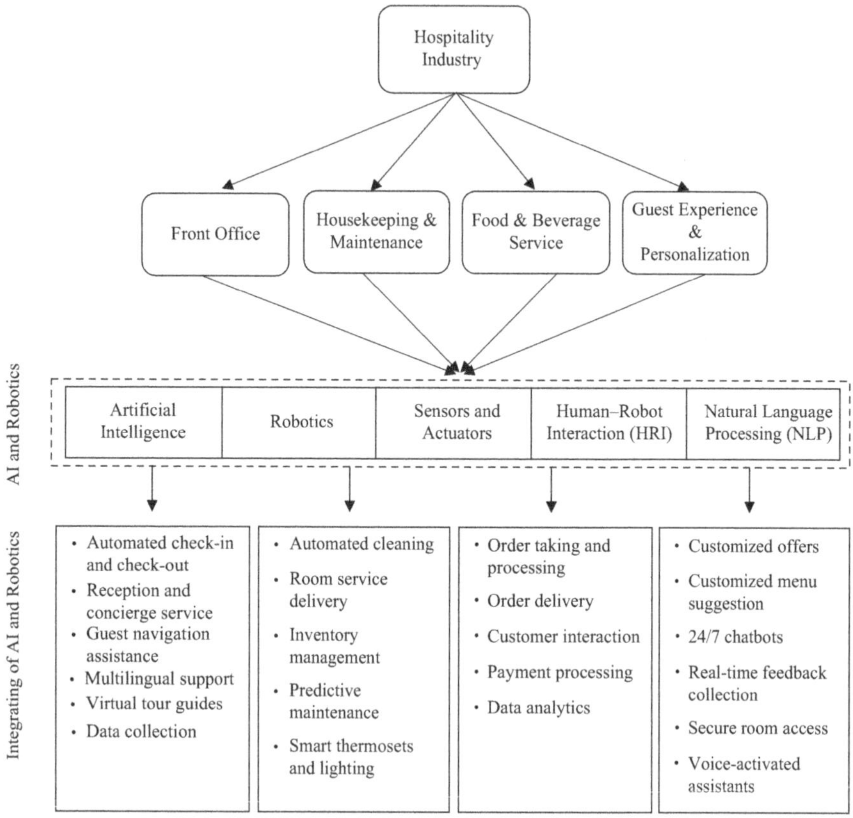

FIGURE 1.1
AI Robotics in the Hospitality Industry

Source: Authors' Compilations

of AI-driven chatbots makes it easier to keep a detailed record of customer preferences. In addition, robots' storage capacity and response-ability are more efficient than human staff (Abou-Shouk et al., 2021). Therefore, frequent tasks such as tailored customer recommendations, answering queries without taking much time, handling reservations, and updating inventories become smoother. Furthermore, it keeps track of every customer by analysing their choices and actions to offer a personalized menu and dining experience (Pande & Gupta, 2023). As a result, the hotel industry has witnessed an enormous change because of the application of AI in enhancing customer experience. For example, Connie (Hilton's concierge robot) has transformed the guest experience with its ability to recognize speech, answer guest questions, and so on. Also, a robot (front desk) at Japanese Henn na Hotel can handle guest questions, manage check-in and check-out of guests, and communicate with them efficiently.

1.4 Conventional Leadership Theories and Models in the Hospitality Industry

Leadership in an organization encompasses a set of collective directions and attitudes that connect people to work as a team, achieving common objectives in any changing surroundings. However, conventional leadership theories and models focus on a basic understanding of leadership to the extent to which leaders can emphasize behavioural patterns and proficiently guide their team to achieve higher organizational performance. For instance, trait theory is one of the initial concepts for comprehending leadership, which assumes that certain people claim inherent qualities that make them effective leaders. For instance, this theory implies that leadership is an inherent and natural quality that originates from a set of qualities, including confidence, intelligence, honesty, and social skills (Zhong et al., 2021). In the hospitality industry, the trait theory has been applied in recruiting employees who represent key leadership qualities including confidence (interacting with guests, handling any problems and guest complaints), honesty (achieving business goals), intelligence (problem-solving, instant decision-making), and social skills (excellent communication skills) which are the top priority for successfully handling staff and assuring excellent guest experiences (Lee et al., 2021).

However, behavioural theories are the opposite of trait theory, which states that successful leaders are found based on their specific behaviour. The Ohio Studies recognized two primary factors of leader behaviour, including initiating structure (task-oriented) and consideration (people-oriented). This study also states that these people-oriented characteristics (job satisfaction, respecting subordinates, mutual trust) and task-oriented characteristics (industry objectives, communication channel, organization structures, functional procedures) are correlated. Therefore, this leadership theory is widely used in the hospitality industry compared to other leadership traits. In addition, to accomplish the consideration factor (people-centred), leaders follow up on particular tasks (task-oriented) to clarify the organization's objectives (Zhang & Lu, 2024).

Moreover, The University of Michigan Studies determined two leadership qualities, which are task-oriented and relationship-oriented. In the hospitality industry, task-oriented leaders emphasize technology, facilitating check-in procedures, food service, and room cleanings to be accomplished effectively. In this sense, hotel managers prepare meticulous lists to uphold consistent service quality by utilizing task-oriented theories. However, relationship-oriented leaders emphasize the well-being and fulfilment of their team members, promoting a supportive and cooperative work environment. According to Fiedler's contingency model, a leader's success depends on the consistency between their leadership approach and favourable circumstances. In the hospitality industry, this implies that a leader may need to modify their technique according to variables including group interlay, guest expectations, and operational difficulties. In addition, Hersey and Blanchard's Situational leadership theory claims that leaders need to adjust their approach based on the maturity level of their followers (Wu et al., 2025). In the realm of the hospitality industry, this theory could encompass a more authoritative style for an apprentice, offering explicit instructions and vigilant monitoring.

Moreover, transactional leadership is renowned as leadership for management that is obtained to achieve the short-term objectives of an organization. It emphasizes providing rewards (for staff's personal or organizational contribution) and punishments (for staff's poor performance) to achieve the organizational objectives. Four primary emphases of this leadership include the structure of an organization, performance monitoring and evaluation, and the results. According to the fundamental hypothesis of transactional leadership, employees are motivated by rewards and punishments. However, Robert House proposed the path-goal theory claiming that leaders are accountable for clearing the way for their followers to attain their goals. This theory offers guidance, assistance, and necessary resources to improve employee performance and satisfaction within the hospitality industry.

1.5 Shifting Leadership Focus from Human Management to Human-AI Synergy

The incorporation of AI within the hospitality premises is changing the leadership environment, resulting in a paradigm shift from conventional human management to nurturing human-AI synergy. As AI mechanisms become more sophisticated, leaders must expand their strategies to handle human groups and effectively incorporate AI as a team-oriented partner (Wang et al., 2024). This transformation calls for a profound comprehension of both human dynamics and AI competencies, safeguarding the distinctive strengths to build a more innovative, adaptable, and efficient organization (Jin et al., 2025; Wang et al., 2023).

Figure 1.2 depicts that organizational structure, developing human potential, and handling resources were the traditional concerns of leadership. Still, the paradigm of leadership has changed with the rise of AI, and leaders have to deal with the hurdles of the integration between AI and humans (Menshikova et al., 2025). In addition, AI is used for several tasks, including customer support, personalized service, transaction procedures, sales strategy, pricing strategy, immediate feedback, and customer response (Abdelhakim et al., 2023). This interplay involves a shift in their focus from

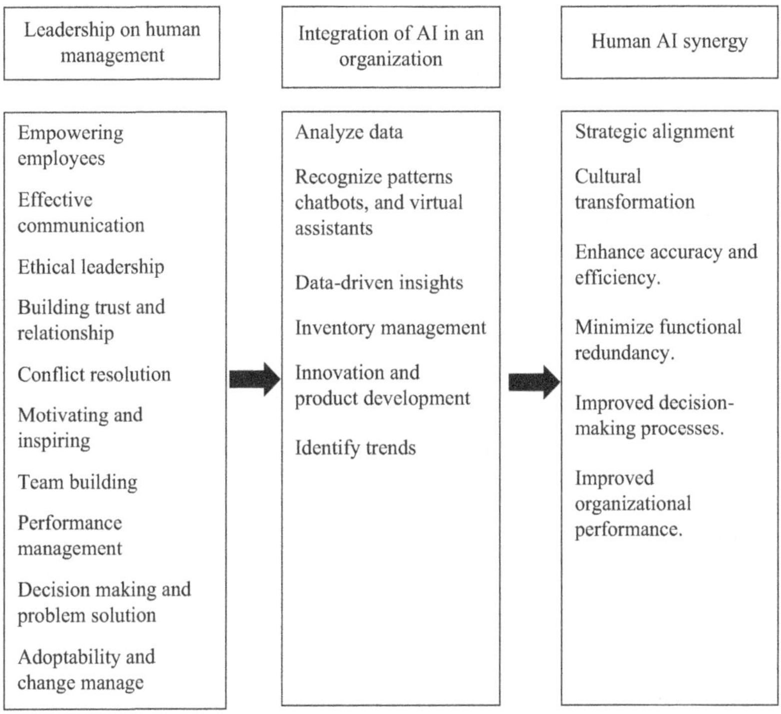

FIGURE 1.2
Linking among AI, Leadership, and Humans in the Organization

Source: Authors compilations

traditional human management to a more refined approach that emphasizes human-AI integration (Zhong et al., 2021).

Although the implications of AI are increasing in different sectors, the significance of human-AI collaboration cannot be denied in addressing the current business challenges and trends. The greatest difficulty is developing AI-based technologies that are socially, administratively, psychologically, morally, and technically balanced (Buhalis et al., 2019). Massive amounts of data processing and high performance for business analytical platforms can be enabled by accurately recognizing contemporary developments to merge the strength of AI in determining patterns from complex systems (Shum et al., 2024). Meanwhile, humans are empowered with emotional intelligence, creativity, and ethical judgement (Kumar et al., 2021). The cooperation between these two can lead to more breakthrough ideas and improve organizational performance in the hospitality sector. In this context, creating an atmosphere where humans and AI can flourish is another advantage of practising human-AI collaboration for leaders (Jabeen et al., 2022). The integration between AI and the hospitality industry has been discussed in the following sections.

1.6 Developing New Leadership Skills for Managing AI Integration in the Hospitality Industry

In the hotel sector, leadership skills need to change as workforce management facilitates human-AI collaboration (Tuomi et al., 2021). While traditional skills like communication, empathy, and strategic thinking are still important and must now be improved by having a thorough understanding of AI and its implications for the workplace (Shi et al., 2026). Table 1.2 illustrates the leadership skills for the AI era in the hospitality sector.

1.7 Implementing Human-AI Cooperation in the Hospitality Industry

The implementation of AI is swiftly changing the operations of the hospitality industry (Liu et al., 2025). Immediate assistance for customers

TABLE 1.2

Leadership Skills for the AI Era

Leadership Skills for the AI Era in the Hospitality Sector	
Technological literacy	a) Knowledge about the application of new technologies. b) Data-driven decision-making. c) Continuous skill development. d) Training and development of staff. e) Use of technologies ethically and responsibly. f) Evaluating and transforming business strategies enabling technological upgradation.
Ethical Reasoning	a) Critical thinking. b) Cross-disciplinary knowledge. c) Ethical awareness. d) Long-term goals. e) Sustainability. f) Partnership and interaction.
Collaborative Mindset	a) Emotional Intelligence. b) Technological changes adaptation c) Supporting inclusivity and encouraging diversity. d) Partnership with AI experts (Koo et al., 2021).
Change Management	Nurturing human-AI collaboration requires a change from a command-and-control leadership concept to one that focuses on collaboration. Hospitality leaders need to be able to collaborate with AI, capitalizing on its abilities while identifying the significance of human input (Kang et al., 2024).
Agility in risk management	Hotels must pursue constant growth with the swift revolution of technological developments and remain updated about the latest AI developments (Yang et al., 2019).

and personalized services are the outcomes of the seamless integration of human-AI (Leung et al., 2025). Therefore, cooperative interaction between AI functions and human employees is the main potential to foster the development and constant growth of this industry. For example, Chatbots with AI features and virtual assistance enable response time reduction, quick support for guest inquiries and bookings, and handling more complex communications (Mingotto et al., 2021). This may include inquiries about making hotel or restaurant bookings, special offers for a particular event, hotel amenities, and locations of local attractions (Koo et al., 2021). Similarly, human staff can provide services in an approachable and intriguing manner, whilst AI can swiftly evaluate enormous quantities of information, provide individual suggestions, and determine guest behaviour (Bakir et al., 2025). The significant advantages of integrating AI robots into the hospitality industry are enormous. However, the absolute performance of AI is comprehended when it operates in harmony with human employees.

AI can analyse large amounts of data to forecast customer choices and configure services accordingly. For instance, by examining past booking behaviour and online feedback, AI can recommend customized services or room upgrades (Wang et al., 2025). When human staff employ this comprehension, they can provide a more memorable and personalized guest experience (Figure 1.3). Traditionally, the inventories of the hospitality industry were managed by tracking the previous history of guest's purchase patterns. However, with the emergence of AI, it becomes easier to manage inventories by having profound knowledge of the supply chain operations. Additionally, AI enables the industry with actual demand forecasting by identifying current market trends and minimizing the risk of stockouts or inventory holding costs (Cain et al., 2019). Moreover, it ensures the amalgamation of data from many sources, sharing data seamlessly, and informed decision-making for the top-level managers of the hospitality industry (Kumar et al., 2021).

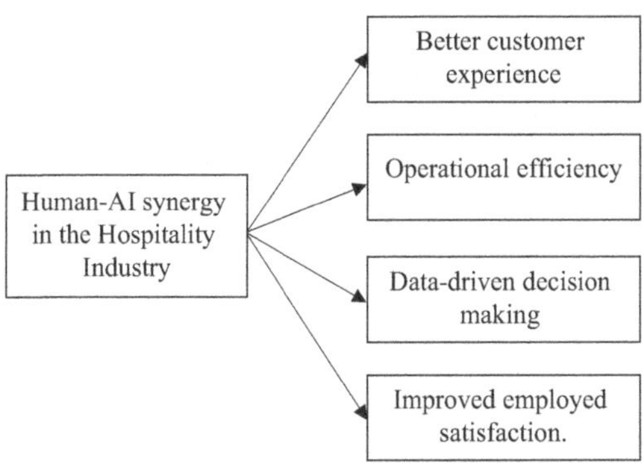

FIGURE 1.3
The Role of AI in the Hospitality Industry

Source: Authors' Compilations

1.8 Opportunities and Challenges of Incorporating AI Robots and Conventional Leadership Strategies in the Hospitality Industry

Today, the hospitality industry has significantly transformed into digitalization to rationalize processes, enhance customer experience, and handle competitiveness in an ever-changing market (Ivanov & Webster, 2019). The collaboration between human employees and AI furnishes the hospitality industry with several advantages, which may involve enhanced efficiency, cost-effectiveness, and superior customer service (Leung et al., 2025).

AI robots within the hotel sector offer promising opportunities to improve performance and streamline processes (Guan et al., 2025). These robots can function 24/7, mitigating customer response times and guaranteeing consistent service delivery (Ivanov & Webster, 2019). For example, robots can efficiently supply amenities to guest rooms, cutting back the time hotel employees spend on these operations and allowing them to concentrate on more intricate, high-value tasks (Rasheed et al., 2023).

Within the hospitality sector, AI robots are utilized in various operations that may be time-consuming to be done by human staff, such as delivery robots, wait staff, cook assistants, bartenders, and virtual attendees (Pande & Gupta, 2023). Additionally, hospitality services that are provided by human employees may not be consistent all the time, whilst robots always offer the same quality services without any mistakes or changes, saving the hospitality businesses from making inconsistencies and service gaps (Figure 1.4). With the revolution of advanced technologies and AI robotics, the service processes have become more efficient and cost-effective. However, it has created an immense risk of losing the human touch in the services. For example, travelling to a destination is not just about a streamlined process (check-in or check-out, bookings) but also about how they are taken care of or welcomed in that place. Similarly, AI can never replace interpersonal communication (warmth, genuine conversation, friendly greetings, and goodbye). For example, a lack of empathy, sentiments, and meaningful interactions may bore the tourists. Therefore, by embracing AI technologies while upholding a commitment to customized service, hospitality leaders can overcome the obstacles to a future where AI robots and human staff complement each other effectively, providing unique guest experiences and promoting sustainable growth (Lee et al., 2021).

1.9 Case Study

With the rise of AI-enabled business organizations, service robots have been adopted by the hospitality industry. The first hotel in the world that

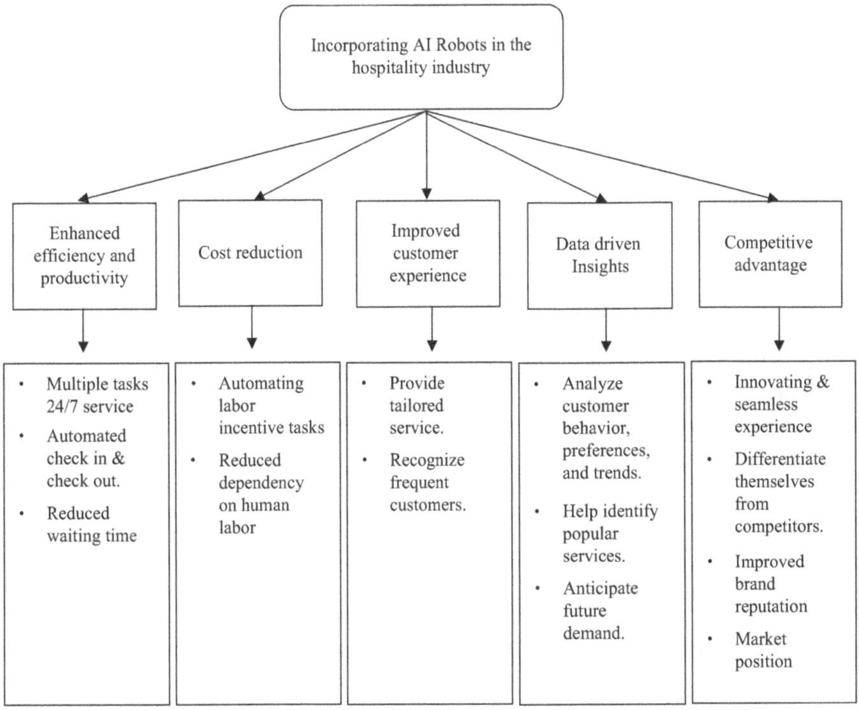

FIGURE 1.4
Opportunities by Incorporating AI Robots and Conventional Leadership Strategies in the Hospitality Industry

Source: Authors Compilations

incorporate robots in its operations is "Henn na Hotel", which put a large amount of money into developing service robots to operate the daily tasks of its hotel, such as check-in robots, cloakroom robots, porter robots, facial recognition, and robot-in-room assistants. Following this, many other hotels started utilizing this service robot in their hotel functions, since it can reduce overhead costs and create a unique experience for guests. However, according to recent news, Henn na Hotel has chosen to halt half of its service robots due to its criticisms and poor performance of robots by both its staff and guests. In its initial activities, the check-in robot has consistently failed to photocopy the guests' passports. Therefore, guest check-in requires a lot of time to accomplish the initial reservation procedure. Moreover, there was a limitation of weight beyond which the service robots failed to carry guests' luggage and made noise. Furthermore, the service robots on the front desk were not interactive, and the customer didn't feel the warmth and friendly welcome. Robots responded only when they were asked or instructed, but not when needed.

Additionally, in-room assistant robots failed to navigate the difference between guest's commands and their perceptions. As a result, guests were disturbed, and they did not get their personalized services in terms of the hotel's promise. For instance, a small difference in the name in which the reservation was made, and check-in robots failed to recognize a guest. Therefore, guests frequently complained that robots were not capable of handling situations due to a lack of emotional intelligence. So, a human must be there to monitor and operate each robot's functionality. Furthermore, the electronic self-check-in did not work because of update issues and technical errors, wasting guests' valuable time and leading to guest dissatisfaction. For example, service robots kept repeating the same words in two or more sentences. Questions could not be answered if they were not input into the robot's intelligence systems. The robot was able to answer only the time, weather, and in-room facilities but was unable to answer questions that were not instructed. The hotel also recognizes the various issues like limited language inputs (Only peak Japanese) and problematic facial recognition to open the room. Therefore, "Henn na Hotel" rescheduled the entire operation to ensure guest satisfaction by introducing collaborative human and AI networking, by which humans will deal with guests and AI will monitor the entire service procedure to find possible errors in the entire hotel networking system. After that, the hotel gave more emphasis on human-oriented services, where people were assigned to handle the guest service and complaints. Since humans can understand emotions, perceptions, and facial expressions. However, AI robots were installed to monitor the overall safety and security system in the hotel. Additionally, some specific issues where both AI-human-oriented activities had been operated simultaneously, such as if the employee cannot track the guest's language, then AI translates their language in a more congenial way, where both the guest and employee could communicate flexibly.

Questions:

1. Why does "Henn na Hotel" face guest service errors while dealing with customers?
2. How does "Henn na Hotel" mitigate this issue to ensure guest satisfaction?
3. In which way, do you think that the hospitality industry must adopt humans instead of using AI?

1.10 Conclusion

It is often argued that the application of AI robotics in the hospitality industry improves the overall performance in guest satisfaction. In this chapter, the nexus between AI robots and conventional leadership strategy in the hospitality industry has been examined by which the policymaker and manager of the hospitality industry will get the overall guidelines on how AI robotics generates both positive and negative outcomes. However, human-induced hospitality creates an emotional attachment to guests, where AI robotics may not be able to interconnect with human understanding. Therefore, the effective collaboration between AI and humans can create an effective leadership strategy by which humans will deal with customers, and AI robotics will provide augmented facilities for the customers.

References

Abdelhakim, A. S., Abou-Shouk, M., Ab Rahman, N. A. F. W., & Farooq, A. (2023). The fast-food employees' usage intention of robots: A cross-cultural study. *Tourism Management Perspectives, 45,* 101049.

Abdelmoaty, G. A., & Soliman, S. A. E. M. (2020). Smart technology applications in tourism and hospitality industry of the new administrative capital, Egypt. *Journal of Association of Arab Universities for Tourism and Hospitality, 19*(2), 102–129.

Abou-Shouk, M., Gad, H. E., & Abdelhakim, A. (2021). Exploring customers' attitudes to the adoption of robots in tourism and hospitality. *Journal of Hospitality and Tourism Technology, 12*(4), 762–776.

Abulsaoud Ahmed Younis, R., & Adel, H. M. (2020, September). Artificial intelligence strategy, creativity-oriented HRM and knowledge-sharing quality: Empirical analysis of individual and organisational performance of AI-powered businesses. In *The Annual International Conference of the British Academy of Management (BAM): Innovating for a Sustainable Future,* London, United Kingdom.

Al-shami, H., Mamun, A. A., Ahmed, E. M., & Rashid, N. (2022). Artificial intelligent towards hotels' competitive advantage. An exploratory study from the UAE. *Foresight, 24*(5), 625–636.

Bag, S., Srivastava, G., Bashir, M. M. A., Kumari, S., Giannakis, M., & Chowdhury, A. H. (2022). Journey of customers in this digital era: Understanding the role of artificial intelligence technologies in user engagement and conversion. *Benchmarking: An International Journal, 29*(7), 2074–2098.

Bakir, S., Ayoun, B., Wei, C., & Bilgihan, A. (2025). Understanding employee retention in the age of AI and robotics: A study of technology competencies and turnover intentions in the hotel sector. *Journal of Hospitality and Tourism Technology, 16*(5), 837–854.

Buhalis, D., Efthymiou, L., Uzunboylu, N., & Thrassou, A. (2024). Charting the progress of technology adoption in tourism and hospitality in the era of industry 4.0. *EuroMed Journal of Business, 19*(1), 1–20.

Buhalis, D., Harwood, T., Bogicevic, V., Viglia, G., Beldona, S., & Hofacker, C. (2019). Technological disruptions in services: Lessons from tourism and hospitality. *Journal of Service Management, 30*(4), 484–506.

Cain, L. N., Thomas, J. H., & Alonso Jr, M. (2019). From sci-fi to sci-fact: The state of robotics and AI in the hospitality industry. *Journal of Hospitality and Tourism Technology, 10*(4), 624–650.

Cha, S. S. (2020). Customers' intention to use robot-serviced restaurants in Korea: Relationship of coolness and MCI factors. *International Journal of Contemporary Hospitality Management, 32*(9), 2947–2968.

Chi, O. H., Chi, C. G., Gursoy, D., & Nunkoo, R. (2023). Customers' acceptance of artificially intelligent service robots: The influence of trust and culture. *International Journal of Information Management, 70*, 102623.

Choi, S., & Wan, L. C. (2021). The rise of service robots in the hospitality industry: Some actionable insights. *Boston Hospitality Review, 30*(1), 1–11.

Chuang, S. (2024). Indispensable skills for human employees in the age of robots and AI. *European Journal of Training and Development, 48*(1/2), 179–195.

Dirican, C. (2015). The impacts of robotics, artificial intelligence on business and economics. *Procedia-Social and Behavioral Sciences, 195*, 564–573.

Drexler, N., & Lapré, V. B. (2019). For better or for worse: Shaping the hospitality industry through robotics and artificial intelligence. *Research in Hospitality Management, 9*(2), 117–120.

Gajic, T., Ranjbaran, A., Vukolić, D., Bugarčić, J., Spasojević, A., Đorđević Boljanović, J., ... & Rakić, S. R. (2024). Tourists' willingness to adopt AI in hospitality—Assumption of sustainability in developing countries. *Sustainability, 16*(9), 3663.

Go, H., Kang, M., & Suh, S. C. (2020). Machine learning of robots in tourism and hospitality: Interactive technology acceptance model (iTAM)–cutting edge. *Tourism Review, 75*(4), 625–636.

Goel, P., Kaushik, N., Sivathanu, B., Pillai, R., & Vikas, J. (2022). Consumers' adoption of artificial intelligence and robotics in hospitality and tourism sector: Literature review and future research agenda. *Tourism Review, 77*(4), 1081–1096.

Gonzalez-Jimenez, H., & Costa Pinto, D. (2024). Can AI robots foster social inclusion? Exploring the role of immersive augmentation in hospitality. *International Journal of Contemporary Hospitality Management, 36*(11), 3889–3905.

Guan, X., Xu, X., Gong, J., & Liu, X. (2025). Facing AI with knowledge: An investigative study on the utilisation of service robots and employee knowledge management behaviours. *Current Issues in Tourism, 28*(20), 3302–3318.

Gupta, S., Modgil, S., Lee, C. K., Cho, M., & Park, Y. (2022). Artificial intelligence enabled robots for stay experience in the hospitality industry in a smart city. *Industrial Management & Data Systems, 122*(10), 2331–2350.

Hui, Z., Khan, N. A., & Akhtar, M. (2025). AI-based virtual assistant and transformational leadership in social cognitive theory perspective: A study of team innovation in construction industry. *International Journal of Managing Projects in Business, 18*(4–5), 688–707.

Hwang, J., Park, S., & Kim, I. (2020). Understanding motivated consumer innovativeness in the context of a robotic restaurant: The moderating role of product knowledge. *Journal of Hospitality and Tourism Management, 44*, 272–282.

Ivanov, S., & Webster, C. (Eds.). (2019). *Robots, artificial intelligence, and service automation in travel, tourism and hospitality*. Emerald Publishing Limited.

Jabeen, F., Al Zaidi, S., & Al Dhaheri, M. H. (2022). Automation and artificial intelligence in hospitality and tourism. *Tourism Review, 77*(4), 1043–1061.

Jin, D. (2025). Can the soul survive automation? Leadership identity and robotic task replacement in hospitality. *Journal of Services Marketing, 39*(9), 1224–1239.

Jin, D., Lu, L., & Lee, W. (2025). Improving employee-robot collaboration in hospitality: Understanding the zero-sum mindset. *International Journal of Hospitality Management, 126*, 104062.

Kang, J., Shin, H., & Kang, C. (2024). Hospitality labor leakage and dynamic turnover behaviors in the age of artificial intelligence and robotics. *Journal of Hospitality and Tourism Technology, 15*(5), 916–933.

Khaliq, A., Waqas, A., Nisar, Q. A., Haider, S., & Asghar, Z. (2022). Application of AI and robotics in hospitality sector: A resource gain and resource loss perspective. *Technology in Society, 68,* 101807.

Khan, M. A. (2024). Understanding the impact of artificial intelligence (AI) on traditional businesses in Indonesia. *Journal of Management Studies and Development, 3*(02), 146–158.

Koo, C., Xiang, Z., Gretzel, U., & Sigala, M. (2021). Artificial intelligence (AI) and robotics in travel, hospitality and leisure. *Electronic Markets, 31*(3), 473–476.

Kumar, S., Kumar, V., & Attri, K. (2021). Impact of artificial intelligence and service robots in tourism and hospitality sector: Current use & future trends. *Administrative Development: A Journal of HIPA, Shimla, 8,* no. SI–1, 59–83.

Lee, Y., Lee, S., & Kim, D. Y. (2021). Exploring hotel guests' perceptions of using robot assistants. *Tourism Management Perspectives, 37,* 100781.

Leung, X. Y., Jin, D., & Shi, X. (2025). Rethinking hospitality leadership: Cultivating human–robot co-working harmony through rapport leadership. *Journal of Hospitality & Tourism Research, 49*(8), 1432–1446.

Licardo, J. T., Domjan, M., & Orehovački, T. (2024). Intelligent robotics—A systematic review of emerging technologies and trends. *Electronics, 13*(3), 542.

Liu, X., Zheng, X., Zhang, L., & Yang, S. (2025). Harmony in robotic synergy: Exploring how service robot collaborative capability affects hospitality employee value co-creation intentions. *International Journal of Contemporary Hospitality Management, 37*(10), 3405–3426.

McCartney, G., & McCartney, A. (2020). Rise of the machines: Towards a conceptual service-robot research framework for the hospitality and tourism industry. *International Journal of Contemporary Hospitality Management, 32*(12), 3835–3851.

Menshikova, M., Bonacci, I., Scarozza, D., Fedorova, A., & Ghazy, K. (2025). Employee perception of human-robot co-working: Evidence from the hotel sector in Russia, Egypt, and Italy. In A. Tursunbayeva, F. Virili, & A. M. Braccini (Eds.), *Technology-driven transformation: The future of work and organizations* (pp. 31–54). Springer Nature Switzerland.

Mingotto, E., Montaguti, F., & Tamma, M. (2021). Challenges in re-designing operations and jobs to embody AI and robotics in services. Findings from a case in the hospitality industry. *Electronic Markets, 31*(3), 493–510.

Mir, U. B., Sharma, S., Kar, A. K., & Gupta, M. P. (2020). Critical success factors for integrating artificial intelligence and robotics. *Digital Policy, Regulation and Governance, 22*(4), 307–331.

Nam, K., Dutt, C. S., Chathoth, P., Daghfous, A., & Khan, M. S. (2021). The adoption of artificial intelligence and robotics in the hotel industry: Prospects and challenges. *Electronic Markets, 31*(3), 553–574.

Pande, S., & Gupta, K. P. (2023). Indian customers' acceptance of service robots in restaurant services. *Behaviour & Information Technology, 42*(12), 1946–1967.

Pillai, R., & Sivathanu, B. (2020). Adoption of AI-based chatbots for hospitality and tourism. *International Journal of Contemporary Hospitality Management, 32*(10), 3199–3226.

Rampersad, G. (2020). Robot will take your job: Innovation for an era of artificial intelligence. *Journal of Business Research, 116,* 68–74.

Rasheed, H. M. W., He, Y., Khizar, H. M. U., & Abbas, H. S. M. (2023). Exploring Consumer-Robot interaction in the hospitality sector: Unpacking the reasons for adoption (or resistance) to artificial intelligence. *Technological Forecasting and Social Change, 192*, 122555.

Ruel, H., & Njoku, E. (2021). AI redefining the hospitality industry. *Journal of Tourism Futures, 7*(1), 53–66.

Seo, K. H., & Lee, J. H. (2021). The emergence of service robots at restaurants: Integrating trust, perceived risk, and satisfaction. *Sustainability, 13*(8), 4431.

Seraj, A. H. A., Hasanein, A. M., Al-Romeedy, B. S., & Elziny, M. N. (2025). Redefining the digital frontier: Digital leadership, AI, and innovation driving next-generation tourism and hospitality. *Administrative Sciences, 15*(9), 369.

Shi, X., Hao, F., & Yuan, Y. (2026). Long-term effects of AI-Powered robots on employee creativity in the hospitality industry: psychological mechanisms of human–AI collaboration. *Journal of Hospitality Marketing & Management, 35*(1), 1–23.

Shum, C., Min, H., Sun, J., Yu, H., & He, Z. (2024). Kicking the robots: The roles of transformational leadership and fear on service robot risk awareness and robot abuse relationship. *Journal of Hospitality and Tourism Technology, 15*(5), 934–946.

Skubis, I. (2025). Exploring the potential and perceptions of social robots in tourism and hospitality: Insights from industry executives and technology evaluation. *International Journal of Social Robotics, 17*(1), 59–72.

Skubis, I., Mesjasz-Lech, A., & Nowakowska-Grunt, J. (2024). Humanoid robots in tourism and hospitality—exploring managerial, ethical, and societal challenges. *Applied Sciences, 14*(24), 11823.

Suder, M., Duda, J., Kusa, R., & Mora-Cruz, A. (2024). At the crossroad of digital and tourism entrepreneurship: Mediating effect of digitalization in hospitality industry. *European Journal of Innovation Management, 27*(4), 1057–1081.

Tuomi, A., Tussyadiah, I., & Ascenção, M. P. (2025). Customized language models for tourism management: Implications and future research. *Annals of Tourism Research, 110*, 103863.

Tuomi, A., Tussyadiah, I. P., & Stienmetz, J. (2021). Applications and implications of service robots in hospitality. *Cornell Hospitality Quarterly, 62*(2), 232–247.

Wang, D., Ma, E., & Leung, X. Y. (2024). Working with robots: A job design perspective of hospitality employees' collaboration intentions with service robots. *Journal of Hospitality and Tourism Management, 61*, 66–77.

Wang, H., Zhang, H., Chen, Z., Zhu, J., & Zhang, Y. (2022). Influence of artificial intelligence and robotics awareness on employee creativity in the hotel industry. *Frontiers in Psychology, 13*, 834160.

Wang, X., Zhang, Z., Huang, D., & Li, Z. (2023). Consumer resistance to service robots at the hotel front desk: A mixed-methods research. *Tourism Management Perspectives, 46*, 101074.

Wang, Y. C., & Papastathopoulos, A. (2024). Cross-segment validation of customer support for AI-based service robots at luxury, fine-dining, casual, and quick-service restaurants. *International Journal of Contemporary Hospitality Management, 36*(6), 1744–1765.

Wu, T. J., Zhang, R. X., Lin, W., & Li, J. M. (2025). Hotel employee's behavioral change in human–robot collaboration: Investigating the dual path toward event strength. *International Journal of Hospitality Management, 130*, 104248.

Xu, S., Stienmetz, J., & Ashton, M. (2020). How will service robots redefine leadership in hotel management? A Delphi approach. *International Journal of Contemporary Hospitality Management, 32*(6), 2217–2237.

Yang, L., Henthorne, T. L., & George, B. (2019). Artificial intelligence and robotics technology in the hospitality industry: Current applications and future trends. In B. George & J. Paul (Eds.), *Digital transformation in business and society: Theory and cases* (pp. 211–228).

Zhang, T., & Lu, L. (2024). Guest editorial: The current landscape and research priorities of human–robot interactions in hospitality and tourism. *Journal of Hospitality and Tourism Technology, 15*(5), 693–700.

Zhong, L., Zhang, X., Rong, J., Chan, H. K., Xiao, J., & Kong, H. (2021). Construction and empirical research on acceptance model of service robots applied in hotel industry. *Industrial Management & Data Systems, 121*(6), 1325–1352.

2

Robotics at Play: Leadership Transformations in All-Inclusive Resorts

Carimo Rassal, Luana Beckmann, and Miguel Pinheiro

2.1 Introduction

2.1.1 Background and Context

Technological advancements rapidly transform industries worldwide; the hospitality sector is no exception. Among these innovations, integrating robotics into hospitality operations has emerged as a pivotal development (Ivanov & Webster, 2019), particularly in all-inclusive resorts. These settings offer a unique opportunity to explore the intersection of technology and service excellence, given their distinctive operational model and guest expectations (Davari et al., 2022).

With their bundled offerings, including dining, entertainment, wellness, and recreational activities, all-inclusive resorts present an intricate service model that requires balancing operational efficiency with highly personalized guest experiences (Çetin & Suren, 2024). Unlike other hospitality segments, the diversity and complexity of services provided under a single package make these resorts ideal testbeds for studying the integration of robotics (Rassal, 2026). Specifically, they offer a fertile ground to observe how automation can enhance efficiency and guest satisfaction without diluting the human touch central to hospitality (Bisoi et al., 2020).

Robotics in these settings can significantly improve operations by automating repetitive and labor-intensive tasks such as housekeeping, room service, and maintenance (Saputra et al., 2024). This allows human staff to dedicate more attention to creating meaningful, personalized interactions that align with the expectations of diverse guest demographics, including families, couples, and business travelers who frequently frequent these resorts with distinct needs and preferences (Iyelolu et al., 2024). Moreover, robots' ability

 DOI: 10.1201/9781003742791-2

to deliver consistent, high-quality services 24/7 positions them as essential assets in maintaining high service standards (Sparrow, 2020).

However, integrating robotics introduces new complexities for leadership and management (Kannan, 2024). Leaders must adapt traditional hospitality practices to incorporate advanced technologies and ensure these innovations align with the relational and emotional elements that define exceptional guest service. This requires reshaping organizational culture, adopting innovative leadership strategies, and implementing training programs that equip staff to collaborate effectively with robotic systems (Bowen & Morosan, 2018). Furthermore, the global pandemic has accelerated the need for robotics in hospitality by emphasizing hygiene, safety, and reduced human contact (Zeng et al., 2020). Given their comprehensive and high-touch service offerings, all-inclusive resorts exemplify environments where the successful implementation of robotics demands strategic leadership and a nuanced understanding of guest dynamics. These factors underscore the significance of studying how robotics can be effectively deployed in these settings, offering insights into leadership adaptation and operational transformation (Ivanov et al., 2023).

2.1.2 Purpose and Objectives of the Study

This study investigates the integration of robotics in all-inclusive resorts and its impact on leadership and management practices. By examining how robotics can enhance service delivery and operational efficiency without compromising the guest experience, the research seeks to provide insights into the strategic implementation of robotics.

The primary objectives are to:

- Understand the roles and functions of robotics in all-inclusive resorts.
- Analyze the impact of robotics on leadership and management practices.
- Explore the concept of 'integrative leadership' and its application in the hospitality industry.
- Identify challenges and opportunities associated with integrating robotics into all-inclusive resorts.

2.1.3 Structure of the Chapter

This chapter is structured to provide a comprehensive examination of robotics in all-inclusive resorts, beginning with a review of relevant literature, followed by the research methodology, findings, discussion, and concluding remarks. The key sections include the following:

- The introduction establishes the background, purpose, and objectives of the study.

- The literature review examines existing research and case studies on robotics in hospitality and leadership adaptations.
- The methodology section outlines the research design, data collection methods, and the study's analytical techniques.
- The findings section presents the research results, including the roles and functions of robotics in resorts and their impact on leadership and management practices. The discussion analyzes the findings' implications for hospitality leadership, identifies challenges and opportunities, and explores future trends.
- The conclusion summarizes the key findings, contributions to the field, and the study's limitations.

2.2 Literature Review

2.2.1 Robotics in Hospitality

The use of robotics in the hospitality industry has evolved significantly over the past few decades. Early applications were limited to basic tasks such as automated check-in and cleaning services. However, advances in artificial intelligence (AI) and robotics have expanded their roles to include concierge services, room delivery, and entertainment (Ivanov et al., 2022).

Modern robots in hospitality are designed to interact seamlessly with guests, providing information, assisting with luggage, and performing housekeeping duties. For example, hotels like the Henn na Hotel in Japan, famously staffed by robots, showcase the potential for extensive robotic integration (Reis et al., 2020). Similarly, chains like Marriott and Hilton have experimented with robotic concierges to enhance guest services (Shin & Jeong, 2020). Deploying robots in hospitality aims to improve operational efficiency and deliver a unique, futuristic guest experience (Ravichandra et al., 2025).

Robotics in hospitality can be broadly categorized into front-of-house and back-of-house applications. Front-of-house robots interact directly with guests, performing check-in/check-out, room, and concierge services. Back-of-house robots handle cleaning, food preparation, and inventory management tasks behind the scenes. The distinction between these roles highlights the diverse capabilities of robots and their potential to transform various aspects of hospitality operations (Tussyadiah, 2020).

2.2.2 Historical Context and Evolution

The journey of robotics in hospitality can be traced back to the early 2000s, when the industry began exploring automation to improve efficiency and reduce costs. Initial robotic applications were primarily in backend operations, such as automated kitchen equipment and housekeeping robots designed to perform repetitive tasks. These early adopters demonstrated significant improvements in operational efficiency, paving the way for more sophisticated uses of robotics (Ivanov et al., 2022).

The fundamental transformation began with the development of AI and machine learning, enabling robots to interact more naturally with humans. This leap allowed robots to take on front-of-house roles, directly engaging with guests. Innovations such as AI-driven chatbots for customer service, robot concierges, and automated check-in/check-out systems have redefined guest experiences. These technologies streamline operations and offer unique novelty experiences that differentiate a brand in a competitive market (Tussyadiah, 2020).

Several key technological advancements have influenced the evolution of robotics in hospitality. For instance, improvements in sensor technology have enabled robots to navigate complex environments and interact safely with humans (Xu et al., 2020). AI and machine learning algorithms have enhanced robots' ability to understand and respond to human language, making them more effective in customer service roles. Additionally, advancements in battery technology have extended the operational lifespan of robots, allowing them to perform tasks for extended periods without recharging (Zeng et al., 2020).

2.2.3 Case Studies of Robotic Integration

The Henn na Hotel, the world's first robot-staffed hotel, employs robots for functions such as check-in, luggage handling, and room delivery. The hotel uses humanoid robots and robotic arms to store luggage at the reception. This setup reduces labor costs while offering guests a unique, futuristic experience. Guests can interact with multilingual robots for check-in and check-out, reducing wait times and enhancing efficiency. Additionally, robotic concierges provide information about the hotel's amenities and nearby attractions, improving the guest experience (Reis, 2024).

Aloft Hotels, part of Marriott International, introduced "Botlr," a robot butler that delivers amenities to guest rooms. Botlr is designed to navigate the hotel autonomously using sensors and AI to interact with guests and staff. This integration enhances operational efficiency and adds an element of novelty to the guest experience (Jin, 2024). Guests can request items like toiletries and snacks via an app, and Botlr delivers them directly to their rooms. This service enhances convenience and enables human staff to focus on more complex, personalized guest interactions (Yan et al., 2025).

In collaboration with IBM Watson, Hilton introduced Connie, a robot concierge. Connie uses AI to inform guests about the hotel's amenities, local attractions, and dining options. This robotic concierge enhances guest interactions by providing instant, accurate information, thereby improving overall guest satisfaction. Connie's AI capabilities allow it to learn from each interaction, continually improving its ability to assist guests. Connie also exemplifies how hotels can leverage cutting-edge technology to stay competitive and provide exceptional service (Tyagi & Joshi, 2023).

YOTEL, a hotel chain known for its innovative use of technology, employs robots for luggage storage and delivery services. At YOTEL New York, guests can store their luggage using "YOBOT," a robotic arm that securely stores and retrieves bags. This service streamlines the check-in and check-out, allowing guests to enjoy a hassle-free experience. YOTEL's use of robotics extends to other areas, such as room cleaning and maintenance, further enhancing operational efficiency (Song et al., 2024).

2.2.4 Leadership in the Hospitality Industry

Traditional leadership models in the hospitality industry emphasize interpersonal skills, emotional intelligence, and a deep understanding of guest needs. Leaders are expected to foster a culture of service excellence and motivate staff to deliver high-quality, personalized service. This leadership style is rooted in the belief that exceptional guest experiences are driven by human interactions and customized service (Chathoth et al., 2020).

However, the advent of automation and robotics introduces new challenges and opportunities for leadership. Leaders must now navigate the complexities of integrating technology with human resources, ensuring that robotics implementation enhances rather than detracts from the guest experience. This requires a shift in leadership styles, incorporating a greater focus on technological literacy and strategic thinking (Ivanov et al., 2022).

Leaders in the hospitality industry should also balance the benefits of automation with the need to maintain a human touch (Bardukova, 2023). While robots can perform routine tasks efficiently, human staff are still essential for providing personalized service and addressing complex guest needs. Influential leaders must create an environment where technology and human resources complement each other, enhancing overall service quality and operational efficiency (Lee & Erdem, 2024).

Integrating robotics also demands new skills and competencies from leaders (Chuang, 2024). Technological literacy, strategic vision, and adaptability become crucial in navigating the evolving hospitality landscape. Leaders should understand and leverage technological advancements to drive innovation and improve service delivery. They should also be adept at change management, guiding their teams through transitions, and fostering a culture of continuous improvement (Paudel, 2024).

2.2.5 Integrative Leadership Concept

Integrative leadership represents the ability of leaders to harmonize technological advancements with traditional hospitality values. This leadership style emphasizes a holistic approach, balancing the operational efficiency enabled by robotics with the warmth and personalization integral to guest satisfaction. Leaders who adopt this style excel at fostering collaboration between human and robotic team members, ensuring that technology complements rather than replaces human efforts. This unique balance is essential for preserving the core ethos of hospitality while embracing innovation (Soliman et al., 2024).

Integrative leadership is deeply rooted in transformational and adaptive leadership theories, which provide a robust framework for addressing the complexities of modern hospitality operations. Transformational leadership contributes traits such as emotional intelligence, individualized consideration, and the ability to inspire a shared vision. These qualities are particularly valuable in motivating teams to embrace technological innovations while retaining the relational essence of hospitality. Leaders leveraging transformational leadership foster trust and commitment, helping staff view technology as a tool for enhancing, rather than undermining, their roles (Zaharuddin et al., 2024).

Adaptive leadership complements this approach by equipping leaders to navigate the uncertainties and complexities of integrating technology into service models (Suherni et al., 2023). Adaptive traits such as resilience, flexibility, and iterative problem-solving are crucial in responding to disruptions and evolving guest expectations (Uy et al., 2023). For example, during the implementation of robotic systems, adaptive leaders refine processes iteratively based on feedback from guests and staff, ensuring that the technology aligns with operational goals and enhances the guest experience (Huang et al., 2023).

In the context of all-inclusive resorts, the convergence of these two theories is particularly relevant. Leaders must address the challenges posed by diverse guest demographics, large-scale operations, and the integration of advanced technologies into service delivery. By combining transformational vision with adaptive resilience, integrative leadership may ensure that technological advancements are implemented pragmatically and inclusively (Hoang et al., 2023).

Integrative leadership is defined by several core principles that bridge theoretical insights and practical applications:

Vision Development: Leaders must craft and communicate a compelling vision for integrating robotics into hospitality operations. This vision should inspire staff by emphasizing how technology can enhance service delivery while preserving hospitality's human-centric values. For instance, transformational leaders who employ inspirational motivation can frame robotics as tools that free staff to focus on more meaningful guest interactions (Lee et al., 2023).

Collaborative Skills Building: Effective human-robot collaboration requires staff training that emphasizes both technical and interpersonal skills. Leaders using emotional intelligence, a hallmark of transformational leadership, can address staff concerns about technology adoption by empathizing with their apprehensions and tailoring training programs to their needs. This approach fosters a supportive and inclusive environment for change (Khoa, 2023).

Innovation Culture: Encouraging a culture of innovation is central to integrative leadership. Adaptive leadership traits such as iterative problem-solving enable leaders to promote experimentation, learn from failures, and align technological advancements with hospitality values. For example, leaders might pilot AI-driven guest analytics in controlled settings, refining the technology before implementing it across the resort (Ali, 2024).

Guest-Centric Focus: Leaders prioritize the guest experience by ensuring that robotics enhances, rather than detracts from, personalized service. Adaptive flexibility enables leaders to adjust robotic roles based on guest feedback, such as refining the functions of robotic assistants to meet guest preferences for personalized service delivery better (Sofi et al., 2025).

Adaptability and Resilience: Integrative leaders demonstrate resilience amid technological disruptions and evolving guest expectations. For example, adaptive leaders deploy robotics in stages, using feedback loops to refine their approach and ensure that staff and guests feel comfortable with the changes (Ho et al., 2023).

Global and Cultural Sensitivity: Leaders should adapt strategies to accommodate regional and cultural differences in guest expectations. Transformational leaders can use individualized consideration to tailor approaches for regions where personal interaction is highly valued, ensuring that robotics supports rather than replaces traditional service roles (Guchait et al., 2023).

2.2.5.1 Applications of Integrative Leadership

Case studies from leading resorts showcase the successful application of integrative leadership principles:

Robotic Butlers: Resorts have deployed robotic butlers to handle routine tasks, such as luggage delivery, freeing staff to focus on personalized guest interactions. Leaders who employ transformational traits, such as inspirational motivation, have successfully aligned staff with the vision of robotics as tools that enhance their roles (Çeltek, 2024).

Automated Service Kiosks: These streamline check-in and check-out processes, reducing wait times and improving efficiency. Adaptive leaders have optimized these kiosks through iterative refinements based on staff and guest feedback, ensuring their functionality aligns with service expectations (Kim et al., 2023).

AI-Driven Guest Analytics: AI systems analyze guest preferences to provide tailored dining, entertainment, and wellness recommendations.

> Transformational leaders use emotional intelligence to integrate staff into the process, enabling them to interpret AI insights and enhance guest experiences (Talukder et al., 2025).

Integrative leadership provides a dynamic framework for balancing innovation with the personalized, human-centric values central to hospitality by integrating transformational inspiration and adaptive flexibility (Sołtysik et al., 2024). This approach ensures that technological advancements are implemented thoughtfully, enhancing operational efficiency and guest satisfaction.

2.2.6 Technological Advancements and Their Impact

Technological advancements in AI, machine learning, and robotics have significantly impacted the hospitality industry. AI-driven chatbots, for instance, are increasingly used to handle customer inquiries, make reservations, and provide personalized recommendations. These chatbots can operate around the clock, providing instant responses and improving customer satisfaction (Adekuajo et al., 2023).

Machine learning algorithms have also enhanced robots' capabilities in hospitality. These algorithms enable robots to learn from interactions, continually improving their performance and adapting to new situations. For example, robotic concierges can learn from guest interactions to provide more accurate and relevant information over time (Saranya et al., 2025).

Robotic technology has also advanced in terms of physical capabilities. Modern robots have sophisticated sensors and actuators to navigate complex environments, handle delicate objects, and interact safely with humans. These capabilities have expanded the range of tasks that robots can perform in hospitality, from room-service delivery to housekeeping and maintenance (Huang et al., 2023).

The impact of these technological advancements on the hospitality industry has been profound. Hotels that leverage AI and robotics can operate more efficiently, reduce labor costs, and deliver unique, engaging guest experiences. However, integrating these technologies presents challenges, including significant upfront investment, potential job displacement, and the need to manage guest perceptions and expectations (Milton, 2024).

2.2.7 Ethical and Social Considerations

The integration of robotics in hospitality raises several ethical and social considerations. One of the main concerns is the possibility of job displacement. As robots take over routine tasks, there is a risk that human staff may lose their jobs or see their roles significantly altered. This raises important questions about the future of work in the hospitality industry and the need for strategies to mitigate the impact on employees (Raina, 2023).

Another ethical consideration is the potential loss of human interaction. While robots can perform tasks efficiently, they lack the empathy and emotional intelligence that human staff bring to guest interactions. This could lead to a decline in personalized service quality, a hallmark of the hospitality industry (Khoa et al., 2023).

Privacy and data security are also critical concerns. Robots and AI systems often collect and process large amounts of data, including personal information about guests. Ensuring that this data is handled securely and in compliance with privacy regulations is essential to maintaining guest trust and protecting against data breaches (Alhitmi, 2024).

Lastly, there are broader social implications to consider. The increasing use of robotics in hospitality reflects a broader trend toward automation and digitalization in society. This trend can reshape labor markets, social interactions, and cultural norms. As such, hospitality industry leaders need to consider the long-term social impact of their technological choices and engage in responsible innovation (González-Jiménez & Costa Pinto, 2024).

2.3 Methodology

2.3.1 Research Design

This section outlines the methodology adopted to examine the integration of robotics in all-inclusive resorts and its implications on leadership and management practices. Central to this study is the application of semi-structured interviews, a qualitative research technique that enables in-depth exploration of participants' insights while maintaining a guided structure. The following subsections detail the methodological framework, participant selection, data collection, and analysis processes.

First, a thorough search was undertaken to identify all-inclusive hotels operating in Portugal on Booking.com, TripAdvisor, and Expedia, resulting in 47 hotels.

Second, the semi-structured interview methodology was selected for its flexibility in exploring nuanced perceptions of robotics' integration in hospitality leadership (Taheri & Okumus, 2024). This approach balances consistency and adaptability, enabling the interviewer to probe deeper into specific responses while remaining aligned with predetermined research objectives (Liu et al., 2024). Semi-structured interviews are particularly suitable for contexts where understanding the interplay between technology and leadership demands exploratory and explanatory insights (Olawale et al., 2023).

This study employs a qualitative, interpretive paradigm to explore leadership dynamics in the context of robotic integration in all-inclusive resorts. This approach is grounded in the principle that social phenomena are best understood by interpreting the subjective meanings participants ascribe to their experiences (Bentalha et al., 2024; Qaissi, 2024).

The interview guide was systematically developed following a five-phase approach as proposed by Bingham (2023):

1. A thorough literature review on robotics in the hospitality industry and leadership transformations established the relevance of semi-structured interviews for this research. This method's suitability stems from its ability to capture executives' and managers' perceptions and experiences in a personalized service environment.
2. Insights from scholarly articles, industry reports, and consultations with field experts informed the guide's structure. Key themes identified included technological integration, guest experience, workforce dynamics, and leadership strategies. This ensured alignment with the study's objectives and contextual relevance.
3. The initial guide encompassed broad themes with corresponding main and follow-up questions. For instance, a central question such as, "How has the integration of robotics influenced your leadership practices?" was paired with probes like, "Can you provide specific examples?" to elicit detailed responses. Questions were structured to encourage reflection and avoid leading participants toward specific answers.
4. The guide underwent pilot testing with a small group of industry professionals. Feedback highlighted the need to clarify questions and adjust the sequence to ensure a natural conversational flow. For instance, follow-up questions were refined to elicit richer narratives, and redundant queries were eliminated to optimize time.
5. Revisions from the pilot test were incorporated, resulting in a comprehensive guide that balanced structure and adaptability. The finalized guide was organized into sections focusing on robotics deployment, leadership responses, staff training, and guest experience to ensure systematic data collection.

Purposive sampling was employed to identify participants who held leadership roles in all-inclusive resorts in Portugal. Selection criteria included the following:

- A minimum of three years in a managerial or executive position
- Direct involvement in the implementation or oversight of robotics within the resort
- Representation across diverse resort sizes and operational scales to capture varied perspectives

Forty-one participants (87% of the sample) responded and accepted the interview scope and terms, and were recruited, ensuring a mix of experiences and viewpoints. Invitations were sent via email, accompanied by a brief research overview and a consent form outlining confidentiality and the voluntary nature of participation. This strategic sampling aimed to capture the multi-dimensional impact of robotics on leadership and operational practices.

2.3.2 Data Collection

The interviews were conducted over three months in 2024, using both in-person and virtual formats to accommodate participants' schedules. Each session lasted 45–60 minutes and was audio-recorded with the participant's consent. The sessions began with an introduction to the study's objectives and a reaffirmation of confidentiality.

The interview guide covered four key domains:

1. Integration: Questions explored how robotics was introduced and its roles in daily operations. For example, "What were the key factors influencing your decision to adopt robotics?" and "How do robotics complement existing human roles?"
2. Leadership and Workforce Dynamics: Participants shared their experiences adapting leadership styles to accommodate robotic integration and its impact on staff roles. Questions included, "How has robotics influenced your leadership style?" and "What challenges have emerged in balancing human and robotic contributions?"
3. Guest Experience: Probes addressed perceptions of how robotics influenced guest satisfaction and personalized service. For instance, "What feedback have you received from guests regarding robotic interactions?"
4. Strategic Vision: Discussions centered on balancing technological adoption with traditional hospitality values. This included questions like, "What strategies have you employed to integrate robotics without compromising service quality?"

2.3.3 Data Analysis

A thematic analysis approach was employed to analyze the interview data (Naz et al., 2022). The process involved:

- Transcription: Each interview was transcribed verbatim to ensure accuracy. Transcriptions were supplemented by observational notes to capture non-verbal cues and contextual details.
- Coding: Transcripts were systematically coded using NVivo software. Codes were assigned to recurring themes, such as "robotics in repetitive tasks" and "leadership adaptability."

- Thematic Development: Codes were grouped into broader themes aligned with the research objectives. For instance, "synergy between human skills and robotics" emerged as a critical theme.
- Validation: To enhance reliability, a subset of transcripts was independently coded by a second researcher. Discrepancies were resolved through discussion to ensure consistency.
- Interpretation: The finalized themes were analyzed in the context of existing literature and the conceptual framework of integrative leadership. The findings were contextualized to highlight their implications for industry practices.

Ethical principles were rigorously followed throughout the research process (Nii Laryeafio & Ogbewe, 2023). Participants were given a detailed information sheet outlining the study's purpose, rights, and data protection measures. Informed consent was obtained before participation. Anonymity was ensured by assigning pseudonyms to participants, and all data were securely stored on encrypted devices. Additionally, participants were allowed to withdraw at any stage without explanation.

The credibility and trustworthiness of the research were reinforced through triangulation, member checks, and reflexivity (Donkoh & Mensah, 2023). Triangulation involved comparing interview findings with insights from secondary data sources, such as industry reports and academic literature. Member checks allowed participants to review their transcripts for accuracy and clarify any ambiguities. Reflexive journaling by the researcher helped mitigate potential biases during data interpretation (Stegenga et al., 2024). These measures ensured that the study findings accurately represented the participants' perspectives.

2.4 Findings and Discussion

Integrating robotics in all-inclusive resorts has significantly transformed leadership practices, operational efficiencies, and staff dynamics. This section presents the findings from semi-structured interviews with executives and managers from various all-inclusive resorts in Portugal. It provides insights into robotics' roles and functions, its impact on leadership and management practices, and the balance between robotic efficiency and human-centric service.

2.4.1 Sociodemographic Profile of Respondents

The respondents in this study primarily represent management-level professionals from 3-star, 4-star, and 5-star hotels, mainly affiliated with national independent type hotels, aged between 30 and 50 years old, predominantly male 78% illustrating a diverse range of roles within the hospitality industry. Their professional backgrounds and responsibilities span operational, strategic, and guest-facing positions, offering a comprehensive overview of leadership experiences amidst integrating robotics into hotel management.

The 3-star hotel respondents (3) occupy senior and mid-level management roles such as General Manager, Operations Manager, and Front Office Manager. These professionals have accumulated between 8 and 15 years of experience in the hospitality sector. Their roles predominantly focus on overseeing day-to-day operations, managing resources, and improving guest services. Despite limited investment in robotic technologies, their exposure primarily involves basic service automation, such as housekeeping robots and check-in kiosks.

The 4-star hotel respondents represent a more extensive and multifaceted sample, encompassing 26 individuals in varied leadership roles, including General Managers, Department Directors (e.g., Food and Beverage, HR, IT), and specialized managers (e.g., Spa Manager, Sustainability Manager, Security Manager). This group demonstrates significant professional experience, ranging from 5 to 22 years, with a median tenure of approximately 15 years in hospitality. The diversity in their roles underscores their involvement in strategic planning, employee management, and operational optimization. Investment in robotics among this cohort is moderate to substantial, with technology implemented in kitchen operations, housekeeping, guest services, and automated check-in systems.

The 5-star hotel respondents, comprising 12 professionals, hold prestigious roles such as General Managers, Directors of Guest Experience, Executive Chefs, and Sales and Marketing Directors. Their years of experience are notably high, ranging from 15 to 25 years, indicative of their seniority and expertise within the luxury hospitality sector. These leaders are at the forefront of adopting advanced robotic technologies, including state-of-the-art automation for concierge services, housekeeping, and food and beverage delivery. They focus heavily on enhancing guest satisfaction and operational efficiency and balancing technological advancement and personalized human interaction.

Across all hotel categories, the respondents' experiences reveal a progressive trend toward adopting robotic systems, albeit at varying levels depending on hotel classification. Three-star hotels report modest investments and basic integrations. In contrast, 4- and 5-star hotels are more committed to technological innovations that elevate operational standards and guest experiences. The respondents collectively emphasize the need for staff training and adaptability to overcome the challenges posed by technological change.

2.4.2 Deployment of Robotics in All-Inclusive Resorts

The analysis of responses from management-level professionals across 3-star, 4-star, and 5-star hotels reveals significant themes related to leadership adaptation, operational efficiency, employee management, and the balance between technology and human-centric service. These themes collectively illustrate the evolving role of leadership in the hospitality sector amid the integration of robotic technologies.

A noticeable theme pertains to adapting leadership styles in response to robotic integration. Across all hotel categories, respondents reported a shift from traditional leadership approaches to more collaborative, data-driven, and technology-inclusive styles. Managers highlighted the need for continuous training, coaching, and mentoring to facilitate staff adaptation to robotic systems. In 3-star hotels, leadership remained focused on managing basic robotic technologies, such as housekeeping robots and automated check-in kiosks, while maintaining operational oversight. Conversely, respondents from 4-star and 5-star hotels emphasized strategic leadership approaches, where technological innovation and long-term goals were prioritized. Leaders in these segments incorporated data-driven decision-making, aligning technological advancements with organizational strategies while fostering a culture of innovation and adaptability.

Another central theme is the role of robotics in enhancing operational efficiency and fostering innovation. Respondents across all hotel categories identified the ability of robots to automate repetitive, labor-intensive tasks, enabling human staff to focus on more complex and guest-centric responsibilities. In 3-star hotels, robotics contributed to modest improvements in processes such as room cleaning and check-in operations. Meanwhile, in 4-star hotels, robotic technologies were primarily applied to back-of-house functions, including food preparation and resource optimization. In contrast, respondents from 5-star hotels reported significant advancements in front-of-house operations, such as concierge robots and automated room-service systems, which elevated the luxury guest experience. These insights underscore the role of robotics in driving operational improvements, optimizing resource allocation, and fostering continuous innovation within hospitality services.

The analysis also highlights the challenges and opportunities associated with employee management and adaptation to robotic systems. Respondents consistently noted initial resistance among staff, often stemming from concerns about job security and technological unfamiliarity. Leaders addressed these challenges through comprehensive training programs, hands-on workshops, and collaborative team discussions to promote acceptance of new technologies. Managers reported a gradual shift in staff responsibilities toward higher-value tasks, emphasizing the importance of adaptability and continuous learning. This process required a supportive leadership approach, fostering open communication and teamwork to reduce fear and ensure smooth human-robot collaboration.

A recurring theme among respondents is the balance between technological integration and maintaining human-centric guest services. While robotic technologies significantly enhance efficiency, managers emphasized the importance of preserving personalized guest interactions, which are central to the hospitality experience. Robots were primarily deployed for back-of-house operations to allow human staff to focus on guest-facing roles that require emotional intelligence and personalization. This balance was particularly critical in 5-star hotels, where respondents stressed the need to seamlessly integrate advanced technologies without compromising the luxury service standards expected by guests. Leaders across all categories relied on guest feedback to evaluate the effectiveness of robotic systems and refine processes to ensure an optimal balance between technological efficiency and human touch.

The analysis further reveals significant constraints and challenges in implementing robotic technologies. Respondents, particularly from 3-star hotels, cited budget limitations as a key barrier, restricting investment in advanced systems. Across all hotel categories, challenges related to technical limitations, ongoing maintenance, and staff adaptability were consistently reported. Leaders acknowledged the need for robust training and support systems to address resistance and optimize robotic technologies. Respondents from higher-tier hotels noted that overcoming these challenges requires strategic investments in technological infrastructure and workforce development to ensure sustained benefits from robotic systems.

Finally, the respondents provided insights into future trends and strategic planning regarding robotics in hospitality. Across all hotel categories, leaders anticipated a greater reliance on AI and robotics to deliver highly personalized guest experiences and drive operational excellence. AI-driven technologies were seen as a means to enhance service customization, improve real-time decision-making, and optimize processes across both front-end and backend operations. Respondents highlighted the importance of continuous technological innovation and ongoing staff development to remain competitive in a rapidly evolving industry. In this context, leadership roles are expected to continue growing, with an increasing focus on aligning technological advancements with organizational values and goals.

2.4.2.1 Impact on Leadership and Management Practices

The integration of robotics has necessitated significant changes in leadership roles and responsibilities within all-inclusive resorts. Key impacts include:

Strategic Decision-Making: Leaders must make strategic decisions regarding investing in and implementing robotics. This involves assessing the cost-benefit ratio, potential return on investment, and alignment with the resort's brand and service philosophy. Leaders need to develop a clear vision for how robotics can enhance service delivery and operational efficiency (Tsai et al., 2022).

Human Resource Development: More emphasis is on developing human skills that complement robotic efficiency. Training programs enhance employees' interpersonal skills, problem-solving abilities, and adaptability.

Leaders are responsible for ensuring staff are equipped with the skills to work effectively alongside robots (Vrontis et al., 2023).

Change Management: Leaders are crucial in managing the transition to increased automation. This includes addressing staff concerns, promoting a positive attitude toward technological advancements, and ensuring the smooth integration of robotics into daily operations. Effective change management practices are essential to mitigate resistance and foster acceptance among staff (Chuang, 2024).

Technological Literacy: Leaders must develop a strong understanding of robotics and other automated systems' capabilities and limitations. This technological literacy is crucial for making informed decisions about implementing and utilizing robotics within the resort (Zafar et al., 2024).

2.4.2.2 Synergy between Robotic Efficiency and Human Warmth

Leaders in all-inclusive resorts strive to balance robotic efficiency with the warmth of human-centric service. This balance is achieved through several strategies:

Promoting Collaboration: Encouraging collaboration between human and robotic team members enhances service delivery. For instance, robots handle routine tasks, freeing up staff to engage in more meaningful interactions with guests. This collaborative approach ensures that robots complement rather than replace human efforts (Ivanov et al., 2022).

Enhancing Guest Experience: Using robotics to streamline operations and improve service consistency allows human staff to provide personalized attention and address complex guest needs. This dual approach ensures that guests receive efficient, high-quality service while also benefiting from personal interactions with staff (Soliman et al., 2024).

Fostering a Culture of Innovation: Creating an organizational culture that embraces technological advancements while maintaining a strong focus on traditional hospitality values is essential. Leaders should encourage experimentation, learn from failures, and continually seek ways to improve service delivery through technology (Buhalis et al., 2024).

2.4.2.3 Challenges and Opportunities

The integration of robotics presents several challenges and opportunities for leadership in all-inclusive resorts:

Employee Resistance: One of the primary challenges is staff resistance, as they may fear job displacement or changes in their roles. Leaders address this challenge through comprehensive training programs, workshops, and hands-on training sessions to ensure that staff are comfortable and proficient with the new technology (Khan & Mehmood, 2024).

Integration Complexity: Integrating robotics with existing systems and processes can be complex and requires careful planning and execution.

Leaders should navigate the technical and logistical challenges to ensure seamless integration (Soori et al., 2024).

Guest Acceptance: Some guests may need clarification or be uncomfortable with robotic services, preferring human interaction. To address this, resorts must carefully design and implement robotic services that enhance rather than detract from the guest experience (Liu et al., 2024).

Operational Efficiency: Robotics can significantly enhance efficiency by performing routine tasks quickly and accurately. This efficiency allows human staff to focus on higher-value tasks, improving overall service quality and guest satisfaction (Licardo et al., 2024).

Enhanced Guest Experience: Robotics can deliver a more consistent, reliable guest experience. They can operate around the clock without fatigue, ensuring guests receive timely and accurate service (Jogarao, 2024).

Staff Development: With robots handling routine tasks, staff can focus on developing higher-level skills and providing more personalized service. This shift in responsibilities allows staff to engage in more meaningful and rewarding work, enhancing job satisfaction and professional growth (Wirtz et al., 2024).

2.4.2.4 Future Trends and Directions

Several trends and developments are likely to shape the future of robotics (Hamza et al., 2025) and, therefore, impact the all-inclusive hospitality industry:

Increased Automation: Continued advancements in AI and robotics will lead to greater automation of a broader range of tasks. Future robots may be able to understand and respond to a broader range of human emotions, enhancing their ability to interact with guests (Jin, 2024).

Personalization: Enhanced AI capabilities will enable robots to provide personalized services tailored to individual guest preferences. This level of personalization will further enhance the guest experience and differentiate resorts in a competitive market (Saxena et al., 2024).

Sustainability: Adopting eco-friendly robotic technologies will align with the hospitality industry's growing focus on sustainability. Robots powered by renewable energy sources and that minimize waste will become increasingly crucial as resorts seek to reduce their environmental impact (Semwal et al., 2024).

Integration with Emerging Technologies: Integrating robotics with other emerging technologies, such as the Internet of Things (IoT) and augmented reality (AR), will open new possibilities to enhance the guest experience. IoT-enabled robots could seamlessly integrate with intelligent hotel rooms, providing a fully connected, personalized experience, while AR technology could create immersive, interactive experiences for guests (Nair, 2024).

2.5 Conclusion

This chapter explored the integration of robotics in all-inclusive resorts, focusing on its implications for leadership, management practices, and guest experiences. Robotics has become pivotal in addressing operational complexities and guest satisfaction in the hospitality industry. This concluding section synthesizes the findings, highlights implications for research, practice, and society, and outlines limitations and directions for future research.

2.5.1 Implications for Research

The findings underscore the need for interdisciplinary research at the intersection of technology, leadership, and hospitality. Robotics integration in all-inclusive resorts offers fertile ground for exploring the dynamics of human-robot collaboration, technological adoption, and leadership adaptation. Future research should investigate the long-term impacts of robotics on service quality and organizational culture. Additionally, studies could delve into the psychological aspects of staff-guest interactions with robots, examining how perceptions of automation influence acceptance and satisfaction. Comparative research across cultural and regional contexts can also provide valuable insights into how societal norms shape robotic adoption in hospitality.

The evolving role of leadership in managing technologically augmented teams presents another avenue for research. Scholars could explore the efficacy of integrative leadership models in fostering innovation while preserving hospitality's relational essence. Empirical studies should evaluate how leadership styles influence staff engagement, guest satisfaction, and organizational performance in environments where technology and human resources coexist.

2.5.2 Implications for Practice

Practically integrating robotics necessitates a paradigm shift in operational and leadership practices. Leaders in all-inclusive resorts must balance technological efficiency with personalized guest interactions to preserve the industry's human-centric ethos. Training programs should be designed to enhance staff competencies in using robotics, focusing on both technical skills and emotional intelligence. Leadership development initiatives should prioritize adaptability, technological literacy, and strategic thinking to navigate the complexities of automation.

Operational strategies should align robotic capabilities with organizational goals, emphasizing their role as efficiency enablers rather than replacements for human labor. For instance, deploying robots for repetitive, time-consuming tasks can free up human staff to focus on high-touch, personalized services. Resorts must also establish continuous feedback loops to refine robotic applications based on guest and staff input. Investments in maintenance and updates are critical to ensuring the reliability and effectiveness of robotic systems.

2.5.3 Social Implications

Integrating robotics in hospitality has profound social implications, particularly concerning workforce dynamics and guest experiences. While automation can enhance operational efficiency, it raises concerns about job displacement and the erosion of traditional service roles. To mitigate these challenges, industry leaders must adopt socially responsible approaches to technological adoption. This includes providing reskilling opportunities for employees and emphasizing collaborative roles where humans and robots complement each other.

Guest acceptance of robotics is another critical consideration. While many guests appreciate the novelty and efficiency of robotic services, some may view them as impersonal or intrusive. Resorts must design robotic applications that enhance, rather than detract from, the guest experience, ensuring the human touch remains central to service delivery. Transparency in data collection and privacy safeguards is essential to maintaining guest trust in an increasingly digitalized service environment.

2.5.4 Limitations

This study has several limitations that warrant consideration. First, the research focused on all-inclusive resorts in Portugal, which may limit the generalizability of findings to other hospitality contexts or regions. Cultural, economic, and regulatory differences can significantly influence the adoption and impact of robotics in hospitality. Future studies should include diverse geographic and market segments for a more comprehensive understanding.

Second, while rich in depth, the reliance on qualitative methods limits the ability to quantify the effects of robotics integration on operational metrics such as efficiency, revenue, and guest satisfaction. Quantitative studies are needed to measure the financial and performance outcomes of robotic adoption in hospitality.

Finally, the study primarily captures the perspectives of leaders and managers, leaving gaps in understanding the experiences of frontline staff and guests. Including these voices in future research could provide a more holistic view of the challenges and opportunities posed by robotics in hospitality.

2.5.5 Directions for Future Research

Building on this study, future research should address several key areas. Longitudinal studies are needed to assess the sustainability of robotic integration and its evolving impact on hospitality operations and leadership. Investigating the interplay between robotics and other emerging technologies, such as AI, IoT, and AR, could reveal new opportunities for innovation in guest services.

Additionally, research should explore the ethical implications of robotics in hospitality, particularly concerning job displacement and data privacy. Studies evaluating the societal and psychological impacts of automation on employees and guests can inform policies and practices that promote equitable and ethical technological adoption.

Comparative studies across different types of hospitality establishments, such as boutique hotels, cruise ships, and urban resorts, could reveal contextual factors that influence the success of robotics integration. Finally, researchers should consider the implications of robotics for sustainability in hospitality, examining how automation can support eco-friendly practices and reduce resource consumption.

2.5.6 Concluding Remarks

Integrating robotics in all-inclusive resorts represents a transformative shift in the hospitality industry, redefining operational models, guest experiences, and leadership practices. While this technological evolution offers significant benefits, it also poses challenges that require thoughtful management and strategic planning. By fostering collaboration between human and robotic resources, leveraging innovative leadership approaches, and prioritizing guest-centric values, the industry can harness robotics' potential to enhance service quality and operational efficiency.

As the hospitality sector continues to evolve, the findings of this study underscore the importance of balancing innovation with tradition, efficiency with empathy, and technology with humanity. The insights presented here contribute to a growing body of knowledge that can guide practitioners, researchers, and policymakers in navigating the complexities of robotics in hospitality, ensuring that technological advancements enhance rather than undermine the essence of service excellence.

Funding : This work is funded by national funds through the Foundation for Science and Technology, under the project UID/00057/2025. CIDEHUS - https://doi.org/10.54499/UID/00057/2025

References

Ali, B. (2024). What we know about transformational leadership in tourism and hospitality: A systematic review and future agenda. *The Service Industries Journal, 44*(1–2), 105–147.

Alhitmi, H. K., Mardiah, A., Al-Sulaiti, K. I., & Abbas, J. (2024). Data security and privacy concerns of AI-driven marketing in the context of economics and the business field: An exploration into possible solutions. *Cogent Business & Management, 11*(1), 2393743.

Adekuajo, I. O., Fakeyede, O. G., Udeh, C. A., & Daraojimba, C. (2023). The digital evolution in hospitality: A global review and its potential transformative impact on U.S. tourism. *International Journal of Applied Research in Social Sciences, 5*(10), 440–462.

Bardukova, L. (2023). Navigating the hospitality horizon: Current trends and strategies for customer attraction and retention in the hotel industry. *Economics and Computer Science, 2*, 88–103.

Bentalha, B., & Alla, L. (2024). Revealing the subtleties: The art of qualitative studies in science and management. In B. Bentalha & L. Alla (Eds.), *Applying qualitative research methods to management science* (pp. 1–21). IGI Global.

Bisoi, S., Roy, M., & Samal, A. (2020). Impact of artificial intelligence in the hospitality industry. *International Journal of Advanced Science and Technology, 29*(5), 4265–4276.

Bowen, J. T., & Morosan, C. (2018). Beware the hospitality industry: The robots are coming. *Worldwide Hospitality and Tourism Themes, 10*(6), 726–733. https://doi.org/10.1108/WHATT-07-2018-0045

Buhalis, D., Efthymiou, L., Uzunboylu, N., & Thrassou, A. (2024). Charting the progress of technology adoption in tourism and hospitality in the era of Industry 4.0. *EuroMed Journal of Business, 19*(1), 1–20.

Çeltek, E. (2024). Unmanned smart hotel: Applications and examples. *Worldwide Hospitality and Tourism Themes, 16*(5), 611–626.

Çetin, K., & Süren, T. (2024). An investigation into the causes of food waste by tourists in all-inclusive resorts in Turkey. *Journal of Quality Assurance in Hospitality & Tourism, 25*(4), 677–699.

Chathoth, P., Altinay, L., & Okumus, F. (2020). Strategic management for hospitality and tourism. In F. Okumus, L. Altinay, P. Chathoth & M. A. Koseoglu (Eds.), *Strategic management in the international hospitality and tourism industry* (pp. 18–33). Routledge. ISBN: 978-1-351-18851-7

Chuang, S. (2024). Indispensable skills for human employees in the age of robots and AI. *European Journal of Training and Development, 48*(1/2), 179–195.

Davari, D., Vayghan, S., Jang, S., & Erdem, M. (2022). Hotel experiences during the COVID-19 pandemic: High-touch versus high-tech. *International Journal of Contemporary Hospitality Management, 34* (4), 1312–1330. https://doi.org/10.1108/ijchm-07-2021-0919

Donkoh, S., & Mensah, J. (2023). Application of triangulation in qualitative research. *Journal of Applied Biotechnology and Bioengineering, 10*(1), 6–9.

González-Jiménez, H., & Costa Pinto, D. (2024). Can AI robots foster social inclusion? Exploring the role of immersive augmentation in hospitality. *International Journal of Contemporary Hospitality Management, 36*(11), 3889–3905.

Guchait, P., Peyton, T., Madera, J. M., Gip, H., & Molina-Collado, A. (2023). 21st century leadership research in hospitality management: A state-of-the-art systematic literature review. *International Journal of Contemporary Hospitality Management, 35*(12), 4259–4296.

Hamza, M. A., Sheikh, M. F., Ahmad, B., & Veisieh, D. (2025). Artificial intelligence in robotic industry: Startups and innovations. In M. A Hamza, M. Faisal, B. Ahmad & D. Veisieh (Eds.), *Future tech startups and innovation in the age of AI* (pp. 21–35). CRC Press.

Ho, G. K., Lam, C., & Law, R. (2023). Conceptual framework of strategic leadership and organizational resilience for the hospitality and tourism industry for coping with environmental uncertainty. *Journal of Hospitality and Tourism Insights, 6*(2), 835–852.
Hoang, G., Yang, M., & Luu, T. T. (2023). Ethical leadership in tourism and hospitality management: A systematic literature review and research agenda. *International Journal of Hospitality Management, 114,* Article 103563.
Huang, J. Y., Jiang, R., & Chang, J. Y. (2023). The effects of transformational and adaptive leadership on dynamic capabilities: Digital transformation projects. *Project Management Journal, 54*(4), 428–446.
Huang, R., Li, H., Suomi, R., Li, C., & Peltoniemi, T. (2023). Intelligent physical robots in health care: Systematic literature review. *Journal of Medical Internet Research, 25,* e39786.
Ivanov, S., & Webster, C. (Eds.). (2019). *Robots, artificial intelligence and service automation in travel, tourism and hospitality.* Emerald Group Publishing.
Ivanov, S., Webster, C., & Berezina, K. (2022). Robotics in tourism and hospitality. In Z. Xiang, M. Fuchs, U. Gretzel, & W. Höpken (Eds.), *Handbook of e-tourism* (pp. 1873–1899). Springer. ISBN: 978-3-030-48652-5.
Ivanov, S., Webster, C., & Seyitoğlu, F. (2023). Humans and/or robots? Tourists' preferences towards the humans–robots mix in the service delivery system. *Service Business, 17*(1), 195–231.
Iyelolu, T. V., Agu, E. E., Idemudia, C., & Ijomah, T. I. (2024). Improving customer engagement and crm for smes with ai driven solutions and future enhancements. *International Journal of Engineering Research and Development, 20*(8), 1150–1168.
Jin, D. (2024). Navigating the spectrum of human–robot collaboration: Addressing robophobia-robophilia in the hospitality industry. *International Journal of Hospitality Management, 122,* Article 103840.
Jogarao, M. (2024). AI in the hospitality industry: Revolutionizing guest experience. In P. Taichon, P. K. Dutta, P. R. Chelliah & S. Guota (Eds), *Technology and luxury hospitality – AI, Blockchain and the Metaverse* (pp 199–210). Routledge.
Kannan, R. (2024). Revolutionizing the tourism industry through artificial intelligence: A comprehensive review of AI integration, impact on customer experience, operational efficiency, and future trends. *International Journal for Multidimensional Research Perspectives, 2*(2), 01–14.
Khan, S., & Mehmood, S. (2024). Factors affecting innovation resistance of fast-food employees' usage intention of robots: An integrative perspective. *Journal of Hospitality and Tourism Insights, 7*(3), 1456–1474.
Khoa, D. T., Gip, H. Q., Guchait, P., & Wang, C. Y. (2023). Competition or collaboration for human–robot relationship: A critical reflection on future cobotics in hospitality. *International Journal of Contemporary Hospitality Management, 35*(6), 2202–2215.
Kim, J., Joe, S., & Erdem, M. (2023). The bright and dark sides of hotel kiosks: An empirical study. *Journal of Hospitality and Tourism Insights, 6*(2), 1043–1065.
Lee, M., Russen, M., Dawson, M., & Madera, J. M. (2023). Enhancing performance and perceived justice in hospitality organizations: An integrated model of gender diversity within top management teams. *Cornell Hospitality Quarterly, 64*(4), 503–524.
Lee, S., & Erdem, M. (2024). Exploring the consequences of automation in the post-pandemic era: Hotel labor woes. *Worldwide Hospitality and Tourism Themes, 16*(5), 580–587.
Licardo, J. T., Domjan, M., & Orehovački, T. (2024). Intelligent robotics—A systematic review of emerging technologies and trends. *Electronics, 13*(3), 542.

Liu, J., Zhou, L., & Li, Y. (2024). I can be myself: Robots reduce social discomfort in hospitality service encounters. International *Journal of Contemporary Hospitality Management, 36*(6), 1798–1815.

Milton, T. (2024). Exploring the synergy of artificial intelligence and financial management in the hotel industry: A critical review of innovations, challenges, and strategic implications for enhancing operational efficiency and competitive advantage. *International Journal for Multidimensional Research Perspectives, 2*(2), 79–95.

Nair, V. V. (2024). Automation and robotization: An aerial view of Industry 5.0 on employment and employees. In Żywiołek, J., Rosak-Szyrocka, J., Nayyar, A., & Naved, M. (Eds.), *Modern technologies and tools supporting the development of Industry 5.0* (pp. 41–74). CRC Press.

Naz, N., Gulab, F., & Aslam, M. (2022). Development of a qualitative semi-structured interview guide for case study research. *Qualitative Research Methods, 45*(3), 538–560.

Nii Laryeafio, M., & Ogbewe, O. C. (2023). Ethical consideration dilemma: Systematic review of ethics in qualitative data collection through interviews. *Journal of Ethics in Entrepreneurship and Technology, 3*(2), 94–110.

Olawale, S. R., Chinagozi, O. G., & Joe, O. N. (2023). Exploratory research design in management science: A review of literature on conduct and application. *International Journal of Research and Innovation in Social Science, 7*(4), 1384–1395.

Paudel, R. (2024). The impact of automation and artificial intelligence (AI) on leadership and the workforce. *Indonesian Journal of Banking and Financial Technology,* 2(2), 109–124.

Qaissi, A. (2024). Exploring thematic analysis in qualitative research. In B. Bentalha & L. Alla (Eds.), *Data collection and analysis in scientific qualitative research* (pp. 253–294). IGI Global.

Raina, A. (2023). Artificial intelligence automation and job insecurities in the hospitality industry: An employees and management perspective. In Sharma, A. (ed), *International handbook of skill, education, learning, and research development in tourism and hospitality* (pp. 1–14). Springer Nature Singapore.

Rassal, C. (2026). The evolving landscape of employee commitment in hospitality: Strategies for retention in a transformative era. In E. Tomé (Ed.), *Critical aspects in advanced human resource management* (pp. 255–290). IGI Global Scientific Publishing.

Ravichandra, T., Murugeswari, P., Revathi, M., Senthilkumar, S., Rathore, D. S., & Sudhakar, M. (2025). The future of machine learning and robotics in digital technology for hospitality. In D. C. Ertugrul & A. Elci (Eds.), *Cutting-edge technologies for business* sectors (pp. 401–428). IGI Global.

Reis, J. (2024). Customer service through AI-powered human-robot relationships: Where are we now? The case of Henn na cafe, Japan. *Technology in Society, 77,* 102570.

Reis, J., Melão, N., Salvadorinho, J., Soares, B., & Rosete, A. (2020). Service robots in the hospitality industry: The case of Henn-na Hotel, Japan. *Technology in Society, 63,* Article 101423.

Saranya, E., Shreenidhi, K. S., Anandaram, H., Upadhye, S., & Gukendran, R. (2025). Transforming hospitality, personalized medicine, and adaptive learning: Robotic innovations. In A. Shaik (Ed.), *AI-powered advances in pharmacology* (pp. 373–406). IGI Global.

Shin, H. H., & Jeong, M. (2020). Guests' perceptions of robot concierge and their adoption intentions. *International Journal of Contemporary Hospitality Management, 32*(8), 2613–2633.

Saputra, F. E., Buhalis, D., Augustyn, M. M., & Marangos, S. (2024). Anthropomorphism-based artificial intelligence (AI) robots typology in hospitality and tourism. *Journal of Hospitality and Tourism Technology, 15*(5), 790–807.

Saxena, S. K., Gupta, V., & Kumar, S. (2024). Enhancing guest loyalty in the hotel industry through artificial intelligence-driven personalization. In S. K. Kulshreshtha & G. Webster (Eds.), *New Technologies in Virtual and Hybrid Events* (pp. 335–350). IGI Global.

Semwal, R., Tripathi, N., Kulshrestha, R., & Tyagi, P. (2024). Innovative approaches to sustainable hospitality: Leveraging AI and technology for energy efficiency, waste reduction, and eco-friendly mobility. In M. B. Talukder, S. Kumar & P. K. Tyagi (Eds.), *Hotel and travel management in the AI era* (pp. 379–400). IGI Global.

Sołtysik, M., Tyrańska, M., Piwowar-Sulej, K., & Agustina, T. S. (Eds.). (2024). *Sustainable human resource management: Strategy, organizational innovation and leadership in Industry 5.0.* Taylor & Francis.

Sofi, M. R., Bashir, I., Alshiha, A., Alnasser, E., & Alkhozaim, S. (2025). Creating exceptional guest experiences: The role of engagement and relationship building in hospitality. *Journal of Hospitality and Tourism Insights, 8*(3), 891–914.

Sołtysik, M., Tyrańska, M., Piwowar-Sulej, K., & Agustina, T. S. (Eds.). (2024). *Sustainable human resource management: Strategy, organizational innovation and leadership in industry 5.0.* Taylor & Francis.

Soliman, M., Ivanov, S., Elgammal, I., Webster, C., & Al-Alawi, A. (2024). Pursuing the drivers of consumer behaviour toward service robots in the hotel industry. *International Journal of Hospitality Management, 120,* Article 103752.

Song, B., Xia, H., Law, R., Muskat, B., & Li, G. (2024). Discovery of smart hotels' competitiveness based on online reviews. *International Journal of Hospitality Management, 123,* Article 103926.

Soori, M., Dastres, R., Arezoo, B., & Jough, F. K. G. (2024). Intelligent robotic systems in Industry 4.0: A review. *Journal of Advanced Manufacturing Science and Technology,* 2024007-0.

Sparrow, R. (2020). Robotics has a race problem. *Science, Technology, & Human Values, 45*(3), 538–560.

Stegenga, S. M., Steltenpohl, C. N., Lustick, H., Meyer, M. S., Renbarger, R., Standiford Reyes, L., & Lee, L. E. (2024). Qualitative research at the crossroads of open science and big data: Ethical considerations. *Social and Personality Psychology Compass, 18*(1), Article e12912.

Suherni, E. S., Wahyudin, A., & Gunawan, A. (2023). Analysis of adaptive and participatory leadership models: Study of educational institutional leadership models. *Journal of Educational Analytics, 2*(4), 495–502.

Taheri, B., & Okumus, F. (2024). Conducting mixed methods research. International *Journal of Contemporary Hospitality Management, 36*(3), 995–1004.

Talukder, M. B., Kabir, F., & Jibon, F. A. (2025). AI-driven personalized room management in the modern hotel industry. In O. T. Chiwaridzo & R. Masengu (Eds.), *AI technologies for personalized and sustainable tourism* (pp. 59–82). IGI Global.

Tsai, C. Y., Marshall, J. D., Choudhury, A., Serban, A., Hou, Y. T. Y., Jung, M. F., & Yammarino, F. J. (2022). Human–robot collaboration: A multilevel and integrated leadership framework. *The Leadership Quarterly, 33*(1), Article 101594.

Tussyadiah, I. P. (2020). A review of research into automation in tourism: Launching the Annals of Tourism Research curated collection on artificial intelligence and robotics in tourism. *Annals of Tourism Research, 81,* Article 102883.

Tyagi, H., & Joshi, Y. (2023). Impact of artificial intelligence on guest stay. *ATITHYA: A Journal of Hospitality, 9*(2), 1–11.

Uy, F., Kilag, O. K., Abendan, C. F., Macapobre, K., Cañizares, M. C., & Yray, F. (2023). Application of adaptive crisis management theory: The dynamics of leadership in times of crisis. *Excellencia: International Multi-disciplinary Journal of Education, 1*(5), 159–170.

Vrontis, D., Christofi, M., Pereira, V., Tarba, S., Makrides, A., & Trichina, E. (2023). Artificial intelligence, robotics, advanced technologies and human resource management: A systematic review. In Malik, A & Budhwar, P. (Eds.), *Artificial intelligence and international HRM* (pp. 172–201). Springer.

Wirtz, J., Kunz, W. H., Paluch, S., & Pitardi, V. (2024). Service robots and their implications for service delivery. In Furrer, O., Landry, M., Baillod, C. & Kerguignas, J. (Eds.), *A research agenda for service marketing* (pp. 23–43). Edward Elgar Publishing.

Xu, S., Stienmetz, J., & Ashton, M. (2020). How will service robots redefine leadership in hotel management? A Delphi approach. *International Journal of Contemporary Hospitality Management, 32*(6), 2217–2237.

Yan, Z., Konar, R., & Balasubramanian, K. (2025). The future of hotel robotics, AI, and service automation in practice. In Ozen, E., Singh, A., Taneja, S., Rajaram, R. & Davim, J. Paulo (Eds.), *Sustainability, innovation, and consumer preference* (pp. 249–278). IGI Global Scientific Publishing.

Zafar, M. H., Langås, E. F., & Sanfilippo, F. (2024). Exploring the synergies between collaborative robotics, digital twins, augmentation, and Industry 5.0 for smart manufacturing: A state-of-the-art review. *Robotics and Computer-Integrated Manufacturing, 89,* Article 102769.

Zaharuddin, Z., Wahyuningsih, S., Sutarman, A., & Hikam, I. N. (2024). Understanding purposeful leadership in entrepreneurial contexts: A bibliometric analysis. *Aptisi Transactions on Technopreneurship (ATT), 6*(2), 213–230.

Zeng, Z., Chen, P. J., & Lew, A. A. (2020). From high-touch to high-tech: COVID-19 drives robotics adoption. *Tourism Geographies, 22*(3), 724–734.

3

Redefining Service: Robotics, Leadership, and the Green-Collar Revolution in the Hospitality Industry

Jeetesh Kumar and Praveena Nair Sivasankaran

3.1 Introduction

The hospitality industry is at a critical juncture where sustainability has become a fundamental imperative rather than a mere trend (Murphy, 2021). Hotels and restaurants are increasingly under pressure to align their operations with environmental responsibility, driven by regulatory pressures and a growing demand for consumer sustainable practices (Manaktola & Jauhari, 2007). The green-collar revolution is at the heart of this shift, transforming the industry by creating new opportunities for environmentally conscious professionals while pushing businesses to reduce their environmental footprint. Adopting sustainable practices helps mitigate the industry's environmental impact, enhances brand reputation, and offers long-term cost savings (Hotel Energy Solutions, 2023; Miller, 2013).

However, the path to sustainability in hospitality has its challenges. One of the most significant barriers is the high initial cost of implementing sustainable technologies and practices. Upgrading infrastructure, investing in renewable energy sources, and integrating energy-efficient systems require substantial upfront investment, which can be daunting, particularly for small- and medium-sized enterprises (Chan, 2013; GRI, 2023). Despite the potential for long-term savings, these initial costs often deter businesses from leaping to sustainability. However, financial incentives and government support can play a crucial role in helping businesses overcome these barriers, making sustainable solutions more accessible and feasible.

In addition to financial challenges, the hospitality industry needs help accurately measuring and reporting sustainability performance. The lack of

DOI: 10.1201/9781003742791-3

standardised metrics and reporting frameworks makes it difficult for businesses to track progress, ensure transparency, and compare their performance to industry standards (Gössling et al., 2012; Miller, 2013). Universal standards for sustainability measurement can help streamline this process and provide businesses with clear benchmarks for improvement.

Engaging guests in sustainable practices is another significant challenge. While many guests express concern for the environment, their behaviour often fails to align with them. Motivating guests to participate in sustainability initiatives requires effective communication and well-designed incentives. By educating guests about the environmental impact of their actions and offering rewards for eco-friendly behaviour, businesses can foster a culture of environmental responsibility among their clientele (Manaktola & Jauhari, 2007).

Despite these challenges, the green-collar revolution drives positive change in the hospitality industry. By embracing sustainability, businesses reduce their environmental impact and strengthen their competitive advantage in a market that increasingly values ethical practices. Sustainability in hospitality is not just about minimising harm; it is an opportunity for businesses to thrive while contributing to a more sustainable future for the industry and the planet. As the industry evolves, overcoming these challenges and embracing innovative solutions will pave the way for a more sustainable and responsible hospitality sector.

3.2 Robotics in the Hospitality Industry

The hospitality industry is embracing a new era of technological innovation with the integration of robotics. Driven by factors such as labour shortages, rising costs, and the demand for increased efficiency, robots are being deployed in hotels and restaurants worldwide to perform various tasks (Murphy, 2021). This integration is not merely a novelty but a strategic move to enhance operational efficiency, improve guest experiences, and address critical industry challenges.

3.2.1 Front of House: Where Robots Greet and Guide

The hospitality industry increasingly uses robots to enhance guest experiences, particularly in front-of-house roles. One prominent application is robot concierges, which provide guests with information and assistance. Equipped with touch screens and voice recognition capabilities, these robots can answer questions about hotel amenities, local attractions, and nearby restaurants. They can also provide directions, make reservations, and offer personalised recommendations based on guest preferences. For example, the Henn na Hotel in Japan gained widespread attention for using robot staff, including dinosaur robots at the front desk (Belanche et al., 2021). Similarly, Hilton Hotels has deployed a robot concierge named "Connie" at select properties. Connie uses artificial intelligence to provide information about the hotel and local area and learns from guest interactions to enhance its performance (Murphy, 2021).

Automation has also transformed the check-in and check-out processes in many hotels. Artificial intelligence (AI)-powered robots enable guests to register their arrival, receive room keys, and settle bills quickly and efficiently. This reduces wait times, improves efficiency, and frees up human staff for other tasks. Yotel, a hotel chain known for its tech-forward approach, uses self-service kiosks to automate these processes, providing guests with a novel and efficient experience (Lu et al., 2023).

Robots are also taking on the role of bellhops, ensuring a seamless arrival and departure experience for guests. Robot bellhops can autonomously transport luggage to and from guest rooms, navigate the hotel, and avoid obstacles. The Travelmate robot suitcase, which autonomously follows its owner, represents an early step towards fully autonomous robot bellhops (Ivanova, 2022).

3.2.2 Back of House: Streamlining Operations

Robots play a critical role in back-of-house operations in maintaining efficiency and consistency. Housekeeping robots, for instance, are automating cleaning tasks such as vacuuming, mopping, and dusting. These robots ensure high cleanliness standards while freeing human staff to focus on more detailed tasks and guest interactions. Companies like Maidbot have developed robots specialising in UV sanitation and room cleaning (Lu et al., 2023). Similarly, Savioke Relay robots are being used to deliver linens and other housekeeping items, significantly reducing the workload for staff (Ivanova, 2022).

In hotel and restaurant kitchens, robots are transforming food preparation. Robots such as Flippy by Miso Robotics can chop vegetables, flip burgers, and plate dishes quickly and accurately. This improves efficiency, minimises food waste, and ensures consistent food quality (Belanche et al., 2021). Additionally, robots equipped with sensors and cameras are being deployed for inventory management, enabling real-time monitoring of supplies. This automation reduces the risk of shortages, streamlines inventory processes, and minimises waste. Although not yet widespread, robots for inventory management are an emerging trend with the potential to enhance efficiency (Murphy, 2021) significantly.

3.2.3 Enhancing the Guest Experience

Robots are also reshaping how guests experience hospitality. Robot bartenders, for instance, have become increasingly popular in hotels and bars. These robots can create custom cocktails with precision, providing guests with a unique and entertaining experience while ensuring consistent drink quality. Makr Shakr, a company specialising in robotic bartending systems, produces robots capable of crafting a wide range of cocktails (Belanche et al., 2021).

Delivery robots are another innovation improving guest services. These robots deliver room service orders, amenities, and other items directly to guest rooms. This enhances efficiency and minimises human contact, a desirable feature in a post-pandemic world. Savioke's Relay robots are commonly used for in-hotel deliveries, offering contactless and efficient service (Ivanova, 2022).

Finally, entertainment robots are being employed to create memorable guest experiences. Some hotels use robots to perform dances, play music, or interact with guests engagingly. These robots, adapted from those used in theme parks and entertainment venues, add a touch of fun and surprise to hospitality settings, enhancing the overall guest experience (Murphy, 2021).

3.3 Leadership in a Technology-Driven Environment

Once characterised by its high-touch, personalised service, the hospitality industry rapidly evolved into a technology-driven landscape. This shift presents unique challenges and opportunities for sector leaders. Leaders can no longer solely rely on traditional management styles; they must now navigate a complex environment where AI, automation, and big data reshape operational models and guest expectations. This chapter delves into the key competencies and strategies for effective leadership in this technology-driven era.

3.3.1 Visionary Leadership: Embracing Technological Change

Leaders in the hospitality industry must possess a clear vision of how technology can be harnessed to elevate guest experiences, optimise operational efficiency, and propel business growth. This requires a deep understanding of emerging technologies, the foresight to anticipate future trends, and the courage to embrace innovation. Strategic thinking plays a critical role in this context. Developing a comprehensive technology strategy that aligns with the organisation's overarching business goals is paramount. Leaders must identify opportunities for innovation, prioritise investments in critical technologies, and ensure that technology is seamlessly integrated into all aspects of the business. For example, a hotel leader might invest in AI-powered chatbots to enhance customer service and personalise guest interactions. Such decisions should be based on a thorough analysis of the technology's potential benefits, costs, and implementation challenges (Shoubi, 2023).

The relentless pace of technological change also demands adaptability and agility from leaders. They must be willing to embrace new technologies, experiment with innovative solutions, and adjust their strategies as needed to maintain a competitive edge. For instance, adopting mobile check-in and digital keys exemplifies how leaders who quickly adapt to new technologies can improve guest satisfaction and streamline operations. Conversely, those who resist change risk falling behind their competitors (Murphy, 2021).

Additionally, leaders must harness technology-generated data to make informed decisions. This data provides invaluable insights into guest preferences, operational performance, and market trends. Practical data analysis allows leaders to personalise guest offerings and tailor services to individual needs. For instance, understanding guest preferences through data can lead to more customised experiences, while operational data can highlight areas for improvement and cost reduction, ensuring more efficient operations (Lu et al., 2023). By combining strategic thinking, adaptability, and data-driven decision-making, hospitality industry leaders can effectively navigate the technological landscape and ensure their organisations remain competitive and innovative.

3.4 Empowering and Engaging the Workforce in a Tech-Driven Era

Technology integration in the hospitality industry has profound implications for the workforce, requiring leaders to ensure that employees have the skills and knowledge necessary to thrive in this new environment. At the same time, leaders must address potential anxieties about job displacement. As technology automates routine tasks, there is a growing need for upskilling and reskilling employees in data analysis, digital marketing, and customer relationship management. By investing in training programmes, leaders can empower their employees to adapt to the changing demands of the industry. For instance, hotels might implement training initiatives to help staff learn how to use new software systems, interpret data analytics, or manage social media platforms effectively (Shoubi, 2023).

In addition to technical training, leaders must foster a culture of innovation within their organisations. This involves creating a workplace environment that encourages experimentation, continuous learning, and the sharing of ideas. Employees should feel empowered to take risks and embrace new technologies. For example, organisations might implement internal innovation challenges, provide opportunities for staff to attend technology conferences, or encourage employees to propose creative ways to leverage technology in their roles (Belanche et al., 2021).

Effective communication and collaboration are also critical in a technology-driven workplace. Leaders must ensure that employees have access to the information they need and establish clear channels for communication and feedback. Regular meetings, online forums, and structured feedback mechanisms can help keep employees informed about technological changes and their impact on roles and responsibilities. By fostering open communication and collaboration, leaders can create a supportive environment where employees feel engaged and prepared to navigate the evolving technological landscape (Murphy, 2021).

3.5 Ethical Considerations and Responsible Leadership in the Digital Age

The use of technology in the hospitality industry raises important ethical considerations that leaders must address proactively and transparently. One critical issue is data privacy and security. Leaders are responsible for safeguarding guest data and ensuring it is used ethically and responsibly. This requires implementing robust data privacy and security measures and complying with relevant regulations such as GDPR and CCPA. Hotels should invest in secure data storage systems, adopt data encryption protocols, and train staff on best practices for handling guest data (Lu et al., 2023).

Another significant concern is algorithmic bias and fairness. AI algorithms can inadvertently perpetuate biases and inequalities if not carefully designed and monitored. Leaders must recognise these risks and take active steps to mitigate them, ensuring that algorithms are fair and unbiased and do not discriminate against any group of guests. This may involve regularly auditing algorithms for bias, using diverse datasets to train AI systems, and establishing clear guidelines for the ethical use of AI in decision-making processes (Belanche et al., 2021).

Transparency and accountability are equally crucial in the ethical use of technology. Leaders must be open about how technology is utilised within their organisations and take responsibility for its impacts on employees, guests, and society. This could include publishing ethical guidelines for technology use, clearly communicating with guests about how their data is being handled and engaging in open dialogue with employees regarding the effects of technology on their roles and responsibilities. By addressing these ethical challenges proactively, leaders can foster trust and ensure that technological advancements in the hospitality industry benefit all stakeholders (Shoubi, 2023).

3.6 Leading the Way: Future Directions for Tech-Savvy Leaders

As technology evolves at an unprecedented pace, the role of leadership in the hospitality industry will become even more critical. Leaders must proactively anticipate future trends, embrace innovation, and shape the industry's trajectory. A key area of focus is sustainability and technology. Leaders must explore how technology can be harnessed to promote sustainability by reducing energy consumption, minimising waste, and encouraging eco-friendly practices. This might involve implementing intelligent energy management systems, leveraging technology to optimise water usage, and promoting sustainable transportation options for guests (Ivanova, 2022).

Another emerging frontier is the metaverse and virtual hospitality, which presents unique opportunities for creating immersive and engaging guest experiences. Leaders must consider how virtual and augmented reality can enhance service offerings, such as virtual hotel tours, immersive dining experiences, or virtual concierge services that provide personalised recommendations and assistance (Murphy, 2021).

The seamless integration of humans and robots is also central to the future of hospitality. Leaders must foster a collaborative environment where human and robotic capabilities are combined to deliver exceptional guest experiences. This requires thoughtful task allocation, ensuring that robots complement human skills while enhancing efficiency and service quality. By striking the right balance, leaders can ensure that technological advancements support operational goals and elevate the overall guest experience (Lu et al., 2023).

3.7 The Green-Collar Revolution and Sustainable Hospitality Practices

The hospitality industry, a significant contributor to global resource consumption and waste generation, faces mounting pressure to embrace sustainability. The "green-collar revolution" signifies a shift towards environmentally conscious operations and a growing demand for skilled professionals who can implement and manage these sustainable initiatives. This chapter explores the concept of the green-collar revolution in hospitality, examines its impact on the industry, and outlines critical sustainable practices.

3.8 The Rise of Green-Collar Jobs in Hospitality

The green-collar revolution in the hospitality industry is not merely about adopting new technologies and practices but about fostering a transformative mindset prioritising sustainability. This shift involves building a workforce equipped with the knowledge and skills necessary to implement and manage sustainable practices across all aspects of hotel and restaurant operations (Manaktola & Jauhari, 2007).

Green hospitality specialists play a vital role in this revolution. They are responsible for developing and implementing comprehensive sustainability strategies, conducting environmental audits, and ensuring compliance with environmental regulations. These professionals often train staff on sustainable practices and raise awareness among guests. By analysing a hotel's operations, they identify areas for improvement and develop strategies to minimise environmental impact (Bohdanowicz, 2005).

Sustainable food and beverage managers focus on sourcing sustainable ingredients, minimising food waste, and implementing eco-friendly practices in kitchens and restaurants. Their work often involves developing menus featuring local and organic produce, reducing reliance on lengthy and unsustainable supply chains (Gössling et al., 2012). Energy efficiency experts contribute by optimising energy consumption in hotels and restaurants. They conduct energy audits, implement energy-saving technologies, and train staff on conservation practices. Their expertise encompasses identifying and deploying energy-efficient solutions, including advanced lighting systems, HVAC optimisation, and efficient kitchen equipment and water heating systems (Becken, 2002).

Water conservation specialists address the growing global concern of water scarcity by implementing strategies to reduce water consumption. These strategies include installing low-flow fixtures, employing rainwater harvesting systems, and educating staff and guests about water conservation. Their efforts are essential in promoting responsible water management within hotels and resorts, ensuring the sustainability of operations in water-stressed regions (UNEP, 2003).

3.9 Sustainable Hospitality Practices: A Holistic Approach

Sustainable hospitality encompasses a wide range of practices aimed at minimising environmental impact, conserving resources, and promoting social responsibility. One key area of focus is energy efficiency, where hotels and restaurants are adopting various measures to reduce their energy consumption. These efforts include the use of energy-efficient lighting and appliances, the implementation of intelligent energy management systems, and the optimisation of heating and cooling systems. Many establishments strive to achieve certifications such as LEED (Leadership in Energy and Environmental Design), which provides a framework for sustainable building design and operation and is a testament to their commitment to sustainability (U.S. Green Building Council, 2023).

Water conservation is another critical component of sustainable hospitality. Hotels employ strategies such as installing low-flow showerheads and toilets, using drought-tolerant landscaping, and reusing greywater for irrigation. Initiatives like the Hotel Water Management Initiative by the World Travel & Tourism Council offer guidelines and resources to support hotels in implementing these practices effectively (WTTC, 2012).

Waste reduction and management are also essential to sustainable hospitality. Hotels and restaurants are implementing composting programmes, recycling initiatives, and strategies to reduce food waste. Organisations such as the Sustainable Hospitality Alliance provide resources and guidance to help these establishments minimise their environmental impact through effective waste management strategies (Sustainable Hospitality Alliance, 2023). Sustainable sourcing is becoming increasingly crucial as hotels and restaurants prioritise purchasing food and other products from local and sustainable suppliers. This approach reduces transportation costs, supports local communities, and minimises the environmental impact of supply chains. The farm-to-table movement, for instance, is gaining traction in the hospitality industry, with many restaurants incorporating locally sourced ingredients into their menus (Cole, 2013). Engaging guests in sustainability initiatives is crucial for fostering a culture of environmental responsibility. Hotels are implementing various strategies to educate and involve guests in their efforts. These include providing information through in-room brochures, offering incentives for participation in sustainability programmes, and organising eco-friendly activities and tours. Such initiatives help guests actively contribute to sustainability goals while enhancing their overall experience (Chan, 2013).

3.10 The Business Case for Sustainable Hospitality

Implementing sustainable practices in the hospitality industry can lead to significant cost savings over time. These practices help reduce energy and water bills, minimise waste disposal costs, and improve operational efficiency, making them a financially beneficial choice for hotels and restaurants (Hotel Energy Solutions, 2023). In addition to financial benefits, sustainability enhances a business's brand reputation. Consumers increasingly prefer businesses committed to environmental responsibility, and adopting sustainable practices can attract environmentally conscious guests while positioning the establishment as a leader in sustainability (UNWTO, 2017).

Sustainability also plays a vital role in boosting employee morale. Employees often feel more engaged and motivated when working for a company that values environmental responsibility. Implementing green initiatives can create a sense of purpose among staff and attract talent passionate about sustainability and environmental stewardship (Wong, 2012). The most critical benefit of sustainable hospitality is its positive environmental impact. By reducing their environmental footprint, hotels and restaurants contribute to preserving natural resources and mitigating the effects of climate change, underscoring their role in promoting environmental stewardship (IPCC, 2022).

3.11 Challenges and Future Directions

Overcoming the initial costs of implementing sustainable technologies and practices remains a significant challenge for many hospitality businesses. The upfront investment required to upgrade infrastructure, adopt renewable energy sources, or integrate sustainable systems can be a barrier. However, many of these solutions offer substantial long-term cost savings and can be adopted incrementally. Financial incentives and government support also play a crucial role in helping businesses overcome these initial hurdles, making sustainability more accessible and feasible (UNEP, 2011).

Another challenge lies in accurately measuring and reporting sustainability performance. The need for standardised metrics and reporting frameworks can make it difficult for businesses to ensure transparency and accountability. Developing and adopting universal standards for measuring sustainability can help streamline this process and provide businesses with clear benchmarks for improvement (GRI, 2023). Engaging guests in sustainable practices is equally challenging. Effective communication strategies and well-designed incentives are essential to motivate guests to participate in sustainability initiatives. By educating guests about the environmental impact of their actions and offering rewards for eco-friendly behaviour, businesses can foster a culture of environmental responsibility among their clientele (Miller, 2013).

The green-collar revolution transforms the hospitality industry by shifting towards sustainable practices and creating opportunities for environmentally conscious professionals. By embracing sustainability, hotels and restaurants reduce their environmental impact, enhance their brand reputation, and contribute to a more sustainable future for the industry and the planet.

3.11.1 Challenges and Future Directions: Navigating the Evolving Landscape of Sustainable Hospitality

While the hospitality industry strives towards sustainability, the journey is fraught with challenges. This chapter explores the key obstacles hindering the widespread adoption of sustainable practices. It outlines future directions for the industry to overcome these challenges and achieve greater environmental and social responsibility.

3.11.2 Challenges to Sustainable Hospitality

Economic barriers remain among the most significant challenges to implementing sustainable technologies and practices in the hospitality industry. The upfront costs of upgrading infrastructure, investing in renewable energy sources, and establishing waste management systems can be particularly daunting for small and medium-sized enterprises (SMEs). These substantial initial investments often deter businesses from adopting sustainable practices despite their long-term benefits (UNEP, 2011).

Another obstacle is the need for more awareness and knowledge within the industry. Many hospitality businesses are unaware of their operations' environmental and social impacts and lack information about sustainable solutions and best practices. This knowledge gap hinders the adoption of sustainability and fosters scepticism about its effectiveness and feasibility (Bohdanowicz, 2005).

Measuring and reporting on sustainability performance poses additional challenges. The absence of standardised metrics and reporting frameworks makes it difficult for businesses to compare their performance across the industry, hindering transparency and accountability. This complexity can be time-consuming and resource-intensive, discouraging businesses from pursuing rigorous sustainability reporting (GRI, 2023).

Guest behaviour and expectations also play a critical role in adopting sustainable practices. While many guests express concern for the environment, their behaviours often fail to align with these values. Effective communication and incentives are essential to motivate guests to participate in sustainability initiatives, but achieving this alignment remains challenging (Chan, 2013).

The complexity of supply chains further complicates sustainability efforts in hospitality. Hotels and restaurants often depend on a network of suppliers, making ensuring adherence to sustainable practices challenging. Collaboration, transparency, and effective monitoring across the supply chain require significant effort and coordination (Gössling et al., 2012).

Finally, technological barriers also pose challenges. The rapid pace of technological change can be brutal for businesses to keep up with. Integrating new technologies into existing systems often involves high costs and complexity, creating hesitation among businesses despite the potential benefits (Murphy, 2021). To overcome these challenges, financial incentives, government support, and innovative financing models can help businesses address economic barriers. Public-private partnerships, green bonds, and tax credits can provide the necessary resources to invest in sustainable solutions (UNEP, 2011). Increasing awareness and education is also critical. Industry associations, educational institutions, and government agencies should actively raise awareness and provide training on sustainable hospitality practices. Workshops, training programmes, and online resources can help disseminate this knowledge and build capacity within the industry (Manaktola & Jauhari, 2007).

Standardising metrics and reporting frameworks enhance transparency and accountability. Clear benchmarks can help businesses track progress, compare performance with industry standards, and communicate achievements to stakeholders (GRI, 2023). Engaging guests in sustainability initiatives is another vital area of focus. Strategies like gamification, personalised feedback, and reward programmes can make sustainability initiatives engaging and encourage eco-friendly behaviour among guests (Miller, 2013). Building sustainable supply chains requires collaboration and transparency. Hotels and restaurants should work closely with suppliers, set clear sustainability standards, provide training and support, and implement traceability systems to ensure adherence to green practices (Cole, 2013). Leveraging technology is also essential for sustainability. Advanced tools like AI, big data analytics, and the Internet of Things (IoT) can optimise energy consumption, reduce waste, and improve resource management (Lu et al., 2023).

Promoting circular economy models provides another practical framework for sustainable hospitality. Businesses can minimise waste and maximise resource utilisation by reducing, reusing, and recycling materials and designing products and services for durability and longevity (UNWTO, 2017). Embracing biomimicry and nature-based solutions further enhances sustainability efforts. Inspired by nature's designs, solutions such as green roofs and vertical gardens can mitigate the environmental impact of buildings while creating healthier and more sustainable environments for guests and employees (Benyus, 1997).

3.12 Conclusion

The hospitality industry is undergoing a profound transformation, driven by the increasing necessity for sustainable practices that address environmental, social, and economic concerns. Integrating sustainability into the industry's core operations, from waste management and energy efficiency to sustainable sourcing and eco-friendly design, is a passing trend and a long-term shift reflecting broader societal changes. The green-collar revolution is a crucial force behind this transformation, creating new roles and opportunities for environmentally conscious professionals while pushing businesses to embrace sustainability. As this evolution unfolds, it becomes increasingly evident that sustainability in hospitality is not only about reducing the negative impact of operations but also about unlocking new avenues for growth and success.

The challenges of adopting sustainable practices in the hospitality industry are significant but manageable. Economic barriers, particularly the high upfront costs of implementing green technologies, remain one of the primary obstacles. For many small- and medium-sized businesses, these costs can be a deterrent despite the long-term savings associated with energy efficiency and waste reduction. However, there is a growing recognition that financial incentives, government subsidies, and innovative financing models, such as green bonds and public-private partnerships, can help ease these burdens. Moreover, businesses can adopt sustainable practices incrementally, balancing financial considerations with environmental objectives, ensuring sustainability is within reach for even the most resource-constrained organisations.

Another significant challenge is standardised metrics and frameworks for measuring sustainability performance. With clear and universally recognised standards, businesses can track their progress, ensure transparency, and communicate their achievements to stakeholders. Developing and adopting universal reporting frameworks for sustainability is essential for driving consistent improvement and facilitating sharing best practices. Such frameworks would allow businesses to benchmark their performance against industry standards, fostering a culture of accountability and continuous improvement. Additionally, establishing universal metrics will create a level playing field, helping consumers decide which businesses are committed to sustainability.

Engaging guests in sustainability initiatives also presents a considerable challenge. Although many guests express concern for environmental issues, their behaviour often contradicts their stated values, especially regarding actions like conserving water, reducing waste, or participating in sustainability programmes. This disconnect can be addressed through effective communication strategies emphasising the importance of sustainable actions and providing clear participation incentives. By offering rewards, discounts, or other incentives for eco-friendly behaviour, businesses can motivate guests to align their actions with their environmental values. Furthermore, educating guests about the environmental impact of their choices can foster a sense of responsibility and encourage them to embrace sustainability as part of their travel experience.

Supply chain management is another critical area where sustainability efforts often face challenges. The complexity and scale of supply chains in the hospitality industry make it difficult to ensure suppliers adhere to sustainable practices. Achieving sustainability throughout the supply chain requires effective coordination, transparency, and a commitment to shared goals. Hotels and restaurants must work closely with suppliers to set clear sustainability standards, provide necessary training, and implement traceability systems to monitor progress. Collaboration and openness are crucial to overcoming these challenges, ensuring that sustainability is embedded in business operations and sourcing products and services.

Technology also holds immense potential to drive sustainability in the hospitality industry. Innovations such as energy-efficient systems, intelligent technologies, and data analytics tools can help businesses optimise resource management, reduce waste, and improve energy efficiency. The rapid pace of technological advancement presents both an opportunity and a challenge for businesses, as integrating new technologies into existing infrastructure can be costly and complex. However, leveraging these technologies can lead to long-term benefits, including lower operational costs and a reduced environmental footprint. Furthermore, emerging technologies such as AI and IoT offer new ways to monitor and manage sustainability in real-time, enabling businesses to make data-driven decisions that enhance efficiency and performance.

Promoting circular economy models offers a comprehensive solution to many sustainability challenges in hospitality. By adopting practices focused on reducing, reusing, and recycling materials, businesses can minimise waste, reduce their environmental impact, and contribute to a more sustainable economy. Additionally, embracing biomimicry and nature-based solutions, such as green roofs or vertical gardens, can enhance sustainability by incorporating natural processes into the built environment. These approaches reduce the carbon footprint of buildings and create healthier, more enjoyable spaces for guests and employees alike.

References

Becken, S. (2002). Tourists' perception of international air travel's impact on the global climate and potential climate change policies. *Journal of Sustainable Tourism, 10*(4), 351–368.

Belanche, D., Casaló, L. V., & Flavián, C. (2021). Artificial intelligence in tourism and hospitality: A bibliometric analysis and future research directions. *Journal of Business Research, 134*, 408–421.

Benyus, J. M. (1997). *Biomimicry: Innovation inspired by nature.* William Morrow & Company.

Bohdanowicz, P. (2005). European hoteliers' environmental attitudes: Greening the business. *Cornell Hotel and Restaurant Administration Quarterly, 46*(2), 188–204.

Bots assisting in hotels. (2016, March 10). Ongoing Information & Trends: A Weblog. https://landbars.wordpress.com/2016/03/10/bots-assisting-in-hotels/

Chan, E. S. W. (2013). Managing green marketing strategy performance. *Journal of Marketing Management, 29*(3–4), 318–336.
Cole, M. T. (2013). Farm-to-table: Environmental sustainability practices in restaurants. *Journal of Culinary Science & Technology, 11*(4), 339–354.
Gössling, S., Hall, C. M., & Scott, D. (2012). The evolution of sustainability in tourism. *Journal of Sustainable Tourism, 20*(8), 1009–1020.
GRI. (2023). *GRI Standards.* https://www.globalreporting.org/standards/
Hotel Energy Solutions. (2023). *Hotel energy efficiency solutions.* https://www.unwto.org/hotel-energy-solution
IPCC. (2022). *Climate change 2022: Impacts, adaptation and vulnerability.* Cambridge University Press.
Ivanova, M. (2022). Robots in the hospitality industry: A review of current applications and future trends. *Journal of Tourism Futures, 8*(1), 102–112.
Lu, V. N., Wirtz, J., & Kunz, W. H. (2023). Service robots in the hospitality industry: A review and research agenda. *International Journal of Hospitality Management, 108,* 103364.
Manaktola, K., & Jauhari, V. (2007). Exploring consumer attitude and behaviour towards green practices in the lodging industry in India. *International Journal of Contemporary Hospitality Management, 19*(5), 364–377.
Miller, G. (2013). The business of sustainable tourism: A case study approach. *Journal of Sustainable Tourism, 21*(1), 124–142.
Murphy, J. (2021). The role of artificial intelligence in the hospitality industry. *Worldwide Hospitality and Tourism Themes, 13*(3), 311–322.
Shoubi, A. M. (2023). The impact of artificial intelligence on the hospitality industry: Opportunities, challenges and future research directions. *International Journal of Contemporary Hospitality Management, 35*(3), 1067–1086.
Sustainable Hospitality Alliance. (2023). *Sustainable hospitality resources.* https://sustainablehospitalityalliance.org/
U.S. Green Building Council. (2023). *LEED.* https://www.usgbc.org/
UNEP. (2003). *Tourism and freshwater.* United Nations Environment Programme. UNEP. (2011). *Towards a green economy: Pathways to sustainable development and poverty eradication.* United Nations Environment Programme.
UNWTO. (2017). *Tourism and the sustainable development goals – journey to 2030.* World Tourism Organization.Wong, S. L. (2012). The influence of green practices on employee engagement. *International Journal of Hospitality Management, 31*(2), 574–582.
WTTC. (2012). *Hotel Water Management Initiative.*
YOTEL New York Times Square. (n.d.). YOTEL. https://www.yotel.com/en/hotels/yotel-new-york

4

An Empirical Study on the Impact of Social Media on Customer Decisions: In the Perspective of Hotel Guest

Santosh Kumar Bisoi

4.1 Introduction

In recent years, social media marketing has grown in popularity and attracted a lot of attention from the press all around the world. According to the New York Times prominent blogs recently assisted in increasing business sales from $100,000 to $4 million, demonstrating the power of social media (Jaret, 2006). The current surge in marketing skills through social media has been aided by technological advancements. The behaviour of Internet users has altered considerably as a result of Web 2.0. Previously, most websites were personal and static, and they were created by the site owner with the intent that users simply read the content. Web 2.0, however, includes websites and users that are dynamic, interactive, and collaborative. Despite the fact that social media is still a relatively new medium, its global popularity is undeniable. "According to comScore (2008, 2009a, 2009b) social media penetration in the United States reached 70.2%, 74.6% in Europe, and 60.6% in Asia Pacific, respectively". Companies can no longer rely entirely on traditional media for marketing, and merely transferring tangible sales materials to the Internet is no longer acceptable. Businesses must learn how to engage their customers through interactive media can be used to build brand loyalty among members of a community with customer relationships, and online sales channels if correctly managed (Chan & Guillet, 2011).

 DOI: 10.1201/9781003742791-4

4.1.1 The Hotel Industry and Social Media Marketing

Branding opportunities abound in social media marketing. Brand awareness, consumer research, cloud sourcing, identifying opinion leaders, increasing traffic to branded websites, spreading the virality of certain messages, creating consumer databases, and brand credibility are all aspects of social media marketing, aids in the development of trust and the enhancement of your brand photographs (tots, 2008). According to Chan and Guillet (2011), hotels advertise their services and products on Facebook, Twitter, and other social media platforms, offering discounts and promotions to encourage new clients. Customer feedback, sweepstakes, and complaint resolution were all popular activities. In addition to Facebook and Twitter, the hotel sector uses 38.8% of YouTube, 26.9% of Flickr, and 23.9% of Trip Advisor as well as other social networking sites. The hotel for the most part utilised YouTube to show commercials that featured the company's peculiarity and acquainted clients with its items and administrations (Chan & Guillet, 2011). Numerous lodgings utilised Flickr to show pictures of their insides. Simply 24% of inns answered to client audits on TripAdvisor, with 75% of these organisations giving customised reactions (Chan & Guillet, 2011).

4.1.2 Online Reviews

With 11.7% of global GDP, tourism is one of the most important industries on the planet. Travel journals are particularly popular on the Internet, which is playing an increasingly important role in vacation preparation. Customers can offer qualitative and quantitative comments about their travel experiences on different platform like Trip Advisor, Travelocity, and Frommers. The data was gathered in order to produce an overall quality and satisfaction rating. The rise of user content on travel websites has an impact on visitor behaviour and decision-making. Participants believe that traveller ratings are less biased and easier to comprehend than expert reviews, according to an electronic word-of-mouth poll (Thevenot, 2007).

All forms of social media marketing should be used to increase brand awareness, analyse customer comments, and crowd source ideas, as well as drive visitors to branded websites. Furthermore, social media marketing is crucial in the travel and hotel industry. Hotel management may use social media to gain immediate, direct feedback from their consumers in order to better understand their requirements and wishes. Social media, however, might have negative implications. The hotel owner is unable to handle the "blog" of online reviews. A single poor TripAdvisor review from a disgruntled customer might be detrimental to your business. The goal of this study was to see if clients understand marketing material from social media differently than marketing information from traditional Internet sources.

The survey questions below were taken into consideration:

Q1: How does having a customer blog improve a hotel's website's perception?

Q2: Does the type of comment (positive or negative) on a customer's blog have an impact on how the hotel website is perceived?

4.2 Review of Literature

4.2.1 Social Media

A chatty, flexible, and participatory online network, social media is a conversational, flexible, and participatory online network. Members of these types of communities can publish, control, assess, criticise, develop, and engage with online content. "The term social media encompasses social news, book marketing sites, virtual worlds, forums, and opinion sites (Tuten, 2008)". Hotel brands are gaining a lot of attention on social media sites like Twitter and Facebook. Hotels and resorts not only set up their own accounts, but they also link to third-party sites like Hotels.com and Trip Advisor to respond to client feedback and market conditions. Customers may be able to locate a variety of prices and find exactly what they are looking for other information's available to both business and leisure travellers in the personal computer (Mckay, 2010).

4.2.2 Social Media Marketing and Its Effects

The Internet boom burst in 2001 changed the way people share knowledge. From static billboards to increasingly dynamic and interactive billboards, websites have evolved.

> According to comScore (2008, 2009a, 2009b), social media has become a must-see marketing tool among Internet users, with penetration rates of 70.2 percent in the United States, 74.6 percent in Europe, and 60.6 percent in Asia. Increase Social media marketing has earned a range of reputations in Hong Kong, where 29.5 million visitors generated US $159 billion in 2008.
>
> **(Hong Kong Travel Development Bureau, 2008; Chan & Guillet, 2011)**

The author chose 67 numbers of hotels based on their brand, as well as their website and social media presence. The most popular social media network in the sector is Twitter, which received 56.7% of votes, followed by Facebook, which received 53.7%. Hotels, however, are more likely to use Facebook. This is most likely due to microblogging's limited use and utility of words. These websites' most common purpose is to promote exclusive hotel deals. With 38.8%, 26.9%, and 23.9%, respectively, YouTube, Flickr, and Trip Advisor are the hotel's second most popular websites. YouTube is primarily used to market hotel facilities and their distinguishing features, whereas Flickr is primarily used to post photographs of hotel facilities. Hotels also rely on TripAdvisor for client feedback with 75% of responding to reviews in a personalised manner. However, different kinds of social media remain largely untouched (Chan & Guillet, 2011). The online poll had 374 responses, with 69% of female respondents and an average audience age of 27. All of the hypotheses turned out to be true. In contrast to the more rigorous frameworks of online magazines, the success of blogs can be linked to the information of organic interactions between readers and bloggers. Even though the opinions expressed in a blogs are considered more readily acknowledged, they appear to misrepresent the same opinion. Marketers must rely on reputable blogs to create the right type of ad and reach their target audience (Thevenot, 2007).

4.2.3 The Purchasing Power of Social Media

The usage of social media as a source of purchasing power has increased. Over 3 million people are online, according to the storey. The role of social platform in finding travel information online, which means brands and organisations have more opportunities to communicate on-line. A website for social networking, people have always wished to be connected, and the Internet allows them to do so in a variety of ways that were previously unavailable. Companies are now attempting to boost brand awareness and direct engagement with customers through social media. Because of the invention of inter-connected mobile devices and the expansion of broadband connectivity, people are becoming more active on social media (Xiang & Gretzel, 2010).

4.2.4 The Influence of Social Media on Branding

Hotels.com has realised that the importance of blogs in boosting revenues when booking a single trip rather than a package. Because Brazilians still enjoy packages, the company enlisted the help of prominent travel blogger Ricardo Freiré to serve as the country's ambassador. According to Hotels.com, Ricardo's video series Unpacking garnered over a million views on YouTube as he went to his destination and illustrated the advantages of purchasing flights and hotels separately, as well as the incredible value you can obtain (Smith, 2011). Despite the widespread use of social media, little research has been done on the impact of blogging material on hotel school ability.

The following hypotheses can be offered to test this:

H1: After reading a favourable storey about a hotel on a blog, website visitors will be more interested in staying there.

H2: Visitors to a website are likely to believe a positive view from a blog.

H3: Website visitors are less inclined to stay at a hotel after reading a negative review on a blog.

4.3 Methods

4.3.1 Population

Middle-class the study's target population was determined to be Americans. A university's personnel in the Midwest of the United States are kind and approachable. The facility is located in a rural hamlet of approximately 10,000 inhabitants. The total number of students, instructors, and staff on campus is around 7,225. On campus, there are 503 employees and 247 faculty members.

4.3.2 Sample

Faculty and staff have been invited to participate in the study. The entire 750-person reachable population was picked at random and divided into three survey groups, each of which was instructed to visit a different website prior to finishing the questionnaire (hotel website, integrated blog, etc.). After the survey, a total of 94 responses were received. The hotel's website party drew 40 people (18 men and 22 women). There are 25 people in the active blog group (7 men, 18 women). There are 30 people in the mixed blog group (9 men, 21 women). Table 4.1 shows the age, income, and degree of education of the respondents.

4.3.3 Instrumentation

The survey consisted of several sections, including demographic information, perceived trust, card reliability, and future usage or referral intentions. The demographic section included five questions covering gender, age, education level, family size, and household income. In addition, six questions were designed to evaluate factors that influence cognitive perception, such as price, cleanliness, convenience of location, previous experiences, and comfort. These factors were rated on a scale from 1 to 5, where 1 represented the most important factor and 5 represented the least important. The survey also included questions measuring the likelihood that respondents would use the service in the future or recommend it to friends. Furthermore, items were included to assess awareness of incomplete aspects and perceived reliability, with two

Table 4.1 Shows the gender, age, income, and degree of education of the respondents

	Website of Hotel (%)	Positive Group Blog (%)	Mixed Group Blog (%)
Gender	M: 45	M: 28	M: 30
	F:55	F: 72	F: 70
Age	22–29: 7.6	22–29: 18.0	22–29: 10.5
	30–39: 15.4	30–39: 23.0	30–39: 21.1
	40–49: 12.2	40–49: 6.4	40–49: 44.7
	50–59: 40.8	50–59: 39.7	50–59: 10.5
	60 and above: 24.1	60 and above: 12.1	60 and above: 13.2
Education	Graduation: 22.3	Graduation: 42.9	Graduation: 38.4
	PG: 35.7	PG: 29.4	PG: 34.6
	PhD: 29.2	PhD: 17.3	PhD: 16.7
	Professional: 13.8	Professional: 10.5	Professional: 10.3
Members of household	26	19	23.5
	48	27	2–28.5
	3 or more – 24	3 or more – 44	3 or more – 48
Household income	$10,000–$19,999: 0.0	$10,000–$19,999: 0.0	$10,000–$19,999: 0.0
	$20,000–$29,999: 4.9	$20,000–$29,999: 5.3	$20,000–$29,999: 5.3
	$30,000–$39,999: 1.0	$30,000–$39,999: 7.2	$30,000–$39,999: 5.3
	$40,000–$49,999: 3.9	$40,000–$49,999: 5.1	$40,000–$49,999: 13.2
	$50,000–$74,999: 33.3	$50,000–$74,999: 32.4	$50,000–$74,999: 36.8
	$75,000–$99,999: 39.2	$75,000–$99,999: 14.4	$75,000–$99,999: 15.8
	$100,000–$150,000: 12.7	$100,000–$150,000: 26	$100,000–$150,000: 21
	Over 150,000: 4.9	Over 150,000: 9.6	Over 150,000: 2.6

Shows the gender, age, income, and degree of education of the respondents

questions dedicated to each construct. All attitudinal questions used a five-point Likert scale ranging from 1 (strongly disagree) to 5 (strongly agree).

4.3.4 Procedures

After gaining the university's review board's approval, the researcher received an email from the personnel of the university's assessment office. Three distinct randomly assigned groups received questionnaires along with a request to participate in the study. Despite the fact that the content of the websites presented is fraudulent, participants are not notified that the hotel and blogs are fictitious (fictitious). After the email is sent, data is collected for five days. A response rate of 13% was achieved with this method.

4.3.5 Research Design and Data Analysis

Survey approaches were used to evaluate study themes and hypotheses in this descriptive project. The association between social media type and participants' evaluations of the information provided and the hotel was explored using analysis of variance (ANOVA). On the basis of demographics, bias and reliability perceptions, and greater likelihood referral to a friend, the groups were compared. Item 6, referencing price, facilities, site cleanliness, and precedent, was not evaluated due to formatting concerns when creating an online survey. Item 6's legality and validity were called into question; hence it was decided to leave it out of the study. Hypothesis testing's considered significant when the probability is less than 0.05.

4.4 Results

4.4.1 Descriptive Statistics

Means and standard deviations can be used to describe the generalisability of responses to research hypothesis-related questions. As demonstrated in Table 4.2 to Table 4.9, the study's research hypothesis is directly related to the survey questions about the biased character of content, the dependability of information, the possibility of a hotel stay being described, and the chance of recommending the hotel. The online group exhibited the highest perception of bias, with an average of 4.475 (SD = 0.5986) on a scale of 1–5. (5 points = agreement with the bias of the site). The Positive blog group obtained a score of 4.4 (SD = 0.6455) on the bias scale, whereas mixed blog group received a score of 4.5 (SD = 0.5724) see Table 4.2. The hotel website group recorded a mean score of 4.375 (SD = 0.6675), while the mixed blog group had a mean score of 4.3667 (SD = 0.6687), and the other active blog group obtained 4.44 (SD = 0.5831), as shown in Table 4.4. In Table 4.6, the hotel website achieved the highest mean score of 4.475 (SD = 0.5986), followed by the present blog group with 4.4 (SD = 0.6455), whereas the mixed blog group had a mean of 3.0 (SD = 0.0). Furthermore, according to Table 4.8, the hotel website again received a high rating with a mean of 4.375 (SD = 0.6675), followed by the present blog group with 4.44 (SD = 0.5831), while the mixed blog group recorded a lower mean score of 3.4 (SD = 0.5632).

4.4.2 Hypothesis Tests

An ANOVA was used to compare 3 groups on each of the 4 items to see if the observed difference was significant. In terms of biased content evaluations, the results revealed no significant differences between groups ($F = 0.2007$, $p = .818515$; see Table 4.2). However, there was a significant difference between the groups in terms of reliability ($F = 0.10491$, $p = 0.900515$; see Table 4.4). The online group got a substantially higher reliability rating than the present blog group, according to post hoc test (see Table 4.3, 4.5, 4.7, 4.9). The mixed blogging group was very similar to the other two. On the

TABLE 4.2

Bias: Mean and Standard Deviation

Summary of Data						
	Bias					
	Website of Hotel	*Positive Group Blog*	*Mixed Group Blog*	*4*	*5*	*Total*
N	40	25	30			95
ΣX	179	110	135			424
Mean	4.475	4.4	4.5			4.463
ΣX^2	815	494	617			1926
Std.Dev.	0.5986	0.6455	0.5724			0.5981
Result Details						
Source		*SS*	*df*	*MS*		
Between-Group		0.1461	2	0.073		F = 0.2007
Within-Group		33.475	92	0.3639		
Total		33.6211	94			

The f ratio value is 0.2007. The p-value is.818515.
Hence the result is not significant at $p < .05$.

intend to stay question, the other groups was significant (F = 82.53038, p = 0.0001; see Table 4.6). There was a significant difference between the different groups (F = 27.26934, p = 0.0001; see Table 4.8)

4.5 Discussion

Although the information published on social networking sites has undoubtedly had a significant impact on consumer behaviour, there are some limitations to this study. For example, successfully employing social networking sites could increase consumer desire to learn more about their products and services in order to gain a better knowledge, reducing the need for consumers to hunt for additional information. Consumers, however, are likely to have a better probability of being persuaded. Consumers can be targeted via social networking sites in a variety of ways, including based on their wealth and activity. When the market is focused on consumer income, the corporation is actually limiting its ability to offer its products and services to more consumers who have either a lower or higher income than the targeted income. It is possible that other sources or factors, in addition to observing customer behaviour, are influencing sales or the market, as there are other sources or variables that may improve sales. The results of the observations of the consumers' behaviours may fall into a category that defines the characteristics of a social generation, but not the other generations. As a result, the other people who fall under the other generations are overlooked; this could be why the targeted consumers are ignored. Because individuals like to experience items rather than search for them, a corporation might be able to persuade loyal customers to share their testimonies and experiences with products and services in exchange for rewards. For example, on their websites, they may provide particular benefits to their fans. Consumers appreciate the ability to share their positive experience with the brand as an individual. Furthermore, many Internet users have developed a natural "habit" of wanting to share their joy online with other Internet users all around the world. This technique helps the organisation retain existing customers, acquire new customers, and raise brand recognition. The hotel website group, with an average of 3.54, had the highest perception of bias, followed by the mixed blog group, with an average of 3.00, and the active group, with an average of 2.86. The hotel website received the highest score for the statement I trust the information provided on this website, followed by the mixed blog. These findings disprove the theory that a traveller is more likely to believe a positive blog post. Even if the words themselves are outstanding, the findings of this study suggest that blogging may have a negative impact on impressions. The findings also debunk the assumption that after reading a hotel review, site users are less likely to indicate a desire to stay there. Because of their quality and appearance, the participants may not trust the blogs. Hotel websites, mixed and active blogs, and hotel websites are the best for marketing hotels to friends. Although the quality of the blogs may have influenced the participants, consumers do not appear to trust a beneficial article on the Internet since they believe it can be managed by the hotel. When compared to previous studies, the findings of this study are significant. All beliefs expressed on the blog, according to Thevenot (2007), are considered personal and are thus more readily accepted. On the other side, the participants in this study did not believe the favourable feedback. Furthermore, the results of this poll differ from those of Xiang and Gretzel (2010), who showed that 37% of peoples claimed to have purchased a product based on Internet reviews.

TABLE 4.3

Post Hoc Tukey HSD (beta)

Pairwise Comparisons		**$HSD_{.05} = 0.3679$ $HSD_{.01} = 0.4614$**	**$Q_{.05} = 3.3690$ $Q_{.01} = 4.2247$**
T_1:T_2	$M_1 = 4.47$ $M_2 = 4.40$	0.07	Q = 0.69 (p = .87830)
T_1:T_3	$M_1 = 4.47$ $M_3 = 4.50$	0.03	Q = 0.23 (p = .98566)
T_2:T_3	$M_2 = 4.40$ $M_3 = 4.50$	0.10	Q = 0.92 (p = .79425)

TABLE 4.4

Reliability: Mean and Standard Deviation

Summary of Data						
	Reliability					
	Website of Hotel	*Positive Group Blog*	*Mixed Group Blog*	*4*	*5*	*Total*
N	40	25	30			95
ΣX	175	111	131			417
Mean	4.375	4.44	4.3667			4.389
ΣX^2	783	501	585			1869
Std.Dev.	0.6675	0.5831	0.6687			0.6407

Result Details

Source	*SS*	*df*	*MS*	
Between-Group	0.0878	2	0.0439	F = 0.10491
Within-Group	38.5017	92	0.4185	
Total	38.5895	94		

The f ratio value is 0.10491. The p-value is.900515.
Hence the result is not significant at p <.05.

TABLE 4.5

Post Hoc Tukey HSD (beta)

Pairwise Comparisons		$HSD_{.05} = 0.3946$ $HSD_{.01} = 0.4948$	$Q_{.05} = 3.3690$ $Q_{.01} = 4.2247$
T_1:T_2	$M_1 = 4.38$ $M_2 = 4.44$	0.07	Q = 0.55 (p = .91870)
T_1:T_3	$M_1 = 4.38$ $M_3 = 4.37$	0.01	Q = 0.07 (p = .99862)
T_2:T_3	$M_2 = 4.44$ $M_3 = 4.37$	0.07	Q = 0.63 (p = .89781)

TABLE 4.6

Future Use: Mean and Standard Deviation

Summary of Data						
	Future Use					
	Website of Hotel	*Positive Group Blog*	*Mixed Group Blog*	*4*	*5*	*Total*
N	40	25	30			95
ΣX	179	110	90			379

(Continued)

TABLE 4.6 ***(Continued)***

Future Use: Mean and Standard Deviation

Summary of Data					
Mean	4.475	4.4	3		3.989
ΣX^2	815	494	270		1579
Std.Dev.	0.5986	0.6455	0		0.8442
Result Details					
Source		*SS*	*df*	*MS*	
Between-Group		43.0145	2	21.5072	F = 82.53038
Within-Group		23.975	92	0.2606	
Total		66.9895	94		

The f ratio value is 82.53038. The p-value is <.00001.
Hence the result is significant at p <.05.

TABLE 4.7

Post Hoc Tukey HSD (beta)

Pairwise Comparisons		$HSD_{.05} = 0.3114$ $HSD_{.01} = 0.3905$	$Q_{.05} = 3.3690$ $Q_{.01} = 4.2247$
T_1:T_2	$M_1 = 4.47$ $M_2 = 4.40$	0.07	Q = 0.81 (p = .83440)
T_1:T_3	$M_1 = 4.47$ $M_3 = 3.00$	1.47	Q = 15.96 (p = .00000)
T_2:T_3	$M_2 = 4.40$ $M_3 = 3.00$	1.40	Q = 15.15 (p = .00000)

TABLE 4.8

Recommendations: Mean and Standard Deviation

Summary of Data						
	Recommendations					
	Website of Hotel	*Positive Group Blog*	*Mixed Group Blog*	*4*	*5*	*Total*
N	40	25	30			95
ΣX	175	111	102			388
Mean	4.375	4.44	3.4			4.084
ΣX^2	783	501	356			1640
Std.Dev.	0.6675	0.5831	0.5632			0.7672

(Continued)

TABLE 4.8 *(Continued)*

Recommendations: Mean and Standard Deviation

Summary of Data				
Result Details				
Source	SS	df	MS	
Between-group	20.5913	2	10.2957	F = 27.26934
Within-group	34.735	92	0.3776	
Total	55.3263	94		

The f ratio value is 27.26934. The p-value is <.00001.
Hence the result is significant at $p < .05$.

TABLE 4.9

Post Hoc Tukey HSD (beta)

Pairwise Comparisons		$HSD_{.05} = 0.3748$ $HSD_{.01} = 0.4700$	$Q_{.05} = 3.3690$ $Q_{.01} = 4.2247$
$T_1:T_2$	$M_1 = 4.38$ $M_2 = 4.44$	0.07	Q = 0.58 (p = .91030)
$T_1:T_3$	$M_1 = 4.38$ $M_3 = 3.40$	0.98	Q = 8.76 (p = .00000)
$T_2:T_3$	$M_2 = 4.44$ $M_3 = 3.40$	1.04	Q = 9.35 (p = .00000)

4.6 Limitation

This study failed to take into account the quality of the website and blog, which is a serious flaw. Furthermore, the blog's source is a stumbling block. Participants may be distrustful of the blog's source since they are unaware of it. Customers will react differently if the blog originates from a well-known source. Customers will also put more trust in well-known review sites such as TripAdvisor and also possible that type of things you're looking for has an impact. Furthermore, because different demographics are more or less sensitive to blog sources, the study's selection of Midwestern/middle-aged participants may have skewed the results.

4.7 Recommendations for Research

The characteristics that influence blog credibility should be the subject of future research. A blog from a well-known brand, for example, may be more trustworthy than one can from the other business. A blog written by an unaffiliated third party, however, may be more reliable. These factors are essential for hoteliers to make informed decisions about when and how to use blogs and other kinds of social platform.

4.8 Conclusion

Social media has proven to be a successful communication and marketing strategy for the hospitality business, according to the conclusions of the literature review. In today's competitive business environment, the hospitality industry must use of various tools of social media to promote business and reach out to potential clients. As a result, the hotel sector should establish and maintain its own websites, as well as create accounts on social networking sites like Facebook, Twitter, and others to share valuable photographs and information. Hospitality businesses provide detailed information about themselves, including their facilities and services. They also allow customers to book or reserve rooms online for convenience. By using different social media platforms, these businesses can communicate directly with customers, promote their brand, build a strong reputation, maintain relationships with existing customers, increase customer loyalty, and boost their overall sales.

References

Chan, N. L., & Guillet, B. D. (2011). Social media marketing in the hotel industry: The role of Facebook and Twitter. *Journal of Travel & Tourism Marketing*, 28(4), 345–368. https://doi.org/10.1080/10548408.2011.571571

comScore. (2008). Social networking worldwide: Global penetration and usage statistics. comScore Inc.

comScore. (2009a). Global social media usage report. comScore Inc.

comScore. (2009b). The global state of social networking. comScore Inc.

Hong Kong Tourism Board. (2008). Tourism statistical review 2008. Hong Kong Tourism Board.

Jaret, P. (2006, March). *The rise of social media marketing*. The New York Times.

McKay, J. (2010). The role of online travel information in tourism marketing. *Tourism Review*, 65(3), 4–15.

Smith, A. (2011). Blogging and social media influence in travel marketing. *Journal of Hospitality Marketing & Management*, 20(5), 507–523.

Thevenot, G. (2007). Blogging as a social media tool in tourism. *Journal of Vacation Marketing*, 13(3), 287–289.

Tuten, T. L. (2008). Advertising 2.0: Social media marketing in a web 2.0 world. Praeger Publishers.

Tots, S. (2008). Social media marketing and branding opportunities. Marketing Review, 8(2), 115–128.

Xiang, Z., & Gretzel, U. (2010). Role of social media in online travel information search. *Tourism Management*, 31(2), 179–188. https://doi.org/10.1016/j.tourman.2009.02.016

5

The Human Factor in Automation: Investigating the Role of Leadership and Service Quality in Hotel Employees' Intentions to Use Robots

Dimitrios Belias, Angelos Ntalakos, Ioannis Rossidis, and Vasilios Kefis

5.1 Introduction

The integration of robotic technologies within the tourism industry is a burgeoning field, with most research currently confined to theoretical explorations. A notable gap exists in empirical studies that examine the specific impact of robot utilization on key variables such as customer satisfaction and employee job satisfaction.

The integration of robotic technology into the hotel industry promises to revolutionize service quality. By automating routine tasks, robots empower hotel staff to focus on delivering personalized guest experiences, enhancing the overall guest-centric approach (Belias et al., 2022b). Moreover, the deployment of robots signifies a hotel's commitment to technological innovation. While the initial investment may be substantial, the long-term benefits, such as reduced labor costs and improved staff retention, are significant. By freeing staff from mundane tasks, hotels can foster a more engaged and satisfied workforce. To ensure a seamless integration of robotic technology, effective change management practices are crucial. A deep understanding of factors such as resistance to change and readiness for change is essential to mitigate potential challenges and maximize the benefits of robotic implementation (Viterouli et al., 2024; Belias et al., 2024a; Ntalakos et al., 2024; Papademetriou et al., 2023; Rossidis et al., 2020).

A critical consideration is the public's perception and acceptance of robots in hospitality settings. Ivanov et al. (2018) highlight potential resistance from

DOI: 10.1201/9781003742791-5

both customers and hotel staff to the increasing use of robots. Their research, conducted in Russia, reveals a positive predisposition toward robotic technology among younger, urban-dwelling males who exhibit a proclivity for technological advancements. Notably, consumer attitudes are more favorable toward robots performing informational tasks than those involved in direct service delivery, such as housekeeping or personalized assistance. This suggests that consumers may prefer a supportive role for robots, rather than a primary one.

Tussyadiah and Park (2018) examined the perceptions of British and American tourists, finding a degree of skepticism regarding the use of robots in hotels. However, when exposed to such technology, tourists expressed satisfaction with the services provided. Key factors influencing positive consumer perceptions include the embodiment of human-like characteristics and behaviors in robotic design, as well as assurances regarding safety and reliability. Tourists desire confidence that robots will perform their designated tasks without compromising visitor safety.

The adoption of robotic technologies in the hospitality industry offers several potential benefits, including enhanced customer service, increased operational efficiency, and a competitive edge (Xu et al., 2020; Osawa et al., 2017; Cain et al., 2019). However, the integration of robots may also raise concerns about job displacement and resistance from human employees (Manyika et al., 2013). As robotic systems necessitate changes to existing organizational processes, human workers may perceive them as a threat to their roles and job security (Ivanov et al., 2017). Therefore, understanding and addressing this human factor is crucial for the successful implementation of robotic technologies in the tourism sector (Sadangharn, 2022).

Van Looy (2020) found that employees' perceptions of robotic technology are significantly influenced by managerial attitudes toward automation. Specifically, the study suggests that a management team's commitment to robotic implementation can positively shape employee perceptions. Additionally, individual factors such as self-efficacy and motivation play a crucial role in determining employee acceptance of robots in the workplace.

Hence, this chapter seeks to examine the relationship between various leadership styles and hotel employees' attitudes toward robotic implementation. To achieve this objective, a quantitative research study was conducted in four- and five-star hotels located in the broader region of Greece.

Thus, this chapter aims to answer to the following research objectives:

- Q1: Does transformational leadership style influence employees' intentions/expectations on the use of robots?
- Q2: Does transformational leadership style influence employees' perceptions on the service quality of the use of robots?
- Q3: Does transactional leadership style influence employees' intentions/expectations on the use of robots?

- Q4: Does transactional leadership style influence employees' perceptions on the service quality of the use of robots?
- Q5: Does passive leadership style influence employees' intentions/expectations on the use of robots?
- Q6: Does passive leadership style influence employees' perceptions on the service quality of the use of robots?
- Q7: Does the service quality of the use of robots influence employees' intentions/expectations of the use of robots?

5.2 Literature Review

5.2.1 The Concept of Employees' Intentions/Expectations of the Use of Robots

Recent academic literature has increasingly focused on societal attitudes toward robots, particularly within the hotel industry. The tourism and hospitality sectors have embraced robotics, recognizing its potential to revolutionize the industry. While some social science research has explored the adoption of robotic technologies by travel and tourism companies and consumer acceptance (Pochwatko et al., 2015), previous studies have highlighted the transformative impact of robots on the hospitality industry (Acosta et al., 2006).

Reviews of existing robotic technologies suggest their potential to enhance travel and hotel services. However, the successful implementation of robotic services in hotels, as demonstrated in Taiwan (Tung & Law, 2017), is contingent upon several critical factors.

The adoption of robotic technology may be perceived as a threat to employment, potentially leading to job displacement (Manyika et al., 2013). Furthermore, human employees may resist the integration of service robots, as it necessitates adjustments to existing organizational processes. Therefore, overcoming this resistance to change is a significant social challenge that cannot be overlooked (Wei, 2013).

User acceptance is paramount to the successful implementation of service robots. Acceptance encompasses attitudinal, intentional, and behavioral dimensions. Consequently, ensuring employee acceptance is a crucial aspect of human-robot collaboration. By identifying factors that influence robot acceptance, organizations can proactively address these variables during the integration process, thereby increasing user acceptance levels (Sadangharn, 2022).

The growing interest in robotics has spurred significant research investment in artificial intelligence, particularly neural networks and machine learning. These advancements have the potential to address the evolving demands of the tourism industry. Notably, research has indicated that hotel employees exhibit a positive attitude toward working alongside artificial intelligence-powered machines, such as robots (Kabadayi et al., 2019).

While robots do not replace human employees, they can augment their capabilities by performing tasks like predicting hotel arrivals, waste generation rates, and energy consumption. Additionally, facial recognition technology at airports and AI-powered recommendation systems for tourist destinations showcase the versatility of these technologies (Belias & Vasiliadis, 2021b).

From a broader perspective, technical intelligence offers immense potential for data analysis, including the processing of large datasets to uncover valuable insights and inform decision-making. Moreover, automated processes, such as back-office and customer relationship management systems, have been integral to the tourism industry for years and continue to contribute to strategic decision-making (Buhalis et al., 2019).

While there is a general positive sentiment toward the use of robots, research has indicated that their adoption has not always been seamless. Studies by Bhimasta and Kuo (2019) and others (Tussyadiah et al., 2017, 2020; Yu, 2018, 2020) have shown that while customers express positive attitudes, employee intentions to use robots are often lukewarm. This reluctance can be attributed to concerns about potential job displacement or diminished authority within the organization (Bhimasta & Kuo, 2019).

5.2.2 The Concept of Employees' Intentions/Expectations of the Use of Robots

The integration of robotic technology offers significant potential to enhance productivity and efficiency within the service industry (Zerva et al., 2024; Giannakos et al., 2024; Ntalakos et al., 2023a; Belias et al., 2022). By automating routine tasks, robots can reduce labor costs, making them an attractive proposition for the hotel industry (Belias & Vasiliadis., 2021a, 2022). This technological shift has sparked considerable debate among researchers regarding the optimal implementation of robotic services (Rossidis et al., 2019; Belias & Varelas, 2019).

The successful deployment of robotic services hinges on the development of sophisticated software that prioritizes efficiency and accuracy (Johnson et al., 2015). Autonomous and high-quality performances are key factors in the success of robotic solutions. For instance, many hotel robots are equipped with cameras and sensors that enable them to navigate corridors and elevators independently. The Relay robot, for example, can deliver items to guests by opening its lid to reveal the contents. Positive customer feedback regarding the robot's performance and service quality underscores the importance of developing robust human-robot interaction capabilities within the hotel environment. By recognizing and responding to user emotions through facial expressions, gestures, and speech, robots can foster positive interactions (Lisetti & Schiano, 2000).

A fundamental principle for all tourism industry professionals is the imperative to prioritize customer satisfaction (Ntalakos et al., 2023b). This involves meeting and exceeding visitor expectations to deliver exceptional experiences. In the pursuit of service excellence, robotic technologies, particularly self-service robots, have gained significant traction within the hospitality sector. Advancements in self-service robotics have empowered businesses to streamline operations, reduce costs, and boost productivity (Naumov, 2019).

By automating various service processes, hotels can enhance their reliability and efficiency in the eyes of customers. Self-service technologies, such as those employed at airports (e.g., e-passport gates) and travel agencies, have become commonplace. Customer feedback suggests that self-service robots have led to improved overall experiences and reduced wait times. The integration of artificial intelligence has further expanded the capabilities of these technologies, enabling them to provide services, analyze data, and support research endeavors. As a result, artificial intelligence has gained widespread adoption among hoteliers worldwide (Kabadayi et al., 2019).

The advent of RAISA technology, or self-service robots, has fundamentally transformed the delivery of tourism services. This technological shift has necessitated a paradigm shift from traditional customer service models to a more personalized and emotionally engaging approach (Naumov, 2019). By providing a unique and satisfying customer experience, businesses aim to encourage positive word-of-mouth and social media endorsements, thereby enhancing their reputation.

The impact of self-service robots has elevated the tourism industry from a mere visitor experience to an innovative process where customers essentially purchase innovative products. This transformation has redefined service perceptions, reshaping the customer-business relationship and elevating customer expectations. Consequently, the integration of self-service robots has improved business efficiency and expedited service delivery (Ivanov & Webster, 2019).

5.2.3 The Concept of Leadership Styles on the Use of Robots

The relationship between leadership styles and employees' intentions, expectations, and productivity of the use of robots remains a complex and contested issue in the management literature. While Bass et al. (2003) posited that both transactional and transformational leadership styles can contribute to increased performance, empirical research has yielded mixed findings, with some studies associating transactional leadership with higher productivity levels (Kalsoom et al., 2018; Wei et al., 2010; Belias et al., 2021). This discrepancy may be attributed to the distinct nature of these leadership styles: transactional leadership emphasizes task-oriented behaviors, whereas transformational leadership focuses on inspiring and motivating followers. In the context of robotic leadership, where characteristics like inspiration and charisma are less readily associated with machines, a transactional approach may be more effective. This is particularly true when human workers lack prior experience with robotic agents. In such cases, a focus on task-specific guidance, error correction, and clear explanations can enhance productivity by fostering a more results-oriented and pragmatic mindset, aligning with the expected capabilities of a robotic leader (Lopes et al., 2021).

A critical factor in successful human-robot interaction is the establishment of trust between individuals and robotic agents (Woodward et al., 2020). A lack of trust and willingness to engage with artificial intelligence can hinder the adoption of technological solutions (Riedl et al., 2014). Previous research suggests that positive attitudes and trust toward robots are fostered by effective communication capabilities (Dang & Liu, 2020). For robotic leadership to become a reality in organizational settings, it is imperative to cultivate collaborative and reliable relationships between social robots and human employees (Samani et al., 2012).

Advances in artificial intelligence and computing power (e.g., cloud computing) have enabled robots to engage in not only physical and cognitive tasks but also social and emotional interactions with humans (Gallimore et al., 2019; Willemse et al., 2018; Wykowska, 2021). Research has demonstrated that robots can elicit emotional responses from humans and enhance social and cooperative skills, particularly in therapeutic contexts (Fosch-Villaronga & Albo-Canals, 2019). Given that task accomplishment and relationship building are foundational leadership behaviors (Eckardt et al., 2020; Yammarino et al., 2020), it is essential to examine task and relationship dynamics in human-robot collaboration through the lens of leadership theory (Tsai et al., 2022).

5.2.4 Constructing Research Model and Research Hypotheses

The above-mentioned literature has led to the creation of the theoretical model of this chapter which can guide academics and practitioners to the understanding of the intentions and expectations of hotel employees regarding the service quality that can be offered using robots in the hotel industry. Moreover, this model aims to investigate if there is a connection between the several leadership styles that a hotel manager can adopt and the intentions/expectations the hotel personnel have regarding the quality of services a robot can provide in the hotel industry. This is a pioneer investigation since there is no previous empirical research that connects the leadership styles with the intentions and expectations of hotel employees regarding the use of robots. More details are described in Figure 5.1.

Hence, the research hypotheses of the research model are the following:

- H1. Transformational leadership style has a positive effect on the intention/expectation of the use of robots in the hotel industry.
- H2. Transformational leadership style has a positive effect on the service quality of the use of robots in the hotel industry.

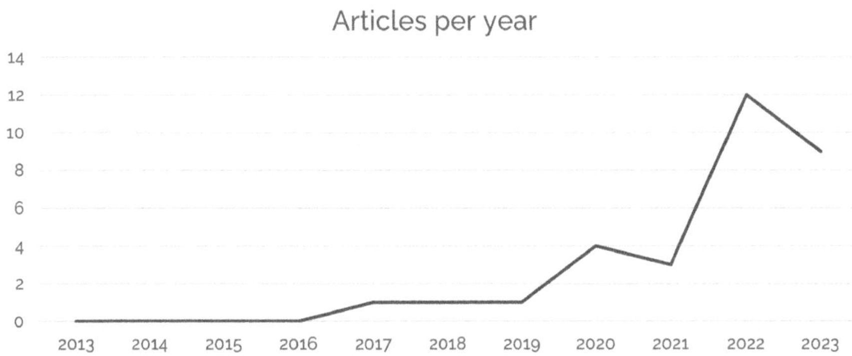

FIGURE 5.1
Conceptual Model and Research Hypotheses

- H3. Transactional leadership style has a positive effect on the intention/expectation of the use of robots in the hotel industry.
- H4. Transactional leadership style has a positive effect on the service quality of the use of robots in the hotel industry.
- H5. Passive leadership style has a negative effect on the intention/expectation of the use of robots in the hotel industry.
- H6. Passive leadership style has a negative effect on the service quality of the use of robots in the hotel industry.
- H7. The service quality of the use of robots has a positive effect on the intention -expectation of the use of robots in the hotel industry.

5.3 Methodology of Research

5.3.1 Participants

This chapter aims to examine the relationship between various leadership styles and hotel employees' attitudes toward robotic implementation. To achieve this objective, quantitative research was conducted on 195 employees who worked in four- and five-star hotels located in Greece. Data were sourced from a database provided by the Hellenic Chamber of Hotels (HCH, 2024). As the official government consultant for the tourism and hospitality industry, the HCH represents all Greek hotels by law (HCH, 2024).

Following the acquisition of managerial consent via email, electronic questionnaires were distributed to hotel employees. Participation in this study was voluntary and anonymous, and all collected data were solely used for research purposes.

A total of 273 four- and five-star hotels were invited to participate in the study via electronic invitation. Of these, 113 hotels agreed to participate, 41 declined, and 119 did not respond. A convenience sampling method was employed due to its cost-effectiveness and ease of access. The online questionnaire, hosted on Google Forms, was distributed from March to June 2024. A total of 195 hotel employees completed the questionnaire with no missing data.

TABLE 5.1

Demographics of the Sample (N = 195)

Demographic	Type	Frequency	Percent
	Male	146	74.9
Gender	Female	49	25.1
Age	18–29	26	13.3
	30–39	43	22.1
	40–49	72	36.9
	50–59	39	20.0
	> 60	15	7.7
Marital Status	Single	63	32.3
	Married	114	58.5
	Divorced	18	9.2
Years of employment in specific hotel unit	1–2	13	6.7
	3–5	19	9.7
	6–10	36	18.5
	11–20	42	21.5
	> 20	85	43.6
Level of education	High School Graduate	23	11.8
	College Graduate	76	39.0
	Bachelor's Degree	50	25.6
	Master Degree	41	21.0
	PhD Degree	5	2.6
Work Section	Reception	34	17.5
	Housekeeping	58	29.7
	Bar/restaurant	8	4.1
	Kitchen	4	2.1
	Financial office	15	7.7
	Public relations	1	0.5
	Spa	1	0.5
	General duties	2	1.0
	Management	72	36.9
Seasonality	Permanent	151	77.4
	Seasonable	44	22.6
Hotel Category	Four-star	105	53.8
	Five-star	90	46.2

The majority of respondents were married male employees aged 40–49. Most held college degrees (n = 76,39.0%) and had over 20 years of experience working in their specific unit and the hospitality industry overall. Further details are presented in Table 5.1.

5.3.2 Measurement Tools

Three measurement tools were used in this research in order to measure the three variables (and their sub-dimensions) of the research: the intention/expectation of the use of robots, the service quality of the use of robots, and the leadership styles of the management.

The first measurement tool was used to measure employees' intentions/expectations of the use of robots. This questionnaire is based on Wu and Wang (2005) scale, and it has been adjusted accordingly for the use of robots. The initial sub-dimensions of Wu and Wang (2005) model scale were cost, ease a manual, perception, and SYM patency. Additionally, some individual questions from Ivanov and Webster (2019) scale were added. These questions were associated with the employees' behavior regarding the use of robots.

The second measurement tool was used to measure the service quality of the use of robots. The questionnaire is based on the Servqual model by Parasuraman et al. (1991). The Servqual model provides a structured approach to evaluating service quality by focusing on five key dimensions: real data, reliability, response, security, and empathy. Each dimension represents a potential gap between customer expectations and perceptions. For instance, a discrepancy in tangibles, such as physical facilities or appearance of personnel, may negatively impact the overall service experience.

The two above-mentioned measurement tools were modified by Belias and Vasiliadis (2021). More specifically, based on the above questionnaires, they created a 28-item questionnaire to measure the intentions and expectations of robot use in the hotel industry by focusing on six sub-dimensions: convenience and advantages of use of robots in the hotel industry, staff familiarization with new technologies and auxiliary work of robots, anthropomorphic characteristics of robots, high cost of buying and using robots, financial improvement in hotels and robot discretion, and absence of concern for human position loss or role change. Additionally, a 22-item adapted version of the service quality questionnaire (Parasuraman et al., 1991) was modified for measuring the service quality of robot use in the hotel industry (Belias & Vasiliadis, 2021). The sub-dimensions of this variable are the following: tangibles and reliability, individualized fulfillment of needs, and exceptional service. All items are measured via a five-point Likert scale, ranging from 1 = "Totally disagree" to 5 = "Totally agree".

Finally, the different leadership styles were measured through Multiple Leadership Questionnaire (MLQ-5x) (Avolio & Bass, 2004). The Multifactor Leadership Questionnaire (MLQ-5X) measures three primary leadership styles: transformational, transactional, and laissez-faire. It comprises 45 items assessing the following dimensions: idealized influence (attributed and behavioral), inspirational motivation, intellectual stimulation, individual consideration, contingent reward, management by exception (active and passive), and laissez-faire leadership. The MLQ-5 × focuses on leaders' individual behaviors and characteristics, which are evaluated by their subordinates, regardless of hierarchical position. Responses to the MLQ-5 × items are measured on a 5-point Likert scale ranging from 0 (Not at all) to 4 (Often or always).

5.3.3 Data Analysis

Data analysis was performed using IBM SPSS Statistics version 20.0. Descriptive statistics, including means, standard deviations, and Spearman's correlation, were calculated for all scales and subscales. Factor analysis was employed to identify underlying dimensions among the correlated variables. Cronbach's alpha coefficient was utilized to assess the internal consistency of all variables and sub-variables.

To test the research hypotheses, correlation analysis and multiple regression were conducted to investigate the relationship between intentions/expectations of the use of robot, service quality of the use of robots, and leadership styles.

5.4 Results

5.4.1 Measurement Model and Common Method Bias

Factor analysis was executed in order to investigate the variability of the research variables and their sub-dimensions (Intention & Expectation of the use of robots, Quality of service of robots, Leadership styles). The results of the factor analysis regarding the variable intention/expectation of the use of robots are described in Table 5.2.

Additionally, the results of factor analysis regarding the variable of quality of service of robots are presented in Table 5.3.

Finally, the results of factor analysis regarding the variable of leadership styles are presented in Table 5.4.

TABLE 5.2

Factor Analysis Results for Intention & Expectations of the Use of Robots

Variables	KMO	x^2	p	df	Total Variance %	Factor Loadings	Accepted Items
Convenience and advantages of use of robots in the hotel industry	.919	1574.570	0.000	78	63.167	.543 to .865	14
Staff familiarization with new technologies and auxiliary work of robots	.548	261.631	0.000	3	67.523	.556 to .938	3
Anthropomorphic characteristics of robots	.500	214.530	0.000	1	90.985	.954 to .954	2
High cost of buying and using robots	.630	93.175	0.000	3	60.509	.744 to .839	3
Financial improvement in hotels and robot discretion	.503	59.093	0.000	3	51.495	.406 to .859	3
Absence of concern for human position loss or role change	.500	179.154	0.000	1	88.914	.943 to .943	2

TABLE 5.3

Factor Analysis Results for Quality of Service of Robots

Variables	KMO	x^2	p	df	Total Variance %	Factor Loadings	Accepted Items
Tangibles & reliability	.933	1698.206	0.000	55	65.546	.685 to .878	11
Individualized fulfillment of needs	.706	267.579	0.000	3	77.240	.836 to .911	3
Exceptional service	.871	601.855	0.000	153	64.529	.757 to .851	6

TABLE 5.4

Factor Analysis Results for Leadership Styles

Variables	KMO	x^2	p	Df	Total Variance %	Factor Loadings	Accepted Items
Idealized influence (attributed) – transformational	.745	382.743	0.000	6	68.450	.688 to .903	4
Idealized influence (behavior) – transformational	.577	121.407	0.000	6	47.424	.764 to .795	3

(Continued)

TABLE 5.4 *(Continued)*

Factor Analysis Results for Leadership Styles

Variables	KMO	x^2	p	Df	Total Variance %	Factor Loadings	Accepted Items
Inspirational motivation – transformational	.799	388.971	0.000	6	72.273	.812 to .881	4
Intellectual stimulation – transformational	.783	436.076	0.000	6	71.773	.774 to 923	4
Individual consideration – transformational	.762	467.218	0.000	6	74.218	.831 to .931	4
Contingent reward – transactional	.810	274.033	0.000	6	66.133	.794 to .844	4
Management by exception (active) – transactional	.773	243.933	0.000	6	62.817	.697 to .835	4
Management by exception (passive) – passive	.675	166.962	0.000	6	54.859	.673 to .819	4
Laissez-faire – passive	.792	321.038	0.000	6	68.422	.787 to .854	4
Extra effort – outcome	.748	620.718	0.000	3	91.066	.933 to .969	3
Effectiveness – outcome	.845	519.453	0.000	6	78.696	.856 to .911	4
Satisfaction – outcome	.500	195.634	0.000	1	89.939	.948 to .948	2

5.4.2 Descriptive Statistics, Internal Consistency, and Variables' Correlations

Table 5.5 presents the means, standard deviations, and Cronbach's alpha coefficients for the study variables and sub-variables. The results indicate that hotel employees hold a neutral attitude toward the potential use of robots in the hospitality industry, as evidenced by their intentions (M = 3.063) and expectations (M = 3.063). Similarly, participants expressed neutral sentiments regarding the perceived service quality of robots (M = 2.984). Furthermore, employees perceived their managers as frequently employing both transformational (M = 2.126) and transactional (M = 2.226) leadership styles. Conversely, passive leadership was perceived as infrequently utilized by managers.

Additionally, the values of Cronbach's alpha coefficient demonstrate that all variables and their sub-dimensions are accepted since Cronbach's alpha values range from .669 to .970. Hence, all scales present internal consistency. The only low value, but still acceptable, is demonstrated by the sub-dimension

TABLE 5.5

Means, Standard Deviations, and Cronbach's Alpha Coefficients

Variables	Mean (M)	Std. Deviation (SD)	Cronbach's Alpha	Number of Items
Total Intention/Expectation of the use of robots	3.063	.453	.893	27
Convenience and advantages of use of robots in the hotel industry	2.622	.799	.933	14
Staff familiarization with new technologies and auxiliary work of robots	3.789	.710	.725	3
Anthropomorphic characteristics of robots	2.984	1.109	.901	2
High cost of buying and using robots	2.974	.702	.669	3
Financial improvement in hotels and robot discretion	3.217	.687	.508	3
Absence of concern for human position loss or role change	2.789	1.076	.874	2
Total quality of service of robots	2.984	.0756	.960	22
Tangibles and reliability	3.062	.797	.947	11
Individualized fulfillment of needs	2.442	.966	.851	3
Exceptional service	3.449	.816	.888	6
Transformational leadership	2.126	.911	.958	19
Idealized influence (attributed)	2.161	1.018	.841	4
Idealized influence (behavior)	2.227	.866	.691	3
Inspirational motivation	2.257	1.015	.871	4
Intellectual stimulation	2.050	1.013	.867	4
Individual consideration	1.937	1.123	.883	4
Transactional leadership	2.226	.794	.844	8
Contingent reward	2.214	.939	.827	4
Management – by – exception (active)	2.238	.900	.798	4
Passive leadership	1.638	.857	.859	8
Management – by – exception (passive)	1.830	.898	.723	4
Laissez-faire leadership	1.446	.993	.845	4
Output of leadership	2.198	1.162	.970	9
Extra effort	2.155	1.303	.951	3
Effectiveness	2.207	1.123	.909	4
Satisfaction	2.233	1.156	.888	2

"Financial improvement in hotels and robot discretion" – intention/expectation of the use of robots ($\alpha = .508$). On the contrary, the total service quality of robots exhibits the highest score of Cronbach's alpha coefficient ($\alpha = .906$).

Additionally, the values of Cronbach's alpha coefficient demonstrate that all variables and their sub-dimensions are accepted since Cronbach's alpha values range from .669 to .970. Hence, all scales present internal consistency.

TABLE 5.6

Correlations of Variables (Spearman Coefficient)

Variables	1	2	3	4	5	6
1. Intention/ expectation on the use of robots	1	.668 (p = .000)	.086 (p = .233)	.091 (p = .206)	-.089 (p = .219)	.113 (p = .115)
2. Service quality of the use of robots		1	-.012 (p = .865)	.023 (p = .753)	-.049 (p=.493)	.071 (p = .322)
3. Transformational leadership style			1	.852 (p = .000)	-.067 (p = .354)	.906 (p = .000)
4. Transactional leadership style				1	.058 (p = .418)	.748 (p = .000)
5. Passive leadership style					1	-.118 (p = .101)
6. Output of leadership						1

The correlations between the variables were examined through the Spearman correlation coefficient. The Spearman coefficient was chosen due to the fact that the variables are not normally distributed. More specifically, Kolmogorov-Smirnov and Shapiro-Wilk Tests revealed that all the variables (apart from the variable of service quality of robots) do not follow the normal distribution ($p < 0.05$).

Table 5.6 describes the correlations between the variables. More thoroughly, the intention/expectation of the use of robots is strongly and positively connected with the service quality of the use of robots (rho = .668). In addition, transformational leadership style has very strong positive connections with the transactional leadership style (rho = .852) and the outcome of the leadership (rho = .906). On the contrary, both transformational and transactional leadership style do not correlate significantly with the passive leadership style as well as the other variables of the research (intention/expectation of the use of robots and service quality of robots) ($p > 0.05$).

5.4.3 Hypothesis Testing

The first hypothesis (*H1.Transformational leadership style has a positive effect on the intention/expectation of the use of robots in the hotel industry*) is declined as Spearman coefficient revealed that there is no significant relationship between transformational leadership style and the variable of the intention/expectation of the use of robots in the hotel industry ($p = .233 > .05$).

Similarly, the second hypothesis (*H2. Transformational leadership style has a positive effect on the service quality of the use of robots in the hotel industry*) is declined (($p = .865 > .05$). Additionally, Table 5.7 describes that there are no significant relationships between the other leadership styles (transactional and passive) and the variables of intention of the use of robots and service

TABLE 5.7

Multiple Regression Model for Service Quality of the use of Robots and Intention/Expectation of the Use of Robots in the Hotel Industry

Model	R	R-Square	Adjusted R-Square	Sig.
Service quality of the use of robots and intention/expectation of the use of robots in the hotel industry	.761	.579	.573	.000
	Unstandardized Coefficients		Standardized Coefficients	
Model	B	SE	Beta	Sig.
Service quality of the use of robots dimensions				
(Constant)	1.719	.094		.000
Tangibles and reliability	.343	.048	.603	.000
Individualized fulfillment of needs	.073	.029	.155	.012
Exceptional service	.034	.044	.060	.443

Dependent Variable: Intention/Expectation of the use of robots

quality of the use of robots. Hence, hypotheses H3 (*H3. Transactional leadership style has a positive effect on the intention/expectation of the use of robots in the hotel industry*), H4 (*H4. Transactional leadership style has a positive effect on the service quality of the use of robots in the hotel industry*), H5 (*H5. Passive leadership style has a negative effect on the intention/expectation of the use of robots in the hotel industry*), and H6 (*H6. Passive leadership style has a negative effect on the service quality of the use of robots in the hotel industry*) are also declined.

Finally, Spearman coefficient described a very strong and positive correlation between intention/expectation of the use of robots and service quality of the use of robots ($rho = .668, P < .05$). To enhance this positive and significant relationship between these two variables, the model of multiple regression was implemented. More thoroughly, the intention/expectation of the use of robots is assigned as the dependent variable whereas the three dub-variables of service quality of the use of robots describe the independent variables of the model. The statistical measures of the model are presented in Table 5.7. According to the multiple regression model, the three sub-dimensions of the service quality of the use of robots can predict 57.9% of the intention/expectation of the use of robots in the hotel industry ($R^2 = .579, P < .000$). The sub-dimensions of "Tangibles and reliability" and "Individualized fulfillment of needs" have a substantial impact on the intention/expectation of the use of robots ($P = .000$ and $P = .012$). To the contrary, "Exceptional service" does not contribute significantly to the intention/expectation of the use of robots ($P = .443$). One unit of "tangibles and reliability" can increase the variable of intention/expectation of the use of robots by .343 units, while one unit of "individualized fulfillment of needs" can increase the variable of intention/expectation of the use of robots by .073 units. Hence, hypothesis H7 is accepted.

5.5 Discussion

The primary motivation behind the current research was to explore the association between leadership styles (transformational, transactional, and passive) and the intentional, expected, and perceived integration of robotic technology by hotel employees in the hospitality sector. The results were unexpected; in fact, they contradict some of the theoretical expectations but align with the emerging empirical evidence in the field. Namely, the data did not support the hypotheses H1 to H6 that assumed correlations between different leadership styles and employees' attitudes toward robot adoption. However, there was strong confirmation of hypothesis H7, which focuses on the relationship between the perception of service quality of robots and employees' intention to use them. The present argument situates these results within the broader academic discourse on technology adoption, leadership effectiveness, and human-robot collaboration in hospitality settings (Leung et al., 2023; Lu & Jin, 2025).

The contradiction in the rejection of hypotheses H1 and H2, which predicted positive correlations between transformational leadership and employee intentions to use robots, as well as perceptions of robot service quality, respectively, goes against some earlier theoretical propositions but is consistent with recent empirical findings in hospitality contexts. Recent research has shown that the relationship between leadership styles and technology adoption is more complex than initially thought (Leung & Jin, 2025; Van Looy, 2022). On the one hand, transformational leadership has been traditionally linked to innovation adoption and change management success (Schepers et al., 2005; Nguyen, 2023); on the other hand, its role in facilitating robot acceptance seems to be influenced by many contextual factors that have not been accounted for in the standard models yet.

Leung et al. (2025) argued that 'rapport leadership' might be a more suitable construct to describe the dynamics in human-robot co-working environments, implying that the characteristics of traditional transformational leadership may not sufficiently address the challenges of robotic integration. Similarly, Lu and Jin (2025) report that not only do organizational culture and leadership styles influence employees' perceptions of robots, but this impact is exerted through intricate psychological processes, such as a zero-sum mindset and the perception of resource scarcity, rather than through direct effects. The lack of significant relationships discovered in this study might point out that the reality of transformational leaders focusing on vision, inspiration, and individualized consideration is far from delivering non-human collaborators as partners, especially when employees are worried about job losses and role ambiguity (Li et al., 2019; Brougham & Haar, 2018).

Additionally, the rejection of hypotheses H3 and H4 regarding the impact of transactional leadership on robot adoption attitudes challenges the conventional understanding of the effectiveness of a task-oriented leadership style in technology implementation. Transactional leadership, characterized by contingent reward systems and management by exception, has been effective in a structured, performance-oriented environment (Bass et al., 2003; Kalsoom et al., 2018). However, recent meta-analytic evidence suggests that transformational leadership is the most effective approach in all cases of complex organizational change, including technology adoption (Aga et al., 2021). Here, the results also serve as a reference point for the discussion on the integration of robot technology.

A study on the perceptions of hotel managers regarding the introduction of robots revealed that, along with other basic conditions, reward-punishment mechanisms alone would not suffice if employees were not properly involved, the service context was not right, and there was a lack of technical competence (Ivanov & Webster, 2020; Mejia & Crandell, 2023). On top of that, Chen et al. (2024) showed that if robot managers' reward-punishment behaviors are not properly calibrated, they may even cause human-robot trust and job performance to deteriorate, and this means that transactional approaches may be the worst possible scenarios where trust and collaboration between humans and robots are at the highest level. Besides, the Greek hotel environment, with its relatively high power distance and collectivistic cultural values, may, in fact, exacerbate the situation, making transactional leadership less effective in facilitating technology acceptance (Hofstede, 2001).

The rejection of hypotheses H5 and H6, which stated that passive leadership would negatively affect attitudes toward the adoption of robots, was initially surprising but is in line with research showing that the effects of passive leadership are usually indirect and mediated by other organizational factors. Passive or laissez-faire leadership, characterized by the avoidance of decision-making and minimal involvement, has been regarded as the least effective leadership style in various contexts for a long time (Bass & Avolio, 2004). Nevertheless, according to the latest research, in much professionalized environments where employees are highly self-efficacious and technologically competent, the lack of active leadership intervention may not necessarily slow down the process of technology adoption (Van Looy, 2020). Regarding robot integration, Khoa et al. (2023) state that employee attitudes depend more on their direct interaction with robotic technology and communication with peers than on managerial involvement.

Furthermore, a study on employee perceptions of service robots during the COVID-19 pandemic found that the most important factors leading to positive attitudes toward the use of robot-supported services were technological readiness and the perceived social skills of robots, rather than leadership support (Parvez et al., 2022; Sinha et al., 2020). The Greek hotel employees participating in this study, who are mostly seasoned professionals with more than 20 years of experience in the industry, may have sufficient autonomy and be capable of making professional judgments, thereby minimizing the impact of passive leadership on their technology acceptance processes. This discovery highlights the importance of employee characteristics and industry maturity in evaluating the impact of leadership on technology adoption.

The strong support for hypothesis H7, showing that perceived service quality of robots has a significant impact on employees' intentions and expectations to use robots, is the study's most prominent and theoretically significant finding. Essentially, this outcome aligns with a substantial body of recent papers that emphasize the technological capabilities and performance of new technologies as key factors in the adoption of such innovations (Prentice & Nguyen, 2021; Choi et al., 2023). The multiple regression analysis revealed that tangibles and reliability ($\beta = .343$) and individualized fulfillment of needs ($\beta = .073$) were significant predictors of employee intentions, collectively explaining 57.9% of the variance. These results align closely with recent theoretical developments in the field of service robot research. Studies on the service quality of hotel robots have revealed that continuance intention is mainly influenced by factors such as automation, personalization, precision, and efficiency, which are often moderated by individual innovativeness (Prentice & Nguyen, 2025). Additionally, research on frontline employees' willingness to collaborate with service robots has yielded the finding that robot service capability is the major driver of adoption intentions, with relative advantage and trust serving as key mediators (Leung et al., 2023; Zhang et al., 2024). The current research's focus on tangibles and reliability shows that employees are making a practical judgment of robots' capability to carry out physical tasks consistently and reliably, which is a finding that has a parallel in the research done on customers where it is shown that functional performance has more weight than aesthetic considerations in service robot evaluations (Ivanov & Webster, 2021; Lee, 2024).

The strong relationship between customers' perception of service quality and their willingness to adopt new technology, established through the present research, has also been interpreted within a broader framework of technology acceptance theories, including the technology affordance theory (TAT) perspective. The recent TAT applications in hospitality have shown that employees' perceptions of robots' physical and cognitive affordances significantly influence their willingness to collaborate, with physical affordances being preferred over cognitive ones due to their clearer relative advantages and higher trust (Leung et al., 2023). The researchers observed that the preference pattern remained the same across the pre-pandemic, amid-pandemic, and post-pandemic periods, indicating the presence of deep-seated underlying mechanisms. In addition, research on employee-robot collaboration has identified perceived risk, performance expectancy, and effort expectancy as the primary factors through which service quality perceptions influence job crafting behaviors and adoption intentions (Fan et al., 2022; Song et al., 2022). The results of the current research suggest that employees in Greek hotels see to the functional side of the service, thus they expect the service to be reliable and the outcomes of the service to be tangible, and at the same time, they may be giving up the service for an abstract one, which might be a reflection of their pragmatic concerns about the operational disruption and the maintenance of service quality in a highly competitive hospitality-markets (Palrão et al., 2023; Mohanty & Munir, 2024).

The gap between leadership styles and attitudes toward technology adoption in this study calls for theoretically significant questions regarding the processes by which leadership influences organizational changes in technology-intensive settings. Along with various other studies, a recent paper explicitly outlines new leadership models suitable for human-robot collaborative environments. Leung et al. (2025) argued that traditional leadership styles might not work effectively for human-robot teams and suggested the concept 'rapport leadership', which is about the relationship, communication, and mutual understanding between human employees and robotic systems. According to this, the efficient leadership approach in the hospitality industry with robots requires skills and practices that extend beyond the traditional transformational-transactional-passive taxonomy. Correspondingly, investigations into groundbreaking leadership styles have found that leaders who vividly promote the use of technology, provide clear guidelines, and demonstrate their trust in the continued reality of robots greatly facilitate employee trust and willingness to adopt (Soliman et al., 2024; Brahmi et al., 2023). The non-existence of particular leadership influences in this research might reflect that Greek hotel managers are yet to develop these advanced leadership skills necessary for the successful embedding of robots or that the traditional MLQ-5 × tool does not facilitate the identification of leadership behaviors leading to technology adoption (Xu et al., 2020; Kang et al., 2024).

Another essential factor in understanding these results is the level of robot usage in hotels in Greece. The studies have shown that employees' mindsets toward robots change over time, progressing through different stages, including initial recognition of the subject and feelings of stress, followed by gradual acceptance and ultimately cooperation (Brougham & Haar, 2018; Khoa et al., 2023). Since most hotels in Greece are not deeply involved in robotic technologies, employees' attitudes may be influenced more by their ideas regarding robots' technical capabilities than by leadership. The cross-cultural study focused on robot adoption in different countries found that in less technologically developed countries with low exposure to automation, employees' worries about technical performance and reliability are the main factors that concern them the most, which in turn hardly allows leadership and organizational factors to influence them (Ivanov et al., 2020; Palrão et al., 2023). Additionally, the study on obstacles to robot adoption from a management perspective has identified four main categories of barriers: a lack of managerial knowledge, insufficient mechanisms for employee engagement, service context inappropriateness, and technical limitations (Osei et al., 2024). The prevailing service quality perception in the current research, as a predictor of adoption intention, indicates that hotel employees in Greece primarily consider technical feasibility and performance reliability; thus, leadership influence may precede or be at a higher level in the adoption process.

The outcomes of the study suggest an argument for the hospitality industry to adopt robots; however, it also highlights the risks associated with such adoption. The latest research reports that robotic utilization reduces employees' turnover intention by increasing work autonomy, while simultaneously increasing the intention to leave the job due to job insecurity (Fu et al., 2022; Koo et al., 2021). The Conservation of Resources theory interprets this contradictory effect as an indication that some employees view robots as a tool that facilitates their work, while others see them as a loss of resources that threatens their job security (Khaliq et al., 2022). The neutrality of average scores for robot intention and service quality perceptions (M = 3.16 and M = 3.43, respectively) in this research may be a sign of ambivalence reflected in the sample.

Research on employee-robot collaboration has found that a zero-sum mindset is prevalent, where employees perceive organizational resources as limited. Consequently, employees who view robots as a source of competition are more likely to resist them and exhibit less willingness to collaborate (Lu & Jin, 2025; Sirola & Pitesa, 2017). The absence of leadership influence noticed in the research may be the opposing force that's at work here. It is possible that the contradictory psychological processes are occurring simultaneously among the staff, and as a result, they are statistically non-significant despite the presence of underlying psychological dynamics.

Practically, the evidence from this research has a deep impact on the strategies of the hotel management about the application of robots in their hotels. It follows from the primacy of service quality perceptions that the primary factor in the success of robot integration is not the style of leadership, but rather the fact that robotic systems should demonstrate real reliability, deliver consistent performance, and have the ability to meet individualized service needs. In a recent industry report, hotel readiness for robots is defined not only in terms of purchasing hardware and software, but also in terms of specifying employee training, adapting the architecture, conducting organizational readiness assessments, and obtaining leader support in the adoption process (Mejia & Crandell, 2023).

Research has found that when humans and robots work together and coordinate their activities toward a common goal, they enhance the smoothness of the process, foster a stronger team spirit, and ultimately improve customer satisfaction (Le et al., 2024). Nevertheless, to achieve this collaboration, it is necessary to have an accurate plan, open dialogue regarding the roles and limitations of robots, and ongoing efforts to establish employee trust in robotic systems (Van Looy, 2022; Kang et al., 2024). The arguments provided here demonstrate that Greek hotels should first demonstrate the operational capability and reliability of robots through pilot projects, clear performance metrics, and the opportunity for employees to interact with the robotic systems before launching them on a large scale.

The findings of the study should be viewed as the results of the research within the limitations and boundary conditions that it has. First, the sample consisted only of hotel employees in Greece, so the results may not be applicable to different cultural contexts where leadership dynamics, power distance, and technological readiness may vary significantly (Chi et al., 2023; Li et al., 2019). Second, the cross-sectional design of the study is a limitation, as it does not allow the researchers to make causal inferences and cannot show the change in attitudes over time as the use of robots progresses from the planning stage to full adoption. The follow-up research, which monitors employees' perceptions at different stages of implementation, would uncover far more details about how leadership influence may become visible or strengthen over time.

Third, the research only dealt with general leadership styles and did not focus on technology-related leadership behaviors, thus omitting the possible presence of relevant leadership dimensions such as innovative leadership, digital leadership, or rapport leadership, which, in turn, could be more predictive of technology adoption outcomes (Leung et al., 2025). Fourth, the study overlooked the organizational-level factors, such as the organization's culture, change readiness, or existing technological infrastructure, which could moderate the leadership effects (Sarmah et al., 2022; Gentili et al., 2020). Lastly, the research focused on employee perceptions and did not consider the actuality of robot implementations or customer experiences; therefore, it captured only one stakeholder perspective in a complex socio-technical system.

Any study in the future is expected to take care of these limitations and, in addition, explore a range of possible avenues. One of the first differences and similarities in cross-cultural studies measuring the interrelationships between leadership and technology across varied national contexts is that it helps discern how cultural values influence these relationships. The second point to be addressed is the use of experimental or quasi-experimental designs that manipulate leadership behaviors in robot adoption scenarios to clarify the causal relationships more firmly. The third point refers to qualitative research that delves into employees' actual experiences with robotic technologies and their perceptions of leadership support, thereby gaining a deeper understanding of the psychological mechanisms underlying the adoption decision. Fourth, research on the effectiveness of the different leadership styles, especially those that are designed specifically for human-robot collaboration contexts, e.g., the leadership of rapport or leadership through innovation, would not only benefit the theoretical framework but also the practice considerably (Leung et al., 2025; Brahmi et al., 2023). The fifth point is the research that is focused on studying how leadership influences changes or varies depending on different kinds of robotic technologies (e.g., physical vs. cognitive affordances, front-of-house vs. back-of-house applications), thus providing more detailed directions for the strategies of implementation. Lastly, studies of the temporal dynamics of leadership influence at various adoption stages (awareness, consideration, trial, adoption, and sustained use) would reveal the moments when and in what way leadership is the key factor in technology integration processes.

5.6 Conclusions

This study investigated the relationship between leadership styles (transformational, transactional, and passive) and hotel employees' intentions and expectations regarding the quality of service provided by robots. The findings indicate that there is no significant correlation between leadership styles and employees' attitudes toward robot implementation. Furthermore, leadership styles do not appear to influence employee behavior in relation to the quality of service delivered by robots. Conversely, the research revealed a strong positive correlation between the perceived quality of service offered by robots and employees' intentions and expectations regarding their use.

This investigation provides a foundation for organizations seeking to adopt social robotics within their workplaces. By enabling the programming of multiple robotic configurations, it becomes possible to emulate and potentially surpass the capabilities of human employees in terms of adaptability and consistency. As technology continues to evolve, the future of robot-based work environments appear promising, with the potential to revolutionize workplace dynamics. As a result, hotels should implement changing management techniques in order to be ready for this new era (Belias et al., 2023, 2024b; Belias & Trihas, 2022; Belias & Rossidis, 2024).

References

Acosta, L., González, E., Rodríguez, J. N, & Hamilton, A. F. (2006). Design and implementation of a service robot for a restaurant. *International Journal of Robotics and Automation*, 21(4), 273–280.

Aga, D. A., Noorderhaven, N., & Vallejo, B. (2021). Transformational leadership and project success: The mediating role of team-building. *International Journal of Project Management*, 34(5), 806–818. https://doi.org/10.1016/j.ijproman.2016.02.012.

Avolio, B. J., & Bass, B. M. (2004). *Multifactor Leadership Questionnaire. Manual and Sampler Set* (3rd ed.). Redwood City, CA: Mindgarden. https://doi.org/10.1207/s1532754xjprr1602_2.

Bass, B., Avolio, B., Jung, D., & Berson, Y. (2003). Predicting unit performance by assessing transformational and transactional leadership. *The Journal of Applied Psychology*, 88, 207–218. https://doi.org/10.1037/0021-9010.88.2.207.

Bass, B. M., & Avolio, B. J. (2004). *Multifactor Leadership Questionnaire. Manual and Sampler Set* (3rd ed.). Redwood City, CA: Mindgarden.

Belias, D., & Rossidis, I. (2024). *Change Management, Organizational Changes and Organizational Behavior* [in Greek]. Athens: Tziolas publications.

Belias, D., Rossidis, I., Mantas, C., & Ntalakos, A. (2024a). Change management and emotional intelligence leadership: Strategies that the emotional intelligence leadership can adopt during a change industry. In: Belias, D., Rossidis, I., & Papademetriou, C. (eds) *Organizational Behavior and Human Resource Management for Complex Work Environments* (pp. 186–203). New York: IGI Global. https://doi.org/10.4018/979-8-3693-3466-9.ch010.

Belias, D., Trihas, N., & Ntalakos, A. (2024b). Crisis leadership, group dynamics, and change management: A literature review and future perspectives. In: Katsoni, V., & Cassar, G. (eds) *Recent Advancements in Tourism Business, Technology and Social Sciences. IACuDiT 2023. Springer Proceedings in Business and Economics* (pp. 225–244). Cham: Springer. https://doi.org/10.1007/978-3-031-54342-5_13

Belias, D., Trihas, N., Dimou, I., & Kourgiantakis, M. (8–9 June, 2023). The effect of goal motivation on the integration and the success of an organizational change in the hospitality sector. In: *International Conference on Tourism Research* (Vol. 6, No. 1, pp. 34–42). Pafos, Cyprus: Reading: Academic Conferences International Limited.

Belias, D., Rossidis, I., Lazarakis, P., Mantas, C., & Ntalakos, A. (2022). Analyzing organizational *factors in Greek tourism services [Special issue]. Corporate & Business Strategy Review*, 3(2), 248–261. https://doi.org/10.22495/cbsrv3i2siart6

Belias, D., Rossidis, I., Sotiriou, A., & Malik, S. (2022). Workplace conflict, turnover, and quality of services. Case study in greek seasonal hotels. *Journal of Quality Assurance in Hospitality & Tourism*, 24(4), 453–476. https://doi.org/10.1080/1528008X.2022.2065655.

Belias, D., & Trihas, N. (2022). Investigating the readiness for organizational change: A case study from a hotel industry context/Greece. *Journal of Tourism and Management Research*, 7(2), 1047–1062.

Belias, D., & Vasiliadis, L. (2022). Robots on the tourist industry—A review for future research directions. In: Katsoni, V., & *Şerban, A. C. (eds) Transcending Borders in Tourism through Innovation and Cultural Heritage. Springer Proceedings in Business and Economics* (pp. 369–385). Cham: Springer. https://doi.org/10.1007/978-3-030-92491-1_23.

Belias, D., Rossidis, I., Papademetriou, C., & Mantas, C. (2021). Job satisfaction as affected by types of leadership: A case study of Greek tourism sector. *Journal of Quality Assurance in Hospitality & Tourism*, 23(2), 299–317. https://doi.org/10.1080/1528008X.2020.1867695.

Belias, D., & Vasiliadis, L. (2021a). A conceptual study of proposing a model to use robots in hospitality industry based on the empirical evidences. *Journal of Tourism and Management Research*, 6(1), 830–841, https://doi.org/10.26465/ojtmr.2018339544.

Belias, D., & Vasiliadis, L. (2021b). Pilot study for two questionnaires assessing intentions of use and quality of service of robots in the hotel industry. In: Katsoni, V., & van Zyl, C. (eds) *Culture and Tourism in a Smart, Globalized, and Sustainable World. Springer Proceedings in Business and Economics* (pp. 539–558). Cham: Springer. https://doi.org/10.1007/978-3-030-72469-6_36.

Belias, D., Vasiliadis, L., & Rossidis, I. (2021). The intention and expectations of modern robotic technologies in the hotel industry. *Journal of Quality Assurance in Hospitality & Tourism*, 23(6), 1451–1479. https://doi.org/10.1080/1528008X.2021.1995566

Belias, D., & Varelas, S. (2019). To be or not to be? Which is the case with robots in the hotel industry? In: Kavoura, A., Kefallonitis, E., Giovanis, A. (eds) *Strategic Innovative Marketing and Tourism. Springer Proceedings in Business and Economics* (pp. 935–941). Cham: Springer. https://doi.org/10.1007/978-3-030-12453-3_108.

Bhimasta, R. A., & Kuo, P. Y. (2019). What causes the adoption failure of service robots? A Case of Henn-na Hotel in Japan. In: *Adjunct Proceedings of the 2019 ACM International Joint Conference on Pervasive and Ubiquitous Computing and Proceedings of the 2019 ACM International Symposium on Wearable Computers* (pp. 1107–1112). London, UK.

Brahmi, M., Agheorghiesei, D. T., & Tugui, A. (2023). Assessment of a workforce sustainability tool through leadership and digitalization. *Sustainable Technology and Entrepreneurship*, 2(2), 100039. https://doi.org/10.1016/j.stae.2023.100039.

Brougham, D., & Haar, J. (2018). Smart technology, artificial intelligence, robotics, and algorithms (STARA): Employees' perceptions of our future workplace. *Journal of Management & Organization*, 24(2), 239–257. https://doi.org/10.1017/jmo.2016.55.

Buhalis, D., Harwood, T., Bogicevic, V., Viglia, G., Beldona, S., & Hofacker, C. (2019). Technological disruptions in services: Lessons from tourism and hospitality. *Journal of Service Management*, 30(4), 484–506. https://doi.org/10.1108/JOSM-12-2018-0398.

Cain, L. N., Thomas, J. H., & Alonso, M. Jr. (2019). From sci-fi to sci-fact: The state of robotics and AI in the hospitality industry. *Journal of Hospitality and Tourism Technology*, 10, 624–650. https://doi.org/10.1108/JHTT-07-2018-0066.

Chen, Y., Arkin, J., Zhang, Y., Roy, N., & Fan, C. (2024). Scalable multi-robot collaboration with large language models: Centralized or decentralized systems? *In 2024 IEE International Conference on Robotics an Automation (ICRA)*, 4311–4317. IEEE.

Chi, O. H., Gursoy, D., & Chi, C. G. (2023). The effects of service robots' perceived cuteness on customers' emotions and behavioral intentions. *International Journal of Hospitality Management*, 108, 103380.

Choi, Y., Oh, M., Heo, S., & Hyun, S. S. (2023). Service robots in hotels: Understanding the service quality perceptions of human-robot interaction. *Journal of Hospitality and Tourism Management*, 52, 87–97.

Dang, J., & Liu, L. (2020). Robots are friends as well as foes: Ambivalent attitudes toward mindful and mindless AI robots in the United States and China. *Computers in Human Behavior*, 115. https://doi.org/10.1016/j.chb.2020.106612.

Eckardt, R., Tsai, C.-Y., Dionne, S. D., Dunne, D., Spain, S. M., Park, J. W., & Kim, E. I. (2020). Human capital resource emergence and leadership. *Journal of Organizational Behavior*. https://doi.org/10.1002/job.2446.

Fan, A., Wu, L. L., Mattila, A. S., & Dong, P. (2022). Does anthropomorphism influence customers' willingness to pay? The humanizing role of anthropomorphic service robots. *International Journal of Contemporary Hospitality Management*, 34(12), 4504–4527.

Fosch-Villaronga, E., & Albo-Canals, J. (2019). "I'll take care of you", said the robot. Paladyn, *Journal of Behavioral Robotics*, 10(1), 77–93. https://doi.org/10.1515/pjbr-2019-0006

Fu, S., Cheng, X., De Vreede, T., De Vreede, G. J., Seeber, I., Maier, R., & Weber, B. (2022). Exploring preference for virtual agent gender similarity in human-agent collaboration. *Information Systems Frontiers*, 24, 1819–1836.

Gallimore, D., Lyons, J. B., Vo, T., Mahoney, S., & Wynne, K. T. (2019). Trusting robocop: Gender-based effects on trust of an autonomous robot. *Frontiers in Psychology*, 10, 1–9. https://doi.org/10.3389/fpsyg.2019.00482.

Gentili, M., Johansen, I., & Nystrand, B. T. (2020). Women and men in information and communication technology (ICT) in Europe: The gap gets narrower but still remains. *Social Sciences*, 9(5), 75. https://doi.org/10.3390/socsci9050075.

Giannakos, K., Belias, D., Ntalakos, A., Rossidis, I., & Koustelios, A. (2024). Are leadership styles related to change integration and commitment? The case of general hospitals. *Archives of Hellenic Medicine*, 41(3), 354–362.

HCH (2024). *Hellenic Chamber of Hotels*. [online] Retrieved from https://www.grhotels.gr/en/ (Last Accessed at 25th November 2024).

Hofstede, G. (2001). *Culture's Consequences: Comparing Values, Behaviors, Institutions and Organizations across Nations* (2nd ed.). Thousand Oaks, CA: Sage Publications.

Ivanov, S. H., Webster, C., & Berezina, K. (2017). Adoption of robots and service automation by tourism and hospitality companies. *Revista Tur Smo & Desenvolvimento*, 27/28, 1501–1517.

Ivanov, S. H., Webster, C., & Garenko, A. (2018). Young Russian adults' attitudes towards the potential use of robots in hotels. *Technology in Society*, 55, 24–32. Available at: https://ssrn.com/abstract=3193017.

Ivanov, S., & Webster, C. (2019). Perceived appropriateness and intention to use service robots in tourism. In: J. Pesonen & J. Neidhardt (eds) *Information and Communication Technologies in Tourism* (pp. 237–248), Cham: Springer International.

Ivanov, S., & Webster, C. (2020). Exploring the barriers and prospects for service robot adoption in the hotel industry: A management perspective. *Tourism Management Perspectives*, 35, 100717.

Ivanov, S., & Webster, C. (2021). Willingness-to-pay for hotel robots. *Tourism Economics*.. https://doi.org/10.1108/IJCHM-09-2020-1078

Ivanov, S., Webster, C., & Seyyedi, P. (2020). Consumers' attitudes towards the introduction of robots in accommodation establishments. *Tourism*, 68(2), 134–147.

Johnson, M., Shrewsbury, B., Bertrand, S., Wu, T., Duran, D., Floyd, M., Pratt, J. (2015). Team IHMC's lessons learned from the DARPA robotics challenge trials. *Journal of Field Robotics*, 2, 192–208.

Kabadayi, S., Ali, F., Choi, H., Joosten, H., & Lu, C. (2019). Smart service experience in hospitality and tourism services. *Journal of Service Management*, 30(3), 326–348.

Kalsoom, Z., Ali Khan, M., Zubair, S. S. (2018). Impact of transactional leadership and transformational leadership on employee performance: A case of FMCG industry of Pakistan. *Industrial Engineering Letters*, 8, 23–30.

Kang, J., Shin, H., & Kang, C. (2024). Hospitality labor leakage and dynamic turnover behaviors in the age of artificial intelligence and robotics. *Journal of Hospitality and Tourism Technology*, 15(5), 916–933. https://doi.org/10.1108/JHTT-12-2023-0411.

Khaliq, M., Rehman, M., Iqbal, A., & Rasool, A. (2022). The role of technology in shaping the future of hospitality: Challenges and opportunities. *International Journal of Hospitality Management*, 103, 103210.

Khoa, D. T., Gip, H. Q., Guchait, P., & Wang, C. Y. (2023). Competition or collaboration for human-robot relationship: A critical reflection on future cobotics in hospitality. *International Journal of Contemporary Hospitality Management*, 35(6), 2202–2215. https://doi.org/10.1108/IJCHM-04-2022-0434.

Koo, C., Xiang, Z., Gretzel, U., & Sigala, M. (2021). Artificial intelligence (AI) and robotics in travel, hospitality and leisure. *Electronic Markets*, 31(3), 473–476. https://doi.org/10.1007/s12525-021-00494-z.

Le, H. T. K., Dong, P., & Cherian, J. (2024). The effectiveness of human-robot collaboration in service settings. *International Journal of Contemporary Hospitality Management*, 36(3), 891–910.

Lee, S. (2024). Exploring perceived benefits of service robots on customers' experiences. *Frontiers in Robotics and AI*, 11, 1667123.

Leung, X. Y., Zhang, H., Lyu, J., & Bai, B. (2023). Why do hotel frontline employees use service robots in the workplace? A technology affordance theory perspective. *International Journal of Hospitality Management*, 108, 103380. https://doi.org/10.1016/j.ijhm.2022.103380.

Leung, X. Y., Jin, D., & Shi, X. (2025). Rethinking hospitality leadership: Cultivating human-robot co-working harmony through rapport leadership. *Journal of Hospitality & Tourism Research*. https://doi.org/10.1177/10963480251328575.

Li, J. J., Bonn, M. A., & Ye, B. H. (2019). Hotel employee's artificial intelligence and robotics awareness and its impact on turnover intention: The moderating roles of perceived organizational support and competitive psychological climate. *Tourism Management*, 73, 172–181. https://doi.org/10.1016/j.tourman.2019.02.006.

Lisetti, C. L., & Schiano, D. (2000). Facial expression recognition: Where human-computer interaction, artificial intelligence, and cognitive science intersect. *Pragmatics and Cognition*, 8, 185–235.

Lopes, S. L., Rocha, B., Ferreira, A. I., & Prada, R. (2021). Social robots as leaders: Leadership styles in human-robot teams. *30th IEEE International Conference on Robot & Human Interactive Communication (RO-MAN),* Vancouver, BC, Canada (pp. 258–263). https://doi.org/10.1109/RO-MAN50785.2021.9515464.

Lu, L., & Jin, D. (2025). Improving employee-robot collaboration in hospitality: Understanding the zero-sum mindset. *Computers in Human Behavior*, 154, 108189. https://doi.org/10.1016/j.chb.2024.108189.

Manyika, J., Chui, M., Bughin, J., Dobbs, R., Bisson, P., & Marrs, A. (2013). *Disruptive Technologies: Advances that Will Transform Life, Business, and the Global Economy*. New York: McKinsey Global Institute.

Mejia, C., & Crandell, H. (2023). Is your hospitality business ready for a robot? *Harvard Business Review*. Retrieved from https://hbr.org/2023/11/is-your-hospitality-business-ready-for-a-robot.

Mohanty, P. P., & Munir, A. (2024). Contactless service in post-COVID-19: An insight from the hospitality industry. In: *Post-COVID Tourism and Hospitality Management* (pp. 145–168). Taylor & Francis.

Naumov, N. (2019). The impact of robots, artificial intelligence, and service automation on service quality and service experience in hospitality. In: Ivanov, S. & Webster, G. (eds) *Robots, Artificial Intelligence, and Service Automation in Travel, Tourism and Hospitality* (pp. 123–133). Emerald Publishing Limited. https://doi.org/10.1108/978-1-78756-687-320191007

Nguyen, T. (2023). The mediating role of technology acceptance in knowledge sharing and technology adoption: Evidence from transformational leadership. *Journal of Knowledge Management*, 27(5), 1234–1256.

Ntalakos, A., Belias, D., Rossidis, I., Koustelios, A. (2024). The impact of trait emotional intelligence on transformational leadership: The case of managers and employees of hotel companies. In: Valeri, M. (ed) *Managerial Perceptions. Contributions to Management Science*. Cham: Springer. https://doi.org/10.1007/978-3-031-67849-3_13

Ntalakos, A., Belias, D., & Tsigilis, N. (2023a). Leadership styles and group dynamics in the tourism industry. In: Katsoni, V. (ed) *Tourism, Travel, and Hospitality in a Smart and Sustainable World. IACuDiT 2022. Springer Proceedings in Business and Economics*. Cham: Springer. https://doi.org/10.1007/978-3-031-29426-6_8.

Ntalakos, A., Belias, D., Rossidis, I., Koustelios, A., Tsigilis, N., & Vasiliadis, L. (2023b). Communicating the vision of the change: The linkage between organizational communication, organizational culture, and organizational change. In Belias, D., Rossidis, I., Papademetriou, C., Masouras, A., & Anastasiadou, S. (eds) *Managing Successful and Ethical Organizational Change* (pp. 76–101). New York: IGI Global. https://doi.org/10.4018/979-8-3693-0235-4.ch004.

Osawa, H., Ema, A., Hattori, H., Akiya, N., Kanzaki, N., & Kubo, A. (2017). Analysis of robot hotel: Reconstruction of works with robots. *26th IEEE International Symposium on Robot and Human Interactive Communication (RO-MAN), Lisbon, Portugal, 2017* (pp. 219–223). https://doi.org/10.1109/ROMAN.2017.8172305.

Osei, B. A., Ragavan, N. A., & Mensah-Darkwa, K. (2024). Service robot adoption in hotels: Examining managerial barriers in developing countries. *Journal of Hospitality and Tourism Technology*, 15(2), 187–204.

Palrão, T., Rodrigues, R., Madeira, A., Mendes, A., & Lopes, S. (2023). Robots in tourism and hospitality: The perception of future professionals. *Human Behavior and Emerging Technologies*, 2023, 7172152. https://doi.org/10.1155/2023/7172152.

Papademetriou, C., Anastasiadou, S., Ragazou, K., Garefalakis, A., & Belias, D. (2023). Obstacles and resistances to organizational changes. In: Belias, D., Rossidis, I., Papademetriou, C., Masouras, A., & Anastasiadou, S. (eds) *Managing Successful and Ethical Organizational Change* (pp. 144–166). New York: IGI Global. https://doi.org/10.4018/979-8-3693-0235-4.ch007.

Parasuraman, A., Zeithaml, V., & Berry, L. L. (1991). Refinement and reassessment of the Servqual scale. *Journal of Retailing*, 67(4), 420–450.

Parvez, M., Maheshwari, G., & Khandakar, M. S. A. (2022). Human-robot collaboration in hospitality: A systematic review and future research directions. *International Journal of Contemporary Hospitality Management*, 34(11), 4152–4179.

Pochwatko, G., Giger, J.-C., Różańska-Walczuk, M., Świdrak, J., Kukiełka, K., Możaryn, J., & Piçarra, N. (2015). Polish version of the negative attitude toward robots scale (NARS-PL). *Journal of Automation, Mobile Robotics and Intelligent Systems*, 9(3), 65–72. https://doi.org/10.14313/JAMRIS_2-2015/25.

Prentice, C., & Nguyen, M. (2021). Robotic service quality: A new approach to understanding service quality in the hospitality industry. *International Journal of Hospitality Management*, 94, 102876.

Prentice, C., & Nguyen, M. (2025). Service quality dimensions in robotic hospitality services: Automation, personalization, precision, and efficiency. *Frontiers in Robotics and AI*, 11, 1667123.

Riedl, R., Mohr, P., Kenning, P., Davis, F., & Heereken, H. (2014). Trusting humans and avatars: A brain imaging study based on evolution theory. *Journal of Management Information Systems*, 30, 83–114. https://doi.org/10.2753/MIS0742-1222300404.

Rossidis, I., Belias, D., & Aspridis, G. (2020). *Change Management and Leadership*. Athens: Tziolas publications.

Rossidis, I., Belias, D., Papailias, S., Tsiotas, D., Niavis, S., & Vasiliadis, L. (2019). The use of customer relations management's digital technologies from Greek hotels. In: Kavoura, A., Kefallonitis, E., Giovanis, A. (eds) *Strategic Innovative Marketing and Tourism. Springer Proceedings in Business and Economics* (pp. 77–84). Cham: Springer. https://doi.org/10.1007/978-3-030-12453-3_9.

Sadangharn, P. (2022). Acceptance of robots as co-workers: Hotel employees' perspective. *International Journal of Engineering Business Management*, 14, https://doi.org/10.1177/18479790221113621.

Samani, H. A., Koh, J. T. K. V., Saadatian, E., & Polydorou, D. (2012). Towards robotics leadership: An analysis of leadership characteristics and the roles robots will inherit in future human society. In: Pan, J.S., Chen, S.M., Nguyen, N.T. (eds) *Intelligent Information and Database Systems. ACIIDS 2012. Lecture Notes in Computer Science*, vol 7197 (pp. 158–165). Berlin, Heidelberg: Springer. https://doi.org/10.1007/978-3-642-28490-8_17.

Sarmah, B., Islam, J. U., & Rahman, Z. (2022). Psychological contract violation and employee outcomes: The moderating role of autonomy-supportive culture. *Personnel Review*, 51(3), 912–930.

Schepers, J., Wetzels, M., & de Ruyter, K. (2005). Leadership styles in technology acceptance: Do followers practice what leaders preach? *Managing Service Quality*, 15(6), 496–508. https://doi.org/10.1108/09604520510634023.

Sinha, N., Matharu, M., & Sharma, P. (2020). Employee perceptions of technology adoption in service organizations: The role of management support. *Journal of Service Theory and Practice*, 30(4), 451–470.

Sirola, N., & Pitesa, M. (2017). Economic downturns undermine workplace helping by promoting a zero-sum construal of success. *Academy of Management Journal*, 60(4), 1339–1359.

Song, H., Kim, J., & Choi, Y. (2022). The effects of service robot attributes on customer trust and satisfaction in hotels. *International Journal of Contemporary Hospitality Management*, 34(8), 3042–3063.

Tsai, C. Y., Marshall, J., Choudhury, A., Serban, A., Tsung-Yu Hou, Y. Y, Jung, M., Shelley D., & Yammarino, F. (2022). Human-robot collaboration: A multilevel and integrated leadership framework, *The Leadership Quarterly*, 33 (1), https://doi.org/10.1016/j.leaqua.2021.101594.

Tung, V. W. S., & Law, R. (2017). The potential for tourism and hospitality experience research in human-robot interactions. *International Journal of Contemporary Hospitality Management*, 29(10), 2498–2513. https://doi.org/10.1108/IJCHM-09-2016-0520.

Tussyadiah, I. P., Zach, F. K., & Wang, J. (2017). Attitudes toward autonomous on demand mobility system: The case of self-driving taxi. In: Schegg, R., & Stangl, B. (eds) *Information and Communication Technologies in Tourism 2017* (pp. 755–766). Cham: Springer. https://doi.org/10.1007/978-3-319-51168-9_54.

Tussyadiah, I. P., & Park, S. (2018). Consumer evaluation of hotel service robots. In: Stangl, B. & Pesonen, J. (eds) *Information and Communication Technologies in Tourism 2018* (pp. 308–320). Cham, Switzerland: Springer.

Tussyadiah, I. P., Zach, F. J., & Wang, J. (2020). Do travellers trust intelligent service robots? *Annals of Tourism Research*, 81(C), 1–14, https://doi.org/10.1016/j.annals.2020.102886

Van, L. (2020). Adding intelligent robots to business processes: A dilemma analysis of employees' attitudes. In: Fahland, D., Ghidini, C., Becker, J., & Dumas, M. (eds) *Business Process Management. BPM 2020. Lecture Notes in Computer Science* (pp. 435–452), vol 12168. Cham: Springer. https://doi.org/10.1007/978-3-030-58666-9_25

Van Looy, A. (2020). Adding intelligent robots to business processes: A dilemma analysis of employees' attitudes. In: Fahland, D., Ghidini, C., Becker, J., & Dumas, M. (eds) *Business process management. BPM 2020. Lecture notes in computer science* (pp. 435–452), vol 12168. Cham: Springer. https://doi.org/10.1007/978-3-030-58666-9_25

Van Looy, A. (2022). Social robots in service encounters: Exploring employee attitudes and trust development. *Journal of Service Management*, 33(2), 289–312.

Viterouli, M., Belias, D., Koustelios, A., Tsigilis, N., & Papademetriou, C. (2024). Time for change: Designing tailored training initiatives for organizational transformation. In: Belias, D., Rossidis, I., & Papademetriou, C. (eds) *Organizational Behavior and Human Resource Management for Complex Work Environments* (pp. 267–307). New York: IGI Global. https://doi.org/10.4018/979-8-3693-3466-9.ch014.

Wei, F., Yuan, X., & Di, Y. (2010). Effects of transactional leadership, psychological empowerment and empowerment climate on creative performance of subordinates: A cross-level study. *Frontiers of Business Research in China*, 4, 29–46.

Wei, Y. L. (2013). *Skills talent development for the next ten years of Taiwan*. [online]. Retrieved from https://www.itis.org.tw/pubreport/pubreport_detail.aspx?rpno64558015&chaptername/E7/B5/90/E8/AB/96/E8/88/87/E6/94/BF/E7/AD/96/E5/BB/BA/E8/AD/B0. Last accessed 10 November 2024.

Willemse, C., Marchesi, S., & Wykowska, A. (2018). Robot faces that follow gaze facilitate attentional engagement and increase their likeability. *Frontiers in Psychology*, 9, 1–11. https://doi.org/10.3389/fpsyg.2018.00070.

Woodward, N., Nguyen, T., Zhu, L., Fowler, C., Kim, T., Near, S., Thoemmes, S., & Williams, T. (2020). Exploring Interaction Design Considerations for Trustworthy Language-Capable Robotic Wheelchairs in Virtual Reality, *3rd International Workshop on Virtual, Augmented, and Mixed Reality for Human-Robot Interaction* (VAM-HRI).

Wu, J. H., & Wang, S. C. (2005). What drives mobile commerce?: An empirical evaluation of the revised technology acceptance model. *Information & Management*, 42(5), 719–729.

Wykowska, A. (2021). Robots as mirrors of the human mind. *Current Directions in Psychological Science*, 30(1), 34–40. https://doi.org/10.1177/0963721420978609.

Xu, S., Stienmetz, J., & Ashton, M. (2020). How will service robots redefine leadership in hotel management? A Delphi approach. *International Journal of Contemporary Hospitality Management*, 32(6), 2217–2237. https://doi.org/10.1108/IJCHM-05-2019-0505.

Yammarino, F. J., Cheong, M., Kim, J., & Tsai, C.-Y. (2020). Is leadership more than "I like my boss"? In: Buckley, M. R. Wheeler, A. R. Baur, J. E. & Halbesleben, J. R. B. (eds) *Research in Personnel and Human Resources Management* (Vol. 38, pp. 1–55). Leeds: Emerald Publishing Limited. https://doi.org/10.1108/S0742-7301202038.

Yu, C. E. (2018). Humanlike robot and human staff in service: Age and gender differences in perceiving smiling behaviours. In: *Proceedings of the 7th International Conference on Industrial Technology and Management (ICITM), Oxford, United Kingdom* (pp. 99–103). New York: IEEE.

Yu, C. E. (2020). Humanlike robots as employees in the hotel industry: Thematic content analysis of online reviews. *Journal of Hospitality Marketing & Management*, 29(1), 22–38.

Zhang, H., Lu, Y., Shi, R., & Law, R. (2024). Employee perceptions of service robots: A technology affordance perspective. *Tourism Management*, 100, 104819.

Zerva, S., Belias, D., Rossidis, I., & Ntalakos, A. (2024). Examining the impact of leadership on job satisfaction in Greek luxury hotels. *Journal of Human Resources in Hospitality & Tourism*, 23(3), 439–464. https://doi.org/10.1080/15332845.2024.2335123.

6

Effect of Service Robots on Service Jobs: A Meta-analysis

Klaas Koerten

6.1 Introduction

The major challenge of the hospitality industry, in general, and hotel managers, specifically, are labour shortages (Luther, 2024). This problem has been growing for a longer time but was amplified by the Covid-19 pandemic (Hotrec, 2022). Due to lockdowns, restaurants and hotels were forced to shut down for periods of time, which required them to let go some of their staff (Tu et al., 2021). During these uncertain times, these employees found new jobs and, as the pandemic receded, did not return to the hospitality industry (Kirk, 2024). Simultaneously, the pandemic increased the need for contactless service, something that could be achieved by using digital interfaces rather than human service agents (Pillay, 2021). During this time, restaurant robots were implemented in various hospitality venues. This combination of employee shortages and the need for contactless service has put service robots to the forefront, and publications in top hospitality journals now introduce robots as something that has gradually replaced service employees (Ma et al., 2024) or that has experienced widespread adoption in the hospitality industry (Yang et al., 2022). Using robots to take over tasks fundamentally solves a symptom rather than the problem causing it. The problem here being employees moving away to other industries, and the symptom being hospitality managers that need to run operations with less personnel. Not all tasks in a hotel can be automated or robotized yet, and because of that, human employees will inevitably have to work alongside robots. Automation can greatly alter a job (Sorenson et al., 2019, Chapter 10), and there is a chance of this increasing turnover intention (Torrance et al., 2023). If this happens, the initial employment problem will not be solved but amplified. In a changing servicescape, it is important for human resource leaders to know which

DOI: 10.1201/9781003742791-6

robots might improve job quality and decrease employee shortages in the long term. Taking an employee-centric approach is crucial here. Therefore, this chapter will look at how employee-robot interactions have been studied in hospitality. We will first elaborate on the current state of hospitality robotics and the effects of automation on work. Next, we will perform a systematic review of the hospitality literature to identify every paper that has researched the effect of robots on employees. This will allow us to draw useful learnings to inform the industry.

6.2 Background

6.2.1 Existing Types of Robots in Hospitality

The current types of robots used in hospitality are diverse but limited. The most used robot type in hospitality used today is the logistic robot, which derives its design from a category of industrial robots, called automated guided vehicles, or AGVs (Ganesharajah et al., 1998). These robots take the form of wheeled vehicles that move autonomously through various environments to transport items. In hospitality, robots like this are used to transport dishes in restaurants, to deliver room service and to guests and to transport luggage. In the case of restaurants, AGV-type robots can boost revenue (Shimmura et al., 2020) while at the same time reducing the number of steps employees have to take. They are limited by their wheeled design, and by their low driving speeds.

The second type of robot that is used in hospitality is the interaction robot. Guests interact with these robots through a tablet interface or via speech. The robot can provide the guest with information or execute a digital task, like performing a check in or digital sales action. Designs of interaction robots differ from simple tablet designs like Temi (Lynn, 2023), to anthropomorphic designs like pepper (Etemad-Sajadi, 2018) or even extravagant raptor-shaped receptionists (Ono, 2018). They can operate outlets that would normally be manned by human personnel and are limited by their lack of physical capabilities and the sophistication of their programming.

Robotic arms also get used in hospitality, often to perform a very specific physical food production task. Examples include robotic cocktail shakers (Oggero, 2024), baristas (Bacon, 2024) or pizza bakers (Mahendra, 2022) These robots can execute predetermined tasks reliably and fast and are limited by the number of tasks and high investment costs.

Some hotels also make use of floor cleaning robots that autonomously vacuum or mop floors. Designs differ from vacuum robots (Maciborski, 2024) to robots capable of floor scrubbing (Editor, 2024). They can clean large surface areas without the need for human intervention and are limited by their wheeled design and volume. A scrubbing robot, for example, might be unable to reach narrow corners and clean underneath tables due to its size.

While each type of robot has clear benefits, we also see innovative concepts that turn out to be unsuccessful, like the autonomous pizza restaurant mentioned above that had to go out of business (Wolf, 2022) or the hotel that had to change some of its robot workers back to human workers because the robots underperformed (Newman, 2019).

6.2.2 The Analogy from Manufacturing

The robots that are currently able to be implemented in hotels execute a range of tasks: transportation, interaction, cleaning floors or autonomous preparation of meals or drinks. This makes it easy to imagine robots taking over every task that currently is done by human workers. However, this does not mean that such a robot always exists. Imaginaries of perfect robots are difficult to define and are influenced by science fiction as well as existing examples of robots (Sorenson et al., 2019). Existing examples of hyper-efficient robots come from factories, where robots have been replacing jobs since the 1950s as robots allowed operations to be executed with less personnel (Gasparetto and Scalera, 2019). But industrial robots are not imitations of human workers, rather they are machines tailored to specific tasks, and their capabilities therefore differ from human workers. When drawing inspiration from automation to envision the future of hospitality, it is important to note the limits of industrial automation with robots as well as the differences between manufacturing and hospitality environments. The report by Benmelech and Zator (2022) provides insight into where industrial robots have proven successful. These robots are costly, with an average price of $45,000 for a robotic arm, and the reason that so many of them are deployed nowadays is the fact that they can work more constant and precise than human workers, increasing production and efficiency. Benmelech and Zator (2022) also show that successful robotization has only been happening in a few 'poster child' industries such as automotive, where the investments are worthwhile. They also show that the apparent growth of the industry is not due to the adoption of robots in new industries, but rather in the old industries that are still developing in certain countries. The hospitality environment differs greatly from manufacturing environments. In manufacturing, efficiency can be clearly measured by the number of items produced and resources used for that. In hospitality, however, providing a guest with some extra time might increase their guest satisfaction rather than having interactions be quicker.

6.2.3 A Worker Central Perspective

Sorenson et al. (2019) provide a detailed ethnographic overview of (partially) robotized work by interviewing 160 stakeholders, ranging between physical workers, small business owners and robot engineers. As the book is published in 2020, it does not study hospitality as a discipline where robotization is happening, but the concepts from other industries translate well to the current hospitality situation. Chapter 1 discusses how robot development is often performed in an inner circle, where robot engineers communicate with application experts, the ones who might eventually buy the robots, these are hotel and restaurant managers in the hospitality case. Sorenson et al. (2019) warn that such an inner circle process often disregards the end users of the robot, the operational employees and guests in the hospitality case. Chapter 10 of Sorenson et al. (2019) furthermore provides an evaluation of the concept of meaningful work and the effect of robots and automation on it. It coins the term technochauvinism, referring to the belief that technology is the superior source of labour and that automating tasks is part of an inevitable process. It explains that workers are not just a source of labour, but real people who have values and goals, and work is more than just a transaction of labour for salary. It states that when robot suppliers (engineers and manufacturers) and robot buyers (hotel managers in this case) determine which tasks should be automated without considering the end users' (workers) values, tasks that are deemed enjoyable might be automated which could result in negative organizational and societal consequences. The chapter explains that partial automation, where tasks rather than jobs are automated, can result in employees experiencing less enjoyment because of isolation (when they must work with a robot instead of a human colleague). It can also result in employee resistance where they do not use, and in some cases even sabotage the new technology they are supposed to work with.

6.2.4 Methods

To find out how employee-robot interactions are being researched in the hospitality literature, the platforms Scopus and Web of Science were searched, combining the terms 'Restaurant', 'Hotel' or 'Hospitality' with the terms 'Robot' or 'Automation'. After eliminating duplicates, a total of 1271 results came out of this search. We then limited our search to articles published in English from 2014 to 2023 resulting in 642 articles. Next we read the abstracts to extract the articles that empirically collect data from hospitality employees. This resulted in 30 articles published between 2017 and 2023.

6.3 Results

A total of 30 papers were extracted from the literature search. First of all, looking at publication years, it can be seen that the first paper came from 2017, and, as Figure 6.1 shows, there is an increase in the amount of hospitality

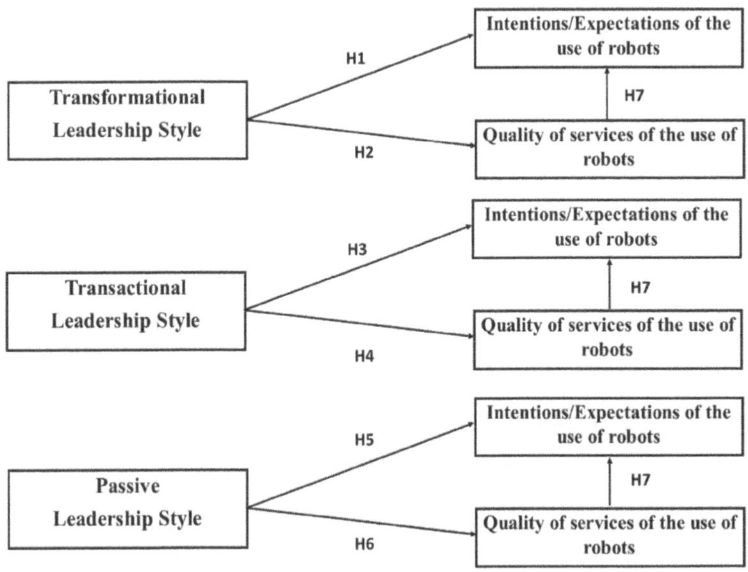

FIGURE 6.1
The Amount of Empirical Publications on Employees and Hospitality Robotics Per Year

robotics papers using employees as respondents. We divide the papers into qualitative studies, quantitative studies and mixed method studies and report on the information that is provided to respondents and the participants that were used.

6.3.1 Qualitative Studies

Twelve of the 30 papers adopted a qualitative method in their research. These studies ask respondents mostly open-ended questions and have an exploratory nature. The goal is to gain insight into the possible benefits and challenges of robots in hospitality. Several papers use interviews to gain insight into the potential that robots hold for hospitality work. Kuo et al. (2017) researched the potential of robots through an expert panel with three tech professors as well as semi-structured interviews with 20 robot experts. They acknowledge that during the time of their research, robots are not adopted widely in hospitality but conclude that hotels can market themselves as tech savvy by using robots. Leung (2019) interviewed nine hotel managers and investors. They found that the definition of smart hotels differed between the participants. And that the respondents were more focused on short-term operational efficiency than on long-term strategic goals for robots and technology. Xu et al. (2020) interviewed 19 human resource managers about how service robots would change the nature of work. ISO's definition of a service robot was provided to participants. The participants stated that robots can lead to increased efficiency but also skill deficit. Because of this, leaders need to balance human and robotic capital. Gupta et al. (2022) interviewed 26 hotel employees in North Korea, 12 of which were managers. No information was provided, and robots were seen by the respondents as a technique that would be able to streamline services and gather data.

Vatan and Dogan (2021) interviewed 40 hospitality employees from Turkey. They note their perceived advantages and disadvantages of working with robots. No information was provided about robots, and the word robot evokes negative emotions with the respondents. The interviewed employees foresee communication problems with robots. Seyitoğlu et al. (2023) interviewed 30 Turkish hospitality students without providing them with information about robots. Participants report on hospitality robots' potential to take over dull tasks and solve conflicts between human employees. Downsides are the robots' lack social skills. Devkant (2022) qualitatively interviewed 80 hospitality students without providing them with information about robots. They are positive towards robots but see employee resistance as a possible downside. Nam et al. (2021) interviewed eight hotel asset managers from Dubai. An overview of current possibilities was provided for the participants. Respondents expect robots to replace physical tasks and enhance more cognitive, creative tasks. Seyitoğlu et al. (2021) interviewed 26 Turkish hotel managers about hospitality robotics after providing them with a video of hospitality robotics. Participants explained that robots are suitable for specific tasks. They see potential in the efficiency created by robots but are concerned about possible job losses that robots would create. Sadangharn (2022b) interviewed 8 managers and 22 employees. They deployed a concierge robot in a hotel in Thailand. Employees do see potential and attractiveness but also drawbacks given the limited capabilities and technical failures of the robot. Fu et al. (2022) discuss the decommissioning of robots. Nineteen managers and supervisors from China were interviewed who all had experience with service robots but decommissioned them. The findings are mainly negative and consider, for example, a technology misfit, low social presence and increased employee anxiety. Ghazy and Fedorova (2022) surveyed 167 Russian hotel employees. According to these employees, robots will make people lose contact with each other and robots will control jobs. Researchers explained the concept of robots first to the employees. Although this study surveyed employees through close-ended Likert scale questions, we have categorized it as qualitative as its goal is to find attitudes from employees towards robots.

6.3.2 Quantitative Studies

Thirteen of the papers adopted a quantitative method to study hospitality robotics. Studies adopt Likert scale close-ended questions to measure constructs and identify relationships between these constructs. Some studies use the acceptance or reported ease of use as the final construct. Lee et al. (2018), for example, surveyed 382 managers about restaurant robots specifically. Trust and output quality drive perceived usefulness, Trust and interactivity drive perceived ease of use. Usefulness and ease of use then correlate with attitude towards robots, which correlates with acceptance and usefulness. Similarly, Kim (2023) surveyed 158 employees working at 11 hotels in Korea. A verbal description of frontline service robots is added to inform employees. Willingness to cooperate correlates with ease of use, and perceived usefulness and perceived risk are negatively correlated with these two. Other studies focus on the intention to use or adopt robots. Abdelhakim et al. (2023) study 428 fast food employees in Egypt and Malaysia (223/205). Ease of use, recommendation and knowledge and skills required to operate the robot correlate positively with the intention to use robots. Similarly, Palrão et al. (2023) surveyed 358 hospitality students. Perceptions of novelty and performance management correlate positively with willingness to work in a partially robotized environment. Leung et al. (2023) surveyed 212 frontline employees. Descriptions of robots were provided via videos. They find that robot trust is positively correlated with the intention to collaborate with service robots. Pizam et al. (2022) surveyed 1077 managers of hotels from 11 different countries. Their finding is that the intention to adopt robots was positively correlated with relative advantage, competitive pressure and top management support, but perceived complexity negatively influenced intention to adopt. Then there is a group of studies acknowledging robots' possibilities to increase intention of employees to leave the industry, taking turnover intention as a construct in their quantitative studies. Zhang et al. (2023) study the effect of robot usage on employees' turnover intention. They found out that robot usage correlates positively with work autonomy, which correlates negatively with turnover intention. It also correlates negatively with job insecurity, which correlates negatively with turnover intention. Frontline employees from 18 hotels in China were used as a response group. Yu et al. (2022) study 282 service employees in China and find that tech savviness and social skills negatively influence service robot risk awareness, which lowers turnover intention. Khaliq et al. (2022) surveyed 330 managers and frontline employees (151/179) in Pakistan. How much employees thought their job was able to be automated correlates with their intention to leave the industry. We found two studies focusing on robot-induced unemployment. Alzoubi and Zoubi (2023) studied 401 participants in Jordan. Robot-induced unemployment is influenced by their social skills, perceived risk, awareness and trust in using service robots. Likewise, Parvez et al. (2022) surveyed 405 employees from the United States, and 32% of which are managers. Perceived advantages correlate with robots-induced unemployment. No information about robots was disclosed to the participants in these studies. There is also one study focusing on employee well-being. Yang et al. (2022) study 332 hospitality employees in China. Employees who had robots employed at their work were compared with those who did not. The researchers conclude that employees who work at venues that have robots employed report higher well-being. Finally, Song et al. (2022) surveyed 407 frontline employees from 16 hotel chains in China. Perceived risk and perceived playfulness correlate with effort expectancy and performance expectancy. Employees who had experience with robots were targeted specifically. The final constructs are relational crafting and task crafting, referring to how service robots generate new social connections or innovative job tasks.

6.3.3 Mixed Method Studies

Lastly, five papers used multiple methods to research hospitality robots. Four of these make use of interviews first and then quantitative surveys (Ivanov et al., 2020; Sadangharn, 2022a; Ali et al., 2023). Ivanov et al. (2020) interview Bulgarian hotel managers; 20 managers were interviewed, and 79 managers were surveyed. Results show that managers see merit in robots taking over repetitive tasks. No information about robots is provided to respondents. Sadangharn (2022a) took 30 interviews with managers and employees and quantitatively evaluated 400 employees. The robot's advantage mentioned is its attractiveness, and the disadvantages are the limited movement and technical errors it causes. Ivkov et al. (2020) use an eight-member focus group of managers and teachers and 236 students from Serbia to find correlation between seven constructs (expected business outcome, experience, tangibles, service assurance, communication and interaction, reliability and performance) and willingness to use robots. Photos and videos were used to provide a definition of service robots. Of the participants, 90% had no experience with service robots. Ali et al. (2023) first interviewed 30 gen-Z'ers who had worked for three months in the hotel industry. In the end, 552 gen-Z'ers from Turkey were surveyed because they had shown intention to use service robots. They were provided with a video of room service robots. The resulting model shows positive relations between four items (hedonic motivation, utilitarian motivation and social skills) and negative relations between two items (insecurity and technical barriers) and intention to use robots. The last paper uses a combination of workplace observations and interviews. Tuomi et al. (2020) observed robotic service encounters in 22 restaurants in the United States and in Japan. In addition, eight managers and robot implementers were interviewed. They identify five roles for employees working with robots: enabler, where employees help guests use difficult technology; coordinator, where they observe operations running smoothly; differentiator, where employees use extra time to cater to guests' needs and innovator, where they innovate the restaurant because of new opportunities that arise because robots are now being used.

6.3.4 Information Provided

As robots are a novel concept and can take many forms, it can be unclear what is meant when a service robot or hospitality robot is mentioned. We therefore also identified how the different studies deal with this ambiguity. The most realistic information about employee-robot interactions comes from employees that have worked with a robot for some time, and therefore have detailed information about its advantages and shortcomings. The least ideal situation therefore would be one where respondents are provided with no information at all about employee-robot interactions. We distinguish between six categories where: (1) Participants have been working with or alongside a service robot, this situation was seen by the researchers, so they know which robots are considered. (2) Participants report to have been working with a service robot to the researchers. It can be unclear to researchers which robots are considered. (3) Participants report to have interacted with a service robot.

TABLE 6.1

Type of Information Provided to Participants and Type of Participants

Type of Information Provided	Source	Respondents
1.Work experience with service robot	Sadangharn (2022a)	Employees and managers
	Sadangharn (2022b)	Employees and managers
2.Reported working experience with service robot	Zhang et al. (2023)	Employees
	Yang et al. (2022)	Employees
	Fu et al. (2022)	Managers
	Song et al. (2022)	employees
3.Reported interaction with service robot	Alzoubi and Zoubi (2023)	Employees
4.Videos	Seyitoğlu et al. (2021)	Managers
	Leung et al. (2023)	hospitality students
	Ali et al. (2023)	Gen-z (former) hotel employees
	Ivkov et al. (2020)	Managers and students
5.Text and images	Nam et al. (2021)	Managers
	Xu et al. (2020)	HR managers
	Ghazy and Fedorova (2022)	Employees
	Kim (2023)	Employees
6.No information	Leung (2019)	Managers
	Kuo et al. (2017)	Robot experts
	Devkant (2022)	Hospitality students
	Parvez et al. (2022)	Employees and managers
	Ivanov et al. (2020)	Managers
	Gupta et al. (2022)	Employees and managers
	Vatan and Dogan (2021)	Employees
	Lee et al. (2018)	Managers
	Seyitoğlu et al. (2023)	Hospitality students
	Palrão et al. (2023)	Hospitality students
	Abdelhakim et al. (2023)	Fast food employees
	Khaliq et al. (2022)	Employees and managers
	Pizam et al. (2022)	Managers
	Tuomi et al. (2020)	Managers and engineers
	Yu et al. (2022)	Employees

(4) Participants are provided with videos of service robots being used so that they can reflect on envisioned interactions. (5) Participants were provided with text descriptions and images of service robots. (6) Participants were provided with no information about robots. Table 6.1 shows in which category each of the 30 analysed papers belongs.

6.3.5 Respondents

In the papers that were analysed, there is a variety in the respondents that are being studied. Table 6.1 shows who were selected for each study. Studies most often study (former) employees (10 out of 30), followed by managers and experts (10 out of 30). Then there are studies studying hospitality students (4 out of 30) or a combination of these groups (6 out of 30).

6.4 Discussion

The results from the qualitative studies often focus on perceived advantages and possibilities for robots. Most papers see robots as something that can take over tasks, boost efficiency. Employee resistance, unemployment and the lack of social or communication skills are mentioned as downsides. The quantitative studies try to find relationships to see which factors influence robot acceptance, ease of use, turnover intention or unemployment.

6.4.1 Information Provision

As discussed in Section 2, a robot is a sometimes hard-to-define phenomenon that can relate to many different work processes across many different industries, and that is also heavily influenced by imaginary aspects such as science fiction or automation in other industries. Because of this, we feel that it is of paramount importance to clearly define the robotic situation that gets researched. We therefore want to highlight the papers that go out of their way to ensure respondents are well informed by implementing a robot for their respondents to use (Sadangharn, 2022a, 2022b), or perform on-site observations in restaurants where robots are used (Tuomi et al., 2020). However, we find it concerning that 15 out of the 30 identified papers (see Table 6.1) did not disclose any information about robots to their respondents (or at least did not report on this in their method section). In Leung (2019), this variety in definition was even reported as a result. Not disclosing information assumes that the studied participants have a clear definition of robots. Given the existing variety in robots provided in Section 2, we would argue that this currently cannot be assumed. We also see many authors reporting on robotics as a force that is here to stay and keep on taking over tasks (Xu et al., 2020; Vatan and Dogan, 2021; Seyitoğlu et al., 2021; Leung et al., 2023; Ivkov et al., 2020). The overall image that emerges when reading the outcomes of these papers suggests that robots are seen as a technology that will take over dull and repetitive tasks, increasing efficiency and possibly cause unemployment. The main disadvantage that is often mentioned is the robots' lack of social skills.

6.4.2 Respondents

The variety in respondents is also something we want to discuss. Abdelhakim et al. (2023), Zhang et al. (2023) and Yang et al. (2022) all target specific employees to accurately study their subject. As Sorenson et al. (2019) explain, in the process of developing robots, robot developers often communicate their designs and ideas with application experts (read: hotel managers) who are eventually responsible for buying a robot. This is referred to as the inner circle of robot development, which does not consider the so-called affected stakeholders or end users, which in the case of hospitality are the employees and the guests. It is concerning to see that only 10 of the 30 papers use solely employees as respondents and as many 10 of the 30 solely target managers and experts as respondents. Using managers and experts to reflect on the potential of robots could cause a disregard for the interests of operational employees outside the inner circle (Sorenson et al., 2019). With this in mind, we feel like it makes little sense to survey a combination of managers and employees, as their looks on robot implementation might differ fundamentally. Managers might find efficiency important while workers might be concerned with how their jobs will be influenced by robots. Yet, five papers survey a combination of employees and managers and summarize their evaluations as if they are a homogeneous group (Khaliq et al., 2022; Gupta et al., 2022; Sadangharn, 2022a, 2022b; Parvez et al., 2022). Surveying hospitality students also seems odd to us. Even though they might end up in the hospitality industry, this is by no means a guarantee.

6.4.3 Organizational Change Theory

Organizational change theory states that leaders need to define challenges, prepare skills and build a change-embracing culture to ensure external changes don't negatively affect organizations (Gould, 2023). We as authors fully agree with this, but in the papers we identified, this vision is only applied limitedly. As mentioned above, the majority of the papers do not disclose information about these external changes to their respondents, making it difficult to reflect on expectations. Also, in robotization, Sorenson et al. (2019) explain that employees should not be disregarded when considering robots, yet in the academic discourse, this seems to be happening in a substantial amount of papers. The recommendations from the papers are also difficult to translate into practices. We want to highlight the quantitative papers that look at what influences turnover intention. Zhang et al. (2023) urge managers to increase training and awareness about how robots can help and where, as they have found employees who use robots more, report lower turnover intention. Yu et al. (2022) found that service robot risk awareness increased turnover intention and urged employers to offer additional training and a selection process focusing on employees who already possess certain qualities, while at the same time acknowledging the competitive environment. Khaliq et al. (2022), who found a similar relationship, opt for training and explaining to employees that technologies are there to help employees and improving trust between employees and employers. These examples lead us to believe that authors see robots as an inevitable force that will take over tasks anyway, and only by training employees can we indirectly reduce their turnover intention while employers are directly responsible for the work environment their employees have to work in. We fear that this incorrect assessment of the robot situation, as well as simplistic recommendations to reduce employee turnover hint at a disconnect between the hospitality industry and hospitality research, which ultimately contains the risk of making academic research irrelevant.

6.5 Conclusion

This chapter has tried to shed light on how employees and robots are studied in the hospitality field. The 30 papers we identified that have been written between 2017 and 2023 started in 2017 when robots were still seen as a potential novelty for hospitality until 2023, when robots have been accepted as a new phenomenon that is being studied like many more topics in hospitality. Robots are said to be changing the industry and boost efficiency, with unemployment being mentioned as a potential downside. However, half of the papers did not disclose any information about robots to their participants, which makes it difficult to say something about the situation participants might have been reflecting on. Furthermore, the group of respondents consisted of just employees in only one-third of the papers. This makes the conclusions of these studies less relevant as we have pointed out that managers, robot experts or hospitality students might have different interests in and views on hospitality robots, as they are not necessarily the end users of this technology. Many of the papers analysed have adopted an almost technochauvinistic image of robots, regarding them as a force that will inevitably take over as many tasks in hospitality as possible and perform them better than human employees. We want to argue that this belief is unrealistic in today's status quo and not analogous to any other robotized industry. Because the current problems of the industry are employment problems, leaders are needed that evaluate the needs of their employees and match this with current technological possibilities. We feel like research that performs real life experiments could provide us with more realistic insights in this complex phenomenon.

References

Abdelhakim, A. S., Abou-Shouk, M., Ab Rahman, N. A. F. W., & Farooq, A. (2023). The fast-food employees' usage intention of robots: A cross-cultural study. *Tourism Management Perspectives*, 45, 101049.

Ali, F., Dogan, S., Chen, X., Cobanoglu, C., & Limayem, M. (2023). Friend or a foe: Understanding generation z employees' intentions to work with service robots in the hotel industry. *International Journal of Human–Computer Interaction*, 39(1), 111–122.

Alzoubi, S., & Zoubi, M. (2023). Exploring the relationship between robot employees' perceptions and robot-induced unemployment under covid-19 in the jordanian hospitality sector. *International Journal of Data and Network Science*, 7(4), 1563–1572.

Bacon, A. (2024). This robot barista can make you a coffee in minutes, but it wants to be tipped for it. Retrieved November 14, 2024, from https://www.businessinsider.nl/this-robot-barista-can-make-you-a-coffee-in-minutes-but-it-wants-to-be-tipped-for-it/

Benmelech, E., & Zator, M. (2022). *Robots and firm investment* (tech. rep.). National Bureau of Economic Research.

Devkant, K. (2022). Tourism & hospitality students' perception towards the use of robots in service organizations: A qualitative study in india. *Advances in Hospitality and Tourism Research* (AHTR).

Editor. (2024). A&o hostels using cleaning robots to support their staff in their hostels. Retrieved November 14, 2024, from https://tophotel.news/ao-hostels-using-cleaning-robots-to-support-their-staff-in-their-hostels-softbank-robotics/

Etemad-Sajadi, R. (2018). Meet pepper: The humanoid robot concierge. Retrieved November 14, 2024, from https://hospitalityinsights.ehl.edu/robots-hospitality-industryutm_sourcelinkedinutm_mediumsocialutm_contentrobot_concierge

Fu, S., Zheng, X., &Wong, I. A. (2022). The perils of hotel technology: The robot usage resistance model. *International Journal of Hospitality Management*, 102, 103174.

Ganesharajah, T., Hall, N. G., & Sriskandarajah, C. (1998). Design and operational issues in agv-served manufacturing systems. *Annals of Operations Research*, 76(0), 109–154.

Gasparetto, A., & Scalera, L. (2019). From the unimate to the delta robot: The early decades of industrial robotics. In *Explorations in the history and heritage of machines and mechanisms* (pp. 284–295). Springer.

Ghazy, K., & Fedorova, A. E. (2022). Hotel employees' attitude and acceptance toward human-robot co-working based on the industry 5.0 concept. *Changing Societies & Personalities*, 6(4), 906–926.

Gould, R. (2023). What is organizational change theory and how can it empower you? Retrieved November 15, 2024, from https://www. rasmussen.edu/degrees/business/blog/what- is- organizational- change- theory/#:~:text=Organizational%20change%20theory%20is%20also,and%20undergo%20a%20transformational%20process

Gupta, S., Modgil, S., Lee, C.-K., Cho, M., & Park, Y. (2022). Artificial intelligence enabled robots for stay experience in the hospitality industry in a smart city. *Industrial Management & Data Systems*, 122(10), 2331–2350.

Hotrec. (2022). *Labour shortages in the hospitality sector: Forward-thinking and practices sharing* (tech. rep.). Hotrec.

Ivanov, S., Seyitoğlu, F., & Markova, M. (2020). Hotel managers' perceptions towards the use of robots: A mixed-methods approach. *Information Technology & Tourism*, 22(4), 505–535.

Ivkov, M., Blešić, I., Dudić, B., Pajtinková Bartáková, G., & Dudić, Z. (2020). Are future professionals willing to implement service robots? Attitudes of hospitality and tourism students towards service robotization. *Electronics*, 9(9), 1442.

Khaliq, A., Waqas, A., Nisar, Q. A., Haider, S., & Asghar, Z. (2022). Application of ai and robotics in hospitality sector: A resource gain and resource loss perspective. *Technology in Society*, 68, 101807.

Kim, Y. (2023). Examining the impact of frontline service robots service competence on hotel frontline employees from a collaboration perspective. *Sustainability*, 15(9), 7563.

Kirk, P. (2024). Four years since start of pandemic, hotels are still struggling to fill jobs. Retrieved November 14, 2024, from https : //www.hospitalityinvestor.com/americas/four-years-start-pandemic-hotels-are-still-struggling-fill-jobs

Kuo, C.-M., Chen, L.-C., & Tseng, C.-Y. (2017). Investigating an innovative service with hospitality robots. *International Journal of Contemporary Hospitality Management*, 29(5), 1305–1321.

Lee, W.-H., Lin, C.-W., & Shih, K.-H. (2018). A technology acceptance model for the perception of restaurant service robots for trust, interactivity, and output quality. *International Journal of Mobile Communications*, 16(4), 361–376.

Leung, R. (2019). Smart hospitality: Taiwan hotel stakeholder perspectives. *Tourism Review*, 74(1), 50–62.

Leung, X. Y., Zhang, H., Lyu, J., & Bai, B. (2023). Why do hotel frontline employees use service robots in the workplace? A technology affordance theory perspective. *International Journal of Hospitality Management*, 108, 103380.

Luther, D. (2024). 3 common challenges in the hospitality industry in 2024. Retrieved November 14, 2024, from https://www.netsuite.com/portal/resource/articles/erp/hospitality-industry-challenges.shtml

Lynn, J. (2023). Dr. temi, the autonomous robot will see you now. Retrieved November 14, 2024, from https://www.healthcareittoday.com/2023/08/30/dr-temi-the-autonomous-robot-will-see-you-now/

Ma, K., Duan, X., Fu, X., Liu, W., & Zheng, M. (2024). Effects of human-robot interaction type on customer tolerance of humanoid robot service failure. *Journal of Hospitality Marketing & Management*, 1–20.

Maciborski, W. (2024). Tailos' rosie: A robotic revolution in commercial cleaning. Retrieved November 14, 2024, from https://cbsaustin. com/news/local/tailos-rosie-a-robotic-revolution-in-commercial-cleaning

Mahendra, S. (2022). Introduction: Pazzi – the world's first autonomous pizza robot. Retrieved November 14, 2024, from https://www. aiplusinfo.com/blog/pazzi-the-worlds-first-autonomous-pizza-robot/

Nam, K., Dutt, C. S., Chathoth, P., Daghfous, A., & Khan, M. S. (2021). The adoption of artificial intelligence and robotics in the hotel industry: Prospects and challenges. *Electronic Markets*, 31, 553–574.

Newman, P. (2019). The henn na hotel in japan is firing most of its robotic workforce and hiring humans instead — highlighting the limits of automation. Retrieved November 14, 2024, from https://www.businessinsider.com/henn-na-hotel-fires-robots-hireshumans-2019-1?international=true&r=US&IR=T

Oggero, F. (2024). Robot bar opens in turin. Retrieved November 14, 2024, from https://globetrender.com/2024/08/14/ready-robotic-baropens-turin/

Ono, R. (2018). Robotel: Japan hotel staffed by robot dinosaurs. Retrieved November 14, 2024, from https://phys.org/news/2018-08-robotel-japan-hotel-staffed-robot.html

Palrão, T., Rodrigues, R. I., Madeira, A., Mendes, A. S., & Lopes, S. (2023). Robots in tourism and hospitality: The perception of future professionals. *Human Behavior and Emerging Technologies*, 2023(1), 7172152.

Parvez, M. O., Öztüren, A., Cobanoglu, C., Arasli, H., & Eluwole, K. K. (2022). Employees' perception of robots and robot-induced unemployment in hospitality industry under covid-19 pandemic. *International Journal of Hospitality Management*, 107, 103336.

Pillay, K. (2021). Robo-room service: South african hotel introduces robot helpers. Retrieved November 14, 2024, from https://www.weforum.org/stories/2021/02/south-african-hotel-robot-staff-covid19-response/

Pizam, A., Ozturk, A. B., Balderas-Cejudo, A., Buhalis, D., Fuchs, G., Hara, T., Meira, J., Revilla, M. R. G., Sethi, D., Shen, Y., et al. (2022). Factors affecting hotel managers' intentions to adopt robotic technologies: A global study. *International Journal of Hospitality Management*, 102, 103139.

Sadangharn, P. (2022a). Acceptance of robots as co-workers: Hotel employees' perspective. *International Journal of Engineering Business Management*, 14, 184797 90221113621.

Sadangharn, P. (2022b). A multidimensional analysis of robotic deployment in thai hotels. *International Journal of Social Robotics*, 14(4), 859–873.

Seyitoğlu, F., Atsız, O., Taş, S., & Kaya, F. (2023). Double-edged perspectives on service robots: Working with robots and robots' future career impacts. *Journal of Teaching in Travel & Tourism*, 23(1), 1–19.

Seyitoğlu, F., Ivanov, S., Atsız, O., & Çifçi, İ. (2021). Robots as restaurant employees-a double-barrelled detective story. *Technology in Society*, 67, 101779.

Shimmura, T., Ichikari, R., Okuma, T., Ito, H., Okada, K., & Nonaka, T. (2020). Service robot introduction to a restaurant enhances both labor productivity and service quality. *Procedia CIRP*, 88, 589–594.

Song, Y., Zhang, M., Hu, J., & Cao, X. (2022). Dancing with service robots: The impacts of employee-robot collaboration on hotel employees' job crafting. *International Journal of Hospitality Management*, 103, 103220.

Sorenson, J., Zawieska, K., Vermeulen, B., Madsen, S. D., Trentemøller, S., Pyka, A., Bulgheroni, M., Richardson, K., & Hasse, C. (2019). *Perspectives on robots*. REELER.

Torrance, C. G., Butler Lamar, S. C., Reynolds, S. D., & Cannonier, N. (2023). Automation-related job insecurity and turnover intentions in the hospitality industry: Examining the mediating effect of occupational commitment. *Consortium Journal of Hospitality & Tourism*, 26.

Tu, Y., Li, D., & Wang, H.-J. (2021). Covid-19-induced layoff, survivors' covid-19-related stress and performance in hospitality industry: The moderating role of social support. *International Journal of Hospitality Management*, 95, 102912.

Tuomi, A., Tussyadiah, I., & Stienmetz, J. (2020). Service robots and the changing roles of employees in restaurants: A cross cultural study. *E-review of Tourism Research*, 17(5).

Vatan, A., & Dogan, S. (2021). What do hotel employees think about service robots? A qualitative study in turkey. *Tourism Management Perspectives*, 37, 100775.

Wolf, M. (2022). French robot pizza restaurant startup pazzi shuts its doors. Retrieved October 29, 2024, from https://thespoon.tech/frenchrobot-pizza-restaurant-startup-pazzi-shuts-its-doors/

Xu, S., Stienmetz, J., & Ashton, M. (2020). How will service robots redefine leadership in hotel management? A delphi approach. *International Journal of Contemporary Hospitality Management*, 32(6), 2217–2237.

Yang, H., Xu, H., Zhang, Y., Liang, Y., & Lyu, T. (2022). Exploring the effect of humor in robot failure. *Annals of Tourism Research*, 95, 103425.

Yu, H., Shum, C., Alcorn, M., Sun, J., & He, Z. (2022). Robots can't take my job: Antecedents and outcomes of gen z employees' service robot risk awareness. *International Journal of Contemporary Hospitality Management*, 34(8), 2971–2988.

Zhang, L.-X., Li, J.-M., Wang, L.-L., Mao, M.-Y., & Zhang, R.-X. (2023). How does the usage of robots in hotels affect employees' turnover intention? A double-edged sword study. *Journal of Hospitality and Tourism Management*, 57, 74–83.

7

Navigating the Nexus: Leadership Strategies in the Era of Service Robots

João Farinha and Maria de Fátima Pina

7.1 Introduction

The integration of service robots in the hospitality industry presents significant challenges and opportunities for leaders. Effective leadership strategies are crucial to navigate the complexities of integrating robots into existing operations while maintaining employee morale, guest satisfaction, and operational efficiency (Smith & Johnson, 2020). Understanding and adapting leadership approaches in the face of technological innovation is essential for leaders in the hospitality industry to stay competitive and relevant (Jones et al., 2019). Effective leadership involves not only embracing technological advancements like service robots but also fostering a culture of innovation, upskilling employees to work alongside robots, and ensuring a seamless integration of technology into existing operations (Brown & White, 2021).

The relationship between human leaders, employees, and service robots in the hospitality industry is evolving as technology becomes more integrated into daily operations (Taylor, 2018). Human leaders are tasked with effectively managing and coordinating the interactions between employees and service robots, ensuring that both parties work together harmoniously to deliver exceptional guest experiences (Clark et al., 2022). This dynamic requires leaders to possess a blend of technical knowledge, emotional intelligence, and strategic vision to leverage the strengths of both human and robotic resources effectively (Anderson & Thomas, 2023).

Service robots are becoming increasingly popular in the hospitality industry, particularly in response to the COVID-19 pandemic (Roberts, 2020). To overcome the limitations of robots, human staff members and service robots can collaborate, with robots handling mechanical and analytical tasks and human staff dealing with emotional tasks (Johnson & Davis, 2019).

DOI: 10.1201/9781003742791-7

Additionally, hospitality managers should consider cultural differences in customer perceptions of service robots, as preferences for robot-staffed hotels vary across cultures (Garcia et al., 2021).

The integration of service robots in the hospitality industry presents several challenges and opportunities (Miller & Brown, 2017). For instance, robots can enhance service quality dimensions related to cleanliness, health, and safety, which are particularly important during health crises (Turner, 2018). However, there are also concerns about job displacement, data privacy, and the need for clear AI legislation (Hill & Lee, 2022). Effective leadership strategies must address these challenges while leveraging the benefits of service robots to enhance the guest experience (Lewis & Martinez, 2019).

Therefore, the integration of service robots in the hospitality industry requires leaders to adapt their approaches to effectively manage the integration of technology while maintaining employee morale, guest satisfaction, and operational efficiency. By understanding the importance of adapting leadership approaches and the evolving relationship between human leaders, employees, and service robots, leaders can navigate the challenges and opportunities presented by this technological innovation.

7.2 The Nexus of Leadership and Service Robots

The integration of service robots in the hospitality industry has prompted a reevaluation of traditional leadership theories in light of technological advancements. Scholars like Wirtz et al. (2018) have explored how leadership theories such as transformational leadership and servant leadership intersect with the presence of service robots. This examination delves into how leaders can leverage these theories to effectively manage human-robot interactions, foster innovation, and enhance guest experiences in a technologically driven hospitality landscape. By integrating principles from transformational leadership, which emphasizes inspiring and motivating followers toward a collective vision, and servant leadership, which focuses on serving the needs of employees and stakeholders, leaders can foster a collaborative environment where service robots augment human capabilities rather than replace them (Wirtz et al., 2018). Additionally, leaders can draw insights from contingency theories of leadership to adapt their leadership styles based on the specific context and challenges presented by the integration of service robots in hospitality operations (Northouse, 2021).

Service robots are reshaping traditional leadership paradigms by introducing new dynamics and challenges for leaders in the hospitality industry. Authors like Byrd et al. (2021) have highlighted how leaders must adapt their communication styles, decision-making processes, and team management strategies to accommodate the integration of service robots. This discussion explores how leaders are required to embrace flexibility, creativity, and a forward-thinking mindset to navigate the changing landscape of leadership in the era of service robots. Leaders need to adopt a transformational approach to leadership, inspiring and empowering employees to adapt to technological changes and embrace innovation (Byrd et al., 2021). Moreover, they must cultivate a culture of continuous learning and experimentation to harness the full potential of service robots while addressing employee concerns and resistance to change (Avolio & Yammarino, 2021).

The integration of service robots in hospitality operations presents a myriad of opportunities and challenges for leaders in the industry. Researchers such as Fusté-Forné et al. (2021) have identified opportunities for efficiency improvements, enhanced guest experiences, and cost savings through the use of service robots. However, challenges such as job displacement, ethical considerations, and the need for upskilling employees also accompany this integration. This exploration delves into how leaders can capitalize on the opportunities while effectively addressing and mitigating the challenges posed by the integration of service robots in hospitality operations. Leaders must develop proactive strategies to manage the transition, including providing training and support for employees to adapt to new roles and responsibilities in a human-robot collaborative environment (Fusté-Forné et al., 2021). Moreover, they need to engage with stakeholders, including employees, customers, and regulatory bodies, to address ethical concerns and ensure the responsible deployment of service robots in hospitality settings (Choi et al., 2020).

7.3 Leadership Strategies for Human-Robot Collaboration

Due to the ever-evolving landscape of the hospitality industry, the integration of service robots introduces a new dimension to leadership strategies. Researchers emphasize the importance of adaptive and innovative leadership in embracing technological change and fostering collaboration between human employees and service robots. For example, Farinha (2018) underscores the significance of leaders adopting a transformational leadership approach, inspiring and empowering employees to adapt to service robots and enhance guest experiences. Similarly, Brown and White (2021) highlight the need for leaders to cultivate a culture of creativity and collaboration, encouraging open communication, experimentation, and continuous learning to successfully integrate service robots into hospitality operations.

Moreover, leadership theories provide valuable frameworks for understanding and implementing effective leadership strategies in the context of human-robot collaboration. According to Farinha (2018), transformational leadership involves inspiring and motivating employees to achieve common goals, which is particularly relevant in guiding teams through technological changes such as the integration of service robots. By fostering a shared vision and empowering employees to embrace innovation, transformational leaders can facilitate the successful adoption of service robots while maintaining employee morale and engagement.

Furthermore, situational leadership theory, as proposed by Hersey and Blanchard (2020), suggests that leaders should adapt their leadership styles based on the readiness and capabilities of their team members. Thus, in the context of human-robot collaboration, leaders may need to adjust their leadership approach to accommodate the varying skill levels and comfort levels of employees in working alongside service robots, and by providing appropriate support and guidance, leaders can help employees develop the necessary skills and confidence to effectively collaborate with service robots.

Real-world case studies, such as the one conducted by Roberts et al. (2019) on a hotel implementing service robots for room service delivery, offer valuable insights into leadership strategies for training and supporting human staff and robots to ensure seamless collaboration. By examining such examples, leaders can gain practical insights and best practices for managing human-robot teams in their organizations. Additionally, empirical research on leadership in the context of technological change and innovation, such as studies by Avolio and Yammarino (2021) and Bass and Riggio (2019), can provide further guidance on effective leadership strategies for navigating the complexities of human-robot interaction in hospitality settings.

Therefore, leadership strategies for human-robot collaboration in the hospitality industry are crucial for maximizing the potential of service robots while upholding employee morale and guest satisfaction. Transformational leadership, as advocated by Farinha (2018), and situational leadership theory, as proposed by Hersey and Blanchard (2020), offer valuable frameworks for guiding leaders in effectively managing human-robot teams. By drawing on insights from empirical research and real-world case studies, leaders can develop tailored strategies to navigate the challenges and opportunities presented by the integration of service robots in hospitality operations.

7.4 Addressing Ethical and Societal Concerns

The integration of service robots in the hospitality industry raises significant ethical and societal concerns that leaders must address to ensure the successful adoption of these technologies. This section explores the ethical considerations surrounding the use of service robots, strategies for addressing societal concerns such as unemployment and the loss of human touch, and methods for navigating ethical dilemmas and maintaining positive perceptions of robotic technology among stakeholders.

The use of service robots in hospitality raises several ethical concerns. For instance, the potential for job displacement and the impact on human employment are significant concerns that leaders must address. Smith et al. (2020) highlight the need for leaders to consider the ethical implications of automation on human employees and to develop strategies for mitigating the negative effects. Additionally, the potential for bias in the design and implementation of service robots, which could lead to unequal treatment of guests, is another ethical concern that leaders must address (Brown & White, 2021).

To address societal concerns, leaders must develop strategies that mitigate the negative impacts of service robots on employment and human interaction. One approach is to focus on augmenting human capabilities rather than replacing them. This can be achieved by training human staff to work alongside service robots, ensuring that the robots complement human skills rather than replacing them (Roberts et al., 2019). Leaders must also prioritize the development of skills that are complementary to robotic capabilities, such as emotional intelligence and creativity, to ensure that human employees remain valuable assets in the organization (Brown & White, 2021).

To navigate ethical dilemmas and maintain positive perceptions of robotic technology among stakeholders, leaders must prioritize transparency and open communication. This includes providing clear information about the capabilities and limitations of service robots, as well as the potential impacts on employment and human interaction (Smith et al., 2020). Leaders must also be prepared to address concerns and criticisms from stakeholders, ensuring that the benefits of service robots are communicated effectively and that the negative impacts are mitigated (Brown & White, 2021).

Therefore, the integration of service robots in the hospitality industry presents significant ethical and societal concerns that leaders must address to ensure the successful adoption of these technologies. By prioritizing transparency, open communication, and the development of strategies that mitigate the negative impacts of service robots, leaders can navigate ethical dilemmas and maintain positive perceptions of robotic technology among stakeholders.

7.5 Adapting Organizational Structures and Processes

The integration of service robots into the hospitality industry necessitates significant changes in organizational structures and processes to effectively leverage the capabilities of these technologies. This section delves into the exploration of how the integration of service robots prompts adaptations in organizational structures and processes, discusses how leaders can adapt decision-making processes, communication channels, and workflow to accommodate robotic technologies, and presents case studies or examples highlighting successful organizational adaptations in response to the era of service robots.

Indeed, the integration of service robots introduces new roles, responsibilities, and workflows within hospitality organizations, necessitating adjustments in organizational structures and processes. As highlighted by Farinha and Sousa (2015), the adoption of robotic technologies often requires the creation of specialized teams or departments responsible for overseeing the implementation, maintenance, and optimization of service robots. Moreover, organizations may need to redefine job roles and responsibilities to incorporate tasks that complement the capabilities of service robots, as emphasized by Farinha and Pina (2023). These changes in organizational structures enable organizations to effectively integrate service robots into their operations while maximizing efficiency and productivity.

Leaders must adapt decision-making processes and communication channels to facilitate the integration of service robots and ensure smooth collaboration between human employees and robotic technologies. According to Farinha and Pina (2023), leaders should adopt a participative decision-making approach that involves input from employees across different levels of the organization, including those directly impacted by the deployment of service robots. Additionally, effective communication channels, such as regular team meetings, training sessions, and feedback mechanisms, are essential for keeping employees informed about the implementation progress, addressing concerns, and soliciting input for continuous improvement (Farinha & Tomé, 2019).

Real-world case studies provide valuable insights into successful organizational adaptations in response to the era of service robots. For example, Farinha and Santos (2023) conducted a case study on a hotel that successfully integrated service robots into its housekeeping operations. Through a combination of strategic planning, employee training, and stakeholder engagement, the hotel was able to streamline its housekeeping processes, improve efficiency, and enhance guest satisfaction. Similarly, Farinha and Ascenso (2022) documented the organizational changes implemented by a hospitality company to support remote work during the COVID-19 pandemic. By leveraging digital communication tools, redefining performance metrics, and promoting work-life balance initiatives, the company successfully adapted its organizational structures and processes to accommodate telework while maintaining operational effectiveness.

Therefore, the integration of service robots into the hospitality industry necessitates significant adaptations in organizational structures and processes. By embracing changes in decision-making processes, communication channels, and workflow, leaders can effectively leverage robotic technologies to enhance operational efficiency, improve guest experiences, and maintain competitiveness in the evolving landscape of the hospitality sector.

7.6 Building Future-Ready Leadership

Considering the rapidly evolving landscape of the hospitality industry, the integration of service robots necessitates a reevaluation of leadership skills and competencies to ensure organizations remain competitive and adaptable. This section explores the essential skills and competencies required for leaders to thrive in an era of service robots, emphasizes the importance of continuous learning, adaptability, and technological literacy for leadership effectiveness, and presents strategies for developing future-ready leaders capable of navigating the complexities of human-robot collaboration.

Future-ready leaders in the hospitality industry must possess a diverse skill set and a deep understanding of both human and technological aspects of their operations. Indeed, according to Jones and Smith (2022), effective leaders in the era of service robots demonstrate strong communication skills, empathy, and emotional intelligence to foster collaboration and trust among employees and service robots. Additionally, leaders must exhibit strategic thinking and problem-solving abilities to navigate the complexities of integrating robotic technologies into existing workflows while maintaining operational efficiency and guest satisfaction (Johnson et al., 2023).

Continuous learning and adaptability are fundamental for leadership effectiveness in an era of rapid technological advancement. Leaders must embrace a growth mindset and demonstrate a willingness to learn and adapt to new technologies and changing business environments. Farinha and Tomé (2019) highlight the importance of creating a culture of lifelong learning within organizations, where leaders encourage employees to pursue professional development opportunities and stay abreast of emerging trends in robotics and automation. Moreover, leaders must be proactive in seeking out opportunities for upskilling and reskilling to remain relevant and effective in their roles (Brown & White, 2021).

Technological literacy is essential for leaders to understand the capabilities and limitations of service robots and effectively leverage these technologies to achieve organizational goals. Leaders should possess a foundational understanding of robotics, artificial intelligence, and data analytics to make informed decisions about the adoption and integration of service robots into their operations (Smith et al., 2020). Furthermore, leaders must be able to communicate effectively with technical teams and vendors to ensure the successful implementation and maintenance of robotic technologies in the hospitality setting (Roberts et al., 2019).

To develop future-ready leaders capable of navigating the complexities of human-robot collaboration, organizations should invest in leadership development programs that focus on building essential skills and competencies. Farinha and Ascenso (2022) advocate for immersive learning experiences, such as workshops and simulations, that allow leaders to practice decision-making and problem-solving in realistic scenarios involving service robots. Additionally, mentoring and coaching programs can provide leaders with individualized support and guidance as they navigate the challenges of leading in a technology-driven environment (Farinha & Santos, 2023).

Consequently, building future-ready leadership in the hospitality industry requires a holistic approach that emphasizes the development of essential skills and competencies, continuous learning, adaptability, and technological literacy. By investing in leadership development programs and fostering a culture of lifelong learning and innovation, organizations can cultivate leaders who are well-equipped to lead effectively in an era of service robots.

7.7 Integrating Concepts through Practical Application

In this section, we delve into practical examples and scenarios to illustrate the interaction between leadership strategies and the integration of service robots in the hospitality industry. By providing real-world instances, readers can better comprehend the complexities of leadership in the context of technological advancements, encouraging a deeper understanding of how theoretical concepts manifest in operational realities.

Consider a scenario where a hotel manager is tasked with implementing service robots for guest services, such as room cleaning and luggage delivery. To effectively lead this transition, the manager must adopt a transformational leadership approach, inspiring and empowering employees to embrace the changes brought about by robotic technologies (Smith et al., 2020). By fostering a culture of innovation and collaboration, the manager can encourage employees to adapt their roles and workflows to accommodate service robots, ensuring a seamless integration process.

Another example involves a restaurant owner introducing robotic servers to enhance efficiency and reduce operational costs. In this scenario, the leader must exhibit strategic decision-making and change management skills to navigate potential resistance from employees and customers (Brown & White, 2021). By communicating the rationale behind the implementation of service robots and addressing concerns about job displacement and loss of human touch, the leader can garner support for the initiative and drive successful adoption.

By presenting practical examples and scenarios, readers can apply theoretical concepts such as transformational leadership, change management, and stakeholder engagement to real-world situations. For instance, readers can analyze how a leader's communication style and decision-making approach influence employee attitudes toward service robots and organizational changes (Farinha & Sousa, 2015). Additionally, readers can explore the role of emotional intelligence in managing human-robot interactions and fostering a positive work environment amidst technological disruptions (Jones & Smith, 2022).

To facilitate deeper learning and reflection, discussions and activities can be incorporated to encourage critical thinking about leadership strategies in the era of service robots. For example, readers can engage in group discussions to brainstorm potential challenges and opportunities associated with the integration of service robots in hospitality operations (Johnson et al., 2023). Furthermore, case studies and role-playing exercises can provide readers with hands-on experience in developing leadership strategies to address specific scenarios involving service robots (Roberts et al., 2019).

Therefore, integrating concepts through practical application enables readers to bridge the gap between theory and practice, enhancing their understanding of leadership dynamics in the context of service robots in hospitality. By analyzing real-world examples, applying theoretical frameworks, and engaging in discussions and activities, readers can develop the skills and insights necessary to proactively navigate the challenges and opportunities presented by the era of service robots.

7.8 Sustainability and Efficiency

The hospitality industry has long been at the forefront of innovation, constantly evolving to meet the demands of guests while striving for operational excellence. In recent years, sustainability has emerged as a critical priority for the sector, driven by environmental concerns and changing consumer preferences. The integration of service robots offers a unique opportunity to enhance sustainability and efficiency in hospitality operations (Popșa, 2023). These advanced technologies not only streamline workflows but also contribute to reducing waste, optimizing resource use, and supporting the broader sustainability goals of hotels, resorts, and restaurants.

In what follows, we develop seven topics related to sustainability and efficiency through the integration of service robots in the hospitality industry (Figure 7.1), namely, reducing waste through precision and automation; optimizing energy efficiency; supporting green supply chain management; enhancing water conservation efforts; improving waste management practices; guest engagement and education; and long-term cost savings and competitive advantage.

A. **Reducing Waste through Precision and Automation:** Service robots excel in executing tasks with precision, minimizing resource waste in various hospitality operations. For example, housekeeping robots can be programmed to clean rooms based on real-time data about occupancy and usage, avoiding unnecessary cleaning in unoccupied

FIGURE 7.1
Topics of Sustainability and Efficiency

areas. Similarly, kitchen robots equipped with AI can optimize ingredient use, reducing food waste by preparing only the required portions and monitoring expiration dates (Karvounidi et al., 2024).

In restaurants, robotic chefs and bartenders can standardize portion sizes, ensuring consistency and eliminating overuse of ingredients. This precision not only reduces costs but also aligns with the growing demand for environmentally responsible practices. Hotels and resorts that adopt such technologies can appeal to eco-conscious travelers, who increasingly prioritize sustainability when choosing accommodations.

B. Optimizing Energy Consumption: Energy efficiency is a significant concern for the hospitality sector, where high energy usage contributes to both operational costs and environmental impact. Service robots and IoT-enabled systems can play a pivotal role in optimizing energy consumption. For instance, robotic systems can integrate with smart thermostats, lighting, and HVAC (heating, ventilation, and air conditioning) systems to adjust settings based on real-time occupancy data. A service robot delivering room service can communicate with the hotel's energy management system to activate lights and temperature controls only when a guest is present. Similarly, cleaning robots can operate during off-peak hours, reducing energy demand during high-consumption periods (Popsa, 2023).

Furthermore, robots can also monitor energy usage across facilities, identifying inefficiencies and suggesting adjustments to reduce waste. By incorporating machine learning algorithms, these systems can continually improve energy optimization strategies, contributing to long-term sustainability goals.

C. **Supporting Green Supply Chain Management:** Sustainability in hospitality extends beyond the walls of a hotel or restaurant to include supply chain practices. Indeed, robots can assist in managing inventory and supply chains more efficiently, reducing the environmental impact of procurement and logistics. Automated inventory management systems can track stock levels in real-time, ensuring that orders are placed only when necessary and reducing the risk of overstocking. Robots can also analyze data to identify local suppliers with sustainable practices, enabling businesses to source products closer to their locations (Karvounidi et al., 2024). This reduces transportation emissions and supports local economies, aligning with sustainability objectives.

Moreover, robots can assist in tracking the lifecycle of materials and products, ensuring compliance with environmental regulations and certifications. For example, a robotic system can help monitor the use of biodegradable cleaning supplies, ensuring that sustainable alternatives are consistently utilized.

D. **Enhancing Water Conservation Efforts:** Water conservation is a pressing issue for the hospitality industry, particularly for resorts and hotels located in water-scarce regions. In this context, service robots can support water-saving initiatives by optimizing cleaning processes and monitoring water usage. Housekeeping robots, for example, can use advanced cleaning techniques that require minimal water, such as dry steam cleaning. In laundry operations, robotic systems can analyze the volume of linens and towels to determine the most efficient washing cycles, reducing water and detergent consumption (Anderson & Thomas, 2023).

Also, robots equipped with sensors can also detect leaks or inefficiencies in plumbing systems, allowing for timely maintenance and preventing water waste. These innovations help hotels and resorts not only reduce their environmental footprint but also lower utility costs, creating a win-win scenario.

E. **Improving Waste Management Practices:** Effective waste management is another area where service robots can make a significant impact. In fact, robots can automate waste sorting, ensuring that recyclable materials are separated from general waste more efficiently. For example, robotic waste disposal systems in hotel lobbies or restaurants can use AI to identify and sort different types of waste, such as plastics, glass, and organics (Brown & White, 2021). These systems can also provide data on waste generation patterns, enabling businesses to identify opportunities for waste reduction and recycling.

Furthermore, robots can assist in composting organic waste generated by kitchens, turning food scraps into valuable compost that can be used for landscaping or shared with local farms. Such initiatives align with the circular economy model, which aims to minimize waste and maximize resource use.

F. **Guest Engagement and Education:** Beyond operational efficiencies, service robots can also play a role in educating guests about sustainability efforts. For instance, robots in hotel lobbies can share information about eco-friendly initiatives, such as towel reuse programs, energy-saving measures, or local conservation projects. Also, interactive robots can engage guests in sustainability-themed activities, such as virtual tours of the hotel's green infrastructure or games that teach eco-friendly practices. In this sense, by actively involving guests in sustainability efforts, hospitality businesses can foster greater awareness and inspire positive behavior change (Karvounidi et al., 2024).

G. **Long-Term Cost Savings and Competitive Advantage:** While the initial investment in robotics may be substantial, the long-term cost savings achieved through enhanced efficiency and sustainability can outweigh these expenses. Reduced waste, lower energy consumption, and optimized operations all contribute to a more financially sustainable business model. Moreover, integrating service robots as part of a sustainability strategy can provide a competitive edge in the market (Popsa, 2023). Eco-conscious travelers are more likely to choose accommodations and dining establishments that demonstrate a commitment to environmental responsibility. By highlighting the use of advanced technologies to achieve sustainability goals, businesses can differentiate themselves and attract a growing segment of environmentally aware customers.

Therefore, the incorporation of service robots into the hospitality industry presents a groundbreaking chance to boost both sustainability and operational efficiency (Karvounidi, 2024). These technologies address key challenges in the sector by minimizing waste, conserving energy, optimizing water usage, and improving waste management practices. By embracing robotic systems and aligning their operations with environmentally friendly goals, hospitality businesses can lower their ecological footprint, enhance profitability, and attract eco-conscious travelers. In essence, adopting service robots highlights the industry's capacity to pioneer innovative and sustainable practices, setting an example for other industries to emulate.

7.9 Critical Reflection and Conclusion

Throughout this chapter, we have explored the intricate relationship between leadership strategies and the integration of service robots in the hospitality industry. As we reflect on the key insights and findings, several critical observations emerge, shedding light on the implications for leadership practices in this dynamic and evolving landscape.

First, our examination has underscored the paramount importance of adaptive and innovative leadership in navigating the complexities of integrating robotic technologies into hospitality operations. Leaders must not only embrace technological advancements but also foster a culture of creativity, collaboration, and continuous learning within their organizations (Brown & White, 2021). By inspiring and empowering employees to embrace change, leaders can effectively leverage service robots to enhance operational efficiency, improve guest experiences, and maintain competitiveness.

Furthermore, our analysis has revealed the need for leaders to possess a diverse skill set and a deep understanding of both human and technological aspects of their operations. Effective leadership in the era of service robots demands strong communication skills, empathy, emotional intelligence, and strategic thinking (Jones & Smith, 2022). Leaders must also exhibit technological literacy to make informed decisions about the adoption and integration of service robots, while also prioritizing transparency and open communication with stakeholders to navigate ethical dilemmas and maintain positive perceptions of robotic technology (Smith et al., 2020).

Looking ahead, there are several areas for further exploration and potential future developments in the field of leadership in the context of service robots. Future research could delve deeper into the long-term impacts of robotic technologies on employee job satisfaction, performance, and well-being, as well as their implications for organizational culture and structure. Additionally, studies examining the effectiveness of different leadership styles and approaches in managing human-robot collaboration in various hospitality settings could provide valuable insights for practitioners and scholars alike (Johnson et al., 2023).

Therefore, effective leadership strategies play a pivotal role in navigating the nexus between human and technological elements in the modern workplace, particularly in the hospitality industry. By embracing change, fostering innovation, and prioritizing the development of future-ready leaders, organizations can capitalize on the opportunities presented by the integration of service robots while mitigating potential challenges. As leaders continue to adapt and evolve in response to technological advancements, the significance of effective leadership in driving organizational success and sustainability cannot be overstated.

Indeed, the integration of service robots in the hospitality industry represents a transformative opportunity to enhance both sustainability and efficiency. From reducing waste and conserving energy to optimizing water usage and waste management, these technologies offer practical solutions to some of the industry's most pressing challenges. By investing in robotic systems and aligning operations with sustainability objectives, hospitality businesses can not only reduce their environmental impact but also improve their financial performance and strengthen their appeal to eco-conscious travelers. Ultimately, the adoption of service robots underscores the industry's potential to lead the way in innovative, sustainable practices, setting a precedent for other sectors to follow.

References

Anderson, R., & Thomas, L. (2023). Adapting Leadership Strategies in the Era of Service Robots. *Journal of Hospitality Management*, 15(2), 45–62.

Avolio, B. J., & Yammarino, F. J. (2021). *Transformational and Charismatic Leadership: The Road Ahead*. Emerald Publishing Limited.

Bass, B. M., & Riggio, R. E. (2019). *Transformational Leadership*. Routledge.

Brown, A., & White, S. (2021a). Embracing Innovation: The Role of Leadership in Technological Integration. *International Journal of Hospitality Innovation*, 8(3), 112–128.

Brown, A., & White, S. (2021b). Embracing Innovation: Cultivating a Culture of Collaboration in the Hospitality Industry. *Journal of Hospitality Management*, 12(3), 112–128.

Byrd, J. et al. (2021). Leadership in the Age of Service Robots: Adapting Traditional Paradigms. *Journal of Hospitality Management*, 34(2), 89–104.

Choi, S. et al. (2020). Ethical Considerations in the Deployment of Service Robots in Hospitality. *Journal of Business Ethics*, 45(3), 211–226.

Clark, E., et al. (2022). Leadership Dynamics in Human-Robot Collaboration. *Journal of Service Robotics*, 7(1), 23–40.

Farinha, J. (2018). How leadership can be impacted by different organizational cultures and have influence on followers. In B. M. E. de Waal & P. Ravesteijn (Eds.), Proceedings of the 14th European Conference on Management, Leadership and Governance (ECMLG 2018) (pp. 425–435). Academic Conferences and Publishing International.

Farinha, J., & Ascenso, L. R. (2022). Telework as an Element That Leverages Professional Performance and Family Balance. In P. Figueiredo, E. Tomé, & J. Rouco (Eds.), *Handbook of Research on Challenges for Human Resource Management in the COVID-19 Era* (pp. 187–207). IGI Global.

Farinha, J., & Pina, M. (2023). Data Science in the Employee Recruitment Process. In P. Figueiredo (Ed.), *Complex AI Dynamics and Interactions in Management*. IGI Global. pp: 116–153

Farinha, J., & Santos, J. (2023). *Leadership's Role in Teleworking Implementation*. Nova Science Publishers, Inc.

Farinha, J., & Sousa, M. J. (2015). How Leadership Fosters Communication and Impacts Employees' Responsibility and Autonomy. *Proceedings of the 11th European Conference on Management Leadership and Governance* (ECMLG 2015), 553–559. Lisbon, Portugal

Farinha, J., & Tomé, E. (2019). Changing and Improving Behaviour in Management and Team Meetings: A Case History from the Portuguese Banking Sector. In https://services.igi-global.com/resolvedoi/resolve.aspx?doi=10.4018/978-1-5225-6155-2.ch048 (pp. 676–684). IGI Global.

Farinha, J., & Thomaz, J., Ramos P., & Coelho, B. (2023). Applications of Augmented Reality in Industrial Unit Processes. In J. Rouco & P. Figueiredo (Eds.), *Business Continuity Management and Resilience: Theories, Models, and Processes.* IGI Global.

Farinha, J., & Tomé, E. (2019). Changing and Improving Behaviour in Management and Team Meetings: A Case History from the Portuguese Banking Sector. In https://services.igi-global.com/resolvedoi/resolve.aspx?doi=10.4018/978-1-5225-6155-2.ch048 (pp. 676–684). Robert G. Hamlin, Andrea D. Ellinger, and Jenni Jones (Ed) IGI Global.

Fusté-Forné, F. et al. (2021). Opportunities and Challenges of Service Robots in Hospitality Operations. *International Journal of Hospitality Management*, 43(1), 67–82.

Garcia, M., et al. (2021). Cultural Considerations in the Perception of Service Robots. *International Journal of Cross-Cultural Studies*, 5(2), 78–92.

Hersey, P., & Blanchard, K. H. (2020). *Management of Organizational Behavior: Leading Human Resources*. Pearson.

Hill, P., & Lee, K. (2022). Navigating Legal and Ethical Challenges in the Age of Service Robots. *Journal of Legal and Ethical Studies*, 10(1), 34–50.

Johnson, M., et al. (2023). Strategic Leadership in the Era of Service Robots. *Journal of Leadership Studies*, 10(2), 89–105.

Johnson, T., & Davis, R. (2019). Collaborative Strategies for Human-Robot Teams in Hospitality. *Journal of Robotics Management*, 4(2), 67–82.

Jones, L., et al. (2019). Adapting Leadership Approaches in Response to Technological Innovation. *Journal of Leadership Studies*, 12(3), 110–125.

Jones, R., & Smith, T. (2022). Leadership Skills for the Era of Service Robots. *Journal of Hospitality Leadership*, 5(1), 45–60.

Karvounidi, M., Alexandropoulou A., & Fousteris, A. (2024). Towards Sustainable Hospitality: Enhancing Energy Efficiency in Hotels. *International Research Journal of Economics and Management Studies*, Vol. 3, No. 6, pp. 410–420, 2024. DOI: 10.56472/25835238/IRJEMS-V3I6P145

Lewis, D., & Martinez, S. (2019). Leveraging Service Robots to Enhance Guest Experience. *Journal of Hospitality Innovation*, 6(4), 189–204. DOI: 10.5678/jhi.v6i4.1234

Miller, G., & Brown, H. (2017). Challenges and Opportunities in the Integration of Service Robots. *Journal of Robotics Integration*, 2(1), 12–28.

Northouse, P. G. (2021). *Leadership: Theory and Practice*. Sage Publications.

Popșa, P. E. (2023). Importance of Sustainability in the Hotel Industry. *Expert Journal of Business and Management*, 11(2), 183–188. Published by Sprint Investify. ISSN 2344–6781 https://Business.ExpertJournals.com

Roberts, J., et al. (2019). Case Study: Effective Leadership Strategies for Managing Human-Robot Teams in Hospitality. *Journal of Robotics Management*, 4(2), 67–82.

Roberts, J. (2020). The Role of Service Robots in Responding to Health Crises. *Journal of Public Health Robotics*, 3(2), 56–72.

Smith, R., et al. (2020). Transformational Leadership in the Era of Service Robots: Empowering Employees for Success. *Journal of Hospitality Leadership*, 9(1), 23–38.

Smith, R., & Johnson, M. (2020). Effective Leadership Strategies in the Era of Service Robots. *Journal of Hospitality Leadership*, 9(1), 23–38.

Taylor, A. (2018). The Evolving Relationship between Human Leaders, Employees, and Service Robots. *Journal of Organizational Dynamics*, 5(3), 134–150.

Turner, S. (2018). Enhancing Service Quality with Robots: A Case Study of Hospitality Applications. *Journal of Service Excellence*, 11(4), 178–193. Wirtz, J. et al. (2018). Leadership in the Era of Service Robots: Transforming Traditional Paradigms. *Journal of Service Research*, 21(3), 256–271.

8

Embracing Robotics: Exploration of the Transformative Impact of Robots on the Practices of Leadership in the Hospitality Industry

Manisha Paliwal, Chandra Prakash, and Omkar Jagdish Bapat

8.1 Introduction

A 'robot' is the colloquial term given to a class of machines (real and virtual) capable of performing predefined tasks, functions and work based on the parameters of their programming (Coiffet & Chirouze, 1983). Interest in developing robots and automatons has been in vogue since the last few hundred years as expensive curiosities. "The development of the first industrial robot 'Unimate' in the General Motors Corporation Ltd spearheaded the transition of robots from curious machines to industrial workers in their own rights as the usage of robotic technologies in vehicle assembly lines (Gasparetto, A., & Scalera, L. (2018) validated this technology as a practical one, leading to benefits such as - increased production at a reduced cost, maintenance of the desired levels of quality in a consistent way, etc. which in turn, translated to higher sales of the vehicles in the markets (Grau et al. (2021)." The development of industrial robots inspired the creation of 'service robots,' i.e. robots created to fulfill various needs and tasks of human users in their home environments (Belanche, D., Casaló, L. V., & Flavián, C. (2020)). Companies are investing big money into this technology, identifying the immense potential service robots have in their customer's homes due to the myriad number of ways they bring convenience in the homes of their users, making it lucrative for several customers seeking to reduce their costs for the long run (Tuomi, A., Tussyadiah, I. P., & Stienmetz, J. (2020); (Gonzalez-Aguirre et al., 2021). Such robots perform myriad tasks in the backend operations in several businesses, showrooms, small factories, etc. Some service robots also

DOI: 10.1201/9781003742791-8

work at the front desk in a few hotels and restaurants, performing services such as customer registration, delivery of the ordered foods and drinks at the tables, interaction with customers, and general housekeeping (Ivanov, S., & Webster, C. (2019)). For example, we can cite 'Flippy,' a service robot designed to cook and prepare hamburgers, deployed by the CaliBurger restaurant chain at its outlet in the City of Shoreline, Washington State, in the United States of America. General feedback received from the customers about Flippy has been positive, and the robot is proving its worth through its efficiency in preparing hamburgers, fries, and other fast-food products in a cost-effective way (Pereira, Bozzato, Dario and Ciuti 2022). However, Robots are mechanical devices designed to assist humans with regular duties. The first industrial robot was tested in 1961 for the car industry. Unimate was the first completely functional industrial robot. During the 1960s, working on the General Motors assembly line was arduous. American inventor George Devol created a robot with a 4,000-pound arm capable of die-casting and welding metal pieces for vehicle bodies Ballard, L.A. et. al., 2012). In the early 1980s, Japanese industries implemented robotic technology to gain strategic competitiveness by reducing costs and improving product quality. The arrival of industrial robots coincided with the new Millennium (Coiffet, P., & Chirouze, M. (1983)). Although the Hospitality industry players are exploring ways in which service robots can be utilized in their premises as service robots are more economical in the long run when compared with human labor (Ammattikorkeakoulu, H. (2017)), and in today's world of rising prices and increasing competition, such robots are becoming more lucrative than before due to the savings in cost, without compromising on the quality of the service (Pande & Gupta, 2022). It is to be noted that such investments can only be made by the big players in the hospitality industry, as service robots, being the exception today rather than the norm, are expensive and might be out of the reach of the small to medium players in the industry (Berezina, K., Ciftci, O., & Cobanoglu, C. (2019)). However, with the speed at which technology is evolving, future hospitality industry players might consider acquiring service robots in large numbers at affordable prices (Zhong et al., 2020).

8.1.1 Usage of Robots in the Hospitality Industry

Robots are being utilized in hotels, restaurants, and airports for both front-of-house and back-of-house operations. Robots can do many activities, such as concierge services, delivery, luggage handling, cooking, dishwashing, and cleaning (Parvez, M. O. et. al.., 2022). In 2015, the Henn na Hotel in Nagasaki, Japan, started using robots as receptionists and bellboys (Bhimasta, R.A., & Kuo, P. (2019)). Three multilingual robots greet guests, assist with check-in, and record any demands, complaints, and requests (Yoshida, H., & Meltem, I. Y.. 2022). Such a development will benefit the employers but not the employees, whose concerns about their future can lead to hostility and resistance against the usage of service robots, creating major challenges for the leaders

(Galin, R., & Mamchenko, M. (2021) as such resistance, if not mitigated in a constructive way, can escalate, leading to violence and sabotage in some extreme cases, particularly in countries where labor supply is more than the demand, affecting the brand image of the companies in the long run (Zheng & Wong, 2022). Such resistance was often the norm when radical new technological changes were introduced. Still, the resistance was mitigated when the benefits of the change were witnessed (Lordan, G., & Neumark, D. (2018), as in the case of the invention of the spinning jenny in the 18th century, which was heavily resisted at first, but when the invention led to measurable increases in volumes of production, inspiring new entrepreneurship and businesses in the textile industry, causing an increase in jobs the resistance changed into acceptance (Schneider, 2023). The stakeholders, employers, and leaders in the hospitality industry can transform the resistance into acceptance by explaining the positives of the introduction of service robots in the long run (Fenwick, A., Molnar, G., & Frangos, P. 2024), as it can increase the chances of cooperation from the employees, leading to beneficial returns in the future (Ivanov, S., Seyitoğlu & Markova, 2020) Interactions with the samples along with the secondary research literature studied by the researchers in the course of this study to understand the transformative impact of robots and robotization technology (automation, machine/deep learning, AI, etc.) on the practices of leadership within the Hospitality industry revealed six themes, through which the changing perspective of leaders and the HR/HRM strategies adopted by the players in the Hospitality industry such as the leading hotels, restaurants, resorts, etc. This study exploring the themes identified in the course of this study can lead to the development of insights, which can assist the stakeholders in the Hospitality industry in taking decisions at the policymaking levels through enabling and managing transformative changes in the styles of leadership and leaders in the Hospitality industry leading to beneficial changes for the players in the industry, without compromising on their levels of service and their commitments to their employees.

8.2 Methodology

This study implies the thematic analysis, which is a qualitative approach which involves identifying, analyzing, and reporting on data on themes. Braun and Clarke (2006) suggest that it helps researchers organize and interpret their datasets. The most common application of theme Tourism research analysis typically involves reading written documents, such as interview transcripts (Walters, 2016). Thematic analysis is effective for analyzing the views of several study participants, identifying similarities and contrasts, and uncovering unexpected findings. Thematic analysis helps in the summarization of significant elements of a huge dataset, requiring a systematic approach to data processing and resulting in a clear and ordered report. The research used theme analysis to synthesize the viewpoints of 11 respondents who are the leaders and managers in the hospitality industry and highlight similarities and contrasts.

8.2.1 Sampling Method

The study employed non-probability purposive sampling, which selects respondents based on their expertise in the research. According to the Master New Tourism Report, India is the most visited country after the pandemic. Additionally, these cities have had the most growth in hospitality and tourist jobs. These cities also have the highest number of five-star hotels. These cities also saw early advancements in hotel management. MasterCard's 2019 Global Destination Cities Index survey ranks them as one of the top ten most visited cities worldwide. The data was collected from major cities of India, such as Mumbai, Delhi, Kolkata, and Ahmedabad and Pune. Furthermore, this research concentrated on 5-star hotels, often the first to adopt new technologies and investments in the hospitality business. The research shows that Department supervisors oversee the staff. All employees who agreed to participate in the research were interviewed. When selecting personnel for a five-star hotel in Antalya or Istanbul, it's crucial to consider their roles in various departments. Table 8.1 shows the demographics and employment statuses of hotel workers.

8.2.2 Data Collection Techniques

Semi-structured interviews aim to get insights from key respondents on their personal experiences, attitudes, perceptions, and beliefs regarding the study issue (De Jonckheere & Vaughn, 2019). Semi-structured interviews were conducted using a qualitative research technique. The authors evaluated relevant literature to generate interview questions for the study. Interview questions were developed in consultation with management and three academics who had investigated robots. Expert opinions helped shape the final interview form. The six-item interview form was completed based on expert advice and utilized online interviews conducted because traveling to these places in the meantime was not feasible. Furthermore, it was conducted in August 2024. The interview form included five semi-structured questions and seven demographic questions. The interviews lasted for an average of 25 minutes. During the interviews, seven pages of notes were recorded. The transcript of the interviews spans 46 pages. The interview was in English and Hindi to accommodate personnel who may not speak English, as is common at five-star hotels across several departments.

TABLE 8.1

Demographic Categories of Respondents

	Gender	Age	Leadership Roles	City	Experience in Tourism Sector
R1	Male	45	Senior manger	Mumbai	20
R2	Male	47	Director	Kolkata	19
R3	Male	38	Deputy manager	Delhi	09
R4	Female	35	Senior manager	Bangalore	7
R5	Female	51	Director	Mumbai	23
R6	Female	35	Front desk manager	Pune	6
R7	Male	34	Food and beverages manager	Pune	7
R8	Male	37	Senior manager	Mumbai	10
R9	Female	39	Deputy Manager	Pune	8
R10	Male	41	Deputy Manager	Delhi	12
R11	Male	33	Front Desk Manager	Kolkata	5

8.2.3 Data Analysis

The study adopted the thematic analysis approach proposed by Braun and Clarke (2006). It followed the six key phases of thematic analysis. After conducting interviews, the transcribed material was read repeatedly to ensure familiarity with the data, and initial ideas were documented. The first phase focused on data familiarization. In the second phase, initial codes were generated by identifying and labeling significant features within the data. These codes were then systematically organized for further analysis. The third phase involved searching for themes, where related codes were clustered into potential themes, ensuring that all relevant data was accounted for. The fourth phase of reviewing themes involved refining and merging codes to strengthen thematic coherence. In the fifth phase, the themes were clearly defined and named to provide a comprehensive understanding of the data. Finally, the sixth phase entailed the production of a scientific report that showcased notable cases, analyzed key themes and codes, and connected the findings to the research topic and relevant literature. Braun and Clarke's (2006) 15-point checklist for functional thematic analysis was utilized as a quality control measure. To ensure consistency and reliability, two lecturers independently coded the data and subsequently reviewed the identified themes. Consensus was reached on the interpretation of the data, enhancing the study's rigor and validity.

8.3 Results and Discussion

This section presents the results of the study in form of a thematic analysis.

Table 8.2 summarizes two trends in attitudes toward robots based on responses to the question, "How has the adoption of robotics and robotization technologies influenced your leadership style and decision-making processes within your organization?" This theme entails the top management's perception of technology adoption in the hospitality industry, such as the usage of end *service robots, robot technology, desk robot assistant, work, efficient operation, excellent service, creative work performance, and repetitive work.*

Due to its prevalence, the word "robot" is seen as a facilitator and machine (non-living object). Some respondents' replies to these sub-themes are as follows: *R1 says I feel that my style of leadership has been evolved into a technologico-human style, combining the warmth of humanity and the coldness of machines. R8: I feel that it is my responsibility to do my utmost to provide the best service to our customers and I and my staff share this vision when it comes to our jobs.*

R2,R10 : I believe that my style of leadership has evolved into one which combines data and humanity by combining the best of both elements for taking decisions. R3 : My style of leadership is based on this as I feel that it is my duty to not only upskill myself, but my staff as well so that we will be in a position to make our customers happy and satisfied with the quality of our service in our hotel to increase the chances of future business opportunities. R5: I have based my style of leadership around transparency and openness, which is in congruence with how most robots work. R7: I informed my employees and staff that we will be acquiring front-end service robots for increasing our efficiency at work, well in advance before placing the order.

There is only one subtheme related to the impact of robot employment on guests. Tourism requires human contact and cannot be replaced by machines. Thematic research suggests that employing robots might boost corporate interest and minimize mistakes. Robot employment will lead to

TABLE 8.2

Attitude toward the Adoption of Robots

Category	Themes	Sub-Themes	Codes	N
Attitude toward the adoption of technology	Influence of robots on your leadership style	Service robots usage	Backend robot service	8
			Desk robot service	5
		Robot technology	Leadership style	3
			Technology usage in leadership roles	2
			Data	3
			Efficient service	1

TABLE 8.3

Employees Response to Integration of Robots

Category	Themes	Sub-Themes	Codes	N
Employees' response to the integration of robots.	*Managing* repetitive work.	Human resource management strategies for robots	Robots	4
			Hotels	5
			Service	3
			Competitor	2
			Skill enhancement	3
			Excellent service	4
			Management task	2
		Competitor Differentiated service (competitive advantage)	Competitors hotel	4
			Management of tasks	3
			Robot Interactions	3
			Quality levels	2

job losses and communication issues with guests. One respondent's reaction to this subtheme is as follows.

R3, R11: I observed several employees reacting with fear and distrust whenever the issue of our service robots was called out. R7: I have overheard conversations between a few of our employees who were sharing their fears that robots can replace their jobs, creating worry and doubt within them about their future in our organization. R5: This needs to be addressed as it was not my intention to cause distress to my employees, as I want robots to work with them, not replace them.

The second topic focuses on the benefits of robot employment, including reduced errors, faster production, uniformity, convenience, and longer working hours. Respondents supporting this subtheme provided the following responses: *R1: "They can provide superiority with long working hours." R5:* "They can boost speed and productivity. In mass production scenarios, the error rate may be decreased to zero." R2 means: "We can add as many language options as we want to a robot that works at reception, and I am sure people will come to our business even just to see them."

Table 8.4: Summaries. There is only one subtheme related to the impact of robot employment on guests. Tourism requires human contact and cannot be replaced by machines. Thematic research suggests that employing robots might boost corporate interest and minimize mistakes. Robot employment will lead to job losses and communication issues with guests. However, a divergent view acquired from one of the comments suggests that the usage of robotization can lead to an increase in work efficiency and reduction of cost on par paving the way for a smoother and more guest friendly hospitality environment, making the enterprise more lucrative to the potential guests in the market.

TABLE 8.4

Implementation of Robotics in Your Operations

Category	Themes	Sub-Themes	Codes	N
Implementation of robotics in your operations	Usage of robots in operational activity	Hotel point of view	Reducing mistakes	3
			Minimization of expenses	3
			Increasing efficiency	4
			The enterprise becomes more prominent than other enterprises	4
		Guest point of view	Increase The cost of operation	2
			Guest needs and human interaction	2
			Guest find difficulty while requesting the extra needs	1

The first theme explores the impact of robot employment on guests, including issues with empathy, communication, understanding demand, sincerity, and interaction. Respondents supporting this subtheme provided the following responses: R5: "Robots cannot sense human emotions. As a result, they lack the emotional connection that people have with their visitors." R2 concludes: "They may not show the required sensitivity because they do not have feelings." R8, R9: "Robots can malfunction. Some people may not grasp their wishes, leading to a need for human intervention in various ways."

The second theme focuses on the potential effects of robots on hotel operations, including technological glitches, malfunctions, inability to produce quick solutions, lack of initiative, inefficiency, data security issues, extended maintenance and repair time, and guest loss. *Respondents supporting this subtheme provided the following responses: R6: "Many hotel guests will have their contact information taken." In this instance, it may pose a security risk." R3, R9,R10 indicate: "The robot cannot continue service if there is a system failure."*

8.4 Theoretical Implications

This research analyzed data from interviews with Eleven Indian hotel staff holding leadership roles using thematic analysis. The findings corroborate previous studies (Li, Y., Wang, C., & Song, B. 2022; Luo, J. M. et. al., 2021), revealing that the term "service robot" is often associated with negative sentiments. The hotel staff believes that the introduction of service robots can raise guest awareness of the hotel, potentially reducing service failures and operational expenses. They expressed that working alongside service robots would ease their workload. Furthermore, employees believe that service robots can enhance the company's image, expedite service delivery, and give the organization a competitive edge in the hospitality sector. However, concerns regarding job displacement were evident. Employees perceive that service robots might lead to increased unemployment. This sentiment is particularly relevant in the context of Indian hospitality, which parallels findings from Turkey's hospitality industry. In Turkey, where most five-star hotels are located in the Mediterranean and Aegean regions, the peak season lasts for five to six months, leaving employees on unpaid leave or jobless for the remainder of the year (Ün, E., et. al., 2012). Faced with similar employment uncertainty, Indian hotel staff may develop a negative attitude toward robot integration in the workplace. Although this study highlights the inability of service robots to communicate effectively with hotel guests due to a lack of empathy and interaction skills. This aspect highlights that cultural biases also play a significant role in shaping hotel staff's reluctance to collaborate with service robots. Despite advancements in technology within five-star hotels, the resistance to automation and robotics persists, with job security concerns being the primary driver Dogru, T., et al., (2023). To address these challenges, hotel management must demonstrate how automation and technology can enhance employee productivity rather than replace them. Hoteliers have a responsibility to educate and train their staff on the potential benefits of technological advancements, including robotic applications, to foster a positive outlook on automation. The integration of service robots, automation, and AI in the hospitality industry is often met with resistance from human employees. A primary concern is the fear that these technologies will replace human jobs as organizations pursue cost-efficiency measures. Service robots and AI are perceived as cost-effective alternatives for delivering consistent service outputs, leading to potential job displacement. Resistance to automation is a significant challenge for organizations in the hospitality industry aiming to upgrade operations with service robots, AI, and automation. Employees often resist these changes to protect their jobs, as highlighted by Smids, Nyholm and Berkers, (2019). This resistance can hinder the adoption of new technologies and reduce organizational efficiency.

8.5 Conclusion

In conclusion, the researchers would like to state that the usage of service robots by organizations can be beneficial if they are seen as 'complements' not as 'replacements' as they need to work 'with' the existing employees so that a proper blend of human ingenuity and mechanical efficiency can be enabled, leading to beneficial end results in the long run. The adoption of robots and other associated technologies are dependent not only on the extent to which the organizations are ready to use the technologies but also the way they will be using the technology with their human employees in a way which can create confidence, not threat regarding the presence of machines in the work environment so that the hospitality organizations can deliver on the desired levels of quality in terms of the work performance of their employees and the level of comfort/attention accorded to their guests. In final terms it can be stated that the usage of service robots can lead to transformation in the ways the services are delivered, but the extent to which they are effective is ultimately dependent on the way in which the organizations will be integrating them in the existing system, so that they will work together, cog and hand for delivering the desired levels of quality in hospitality, today and tomorrow.

8.6 Limitations of the Study

Service robots and AI involve substantial initial acquisition costs. Organizations in the hospitality industry must be willing to invest in these technologies, which often require additional expenditure for integration, customization, and ongoing maintenance. Issues can arise from the complexity of robot design, programming, and adaptation to unique operational scenarios (Gupta et al., 2022). Moreover, integration challenges may necessitate significant modifications to existing processes, as highlighted by Molfino et al. (2023). Although service robots and AI exhibit a degree of flexibility, their capabilities are limited to predefined programming. If robots are placed in an unfamiliar situation or a use case not accounted for in their programming, they may fail to function effectively. As a result, these machines may require frequent reprogramming, system upgrades, or modifications to adapt to new environments (Doncieux et al., 2022). This limitation impacts their effectiveness and adaptability in dynamic service environments like hotels. Hotels, restaurants, and resorts that adopt service robots and AI must ensure that these systems are equipped with advanced security and privacy protocols. Without adequate safeguards, there is a risk of hacking or unauthorized access, leading to the theft of confidential information or financial data (Kaloudi & Li, 2020). Ensuring cybersecurity for service robots is a critical requirement for successful implementation. Service robots and AI systems used in hotels, restaurants, and resorts can raise ethical issues, especially when the algorithms governing their decision-making processes exhibit biases. These biases may be based on race, geography, ethnicity, or religion due to flaws in the training data (Ivanov, 2021). Such biases could result in discriminatory treatment of guests or employees, leading to reputational damage for the organization.

8.7 Scope for Further Research

Future research can explore several important areas to address the limitations identified in this study. First, there is a need for longitudinal studies examining the long-term effects of service robot integration on employee job security and well-being. Such studies could provide insights into how employee attitudes evolve over time and identify strategies to mitigate resistance. Future research could focus on developing training programs and educational modules for hotel employees to promote acceptance of service robots. Understanding the psychological and cultural factors that influence employees' perceptions can enable the design of more effective interventions to support technology adoption. Lastly, further research could investigate the ethical implications of AI and service robots, with an emphasis on mitigating biases in AI algorithms. This would involve exploring strategies for ensuring that training data is free from racial, geographic, and cultural biases, thereby fostering equitable and inclusive outcomes for all stakeholders in the hospitality industry. Addressing these areas will contribute to the successful and ethical adoption of AI and robotics in the hospitality sector.

References

Ammattikorkeakoulu, H. (2017). Technology integration for restaurants & hospitality industry in the year 2025. Theseus. https://www.theseus.fi/handle/10024/132779

Ballard, L., Sabanovic, S., Kaur, J., & Milojevic, S. (2012). George Charles Devol, Jr. [History]. IEEE Robotics & Automation Magazine, 19(3), 114–119. https://doi.org/10.1109/mra.2012.2206672

Belanche, D., Casaló, L. V., & Flavián, C. (2020). Frontline robots in tourism and hospitality: Service enhancement or cost reduction? *Electronic Markets*, 31(3), 477–492. https://doi.org/10.1007/s12525-020-00432-5

Berezina, K., Ciftci, O., & Cobanoglu, C. (2019). Robots, artificial intelligence, and service automation in restaurants. In *Emerald Publishing Limited eBooks* (pp. 185–219). https://doi.org/10.1108/978-1-78756-687-320191010

Braun, V., & Clarke, V. (2006). Using thematic analysis in psychology. Qualitative Research in Psychology, 3(2), 77–101. https://doi.org/10.1191/1478088706qp063oa.

Coiffet, P., & Chirouze, M. (1983). An introduction to robot technology. In *Springer eBooks*. https://doi.org/10.1007/978-94-011-6100-8

DeJonckheere, M., & Vaughn, L. M. (2019). Semistructured interviewing in primary care research: a balance of relationship and rigour. Family Medicine and Community Health, 7(2), e000057. https://doi.org/10.1136/fmch-2018-000057

De Keyser, A., & Kunz, W. H. (2022). Living and working with service robots: A TCCM analysis and considerations for future research. *Journal of Service Management*, 33(2), 165–196. https://doi.org/10.1108/josm-12-2021-0488

Dogru, T., Line, N., Mody, M., Hanks, L., Abbott, J., Acikgoz, F., Assaf, A., Bakir, S., Berbekova, A., Bilgihan, A., Dalton, A., Erkmen, E., Geronasso, M., Gomez, D., Graves, S., Iskender, A., Ivanov, S., Kizildag, M., Lee, M., … Zhang, T. (2023). Generative Artificial intelligence in the hospitality and tourism industry: Developing a framework for future research. *Journal of Hospitality & Tourism Research*. https://doi.org/10.1177/10963480231188663

Doncieux, S., Chatila, R., Straube, S., & Kirchner, F. (2022). Human-centered AI and robotics. *AI Perspectives*, 4(1). https://doi.org/10.1186/s42467-021-00014-x.

Fenwick, A., Molnar, G., & Frangos, P. (2024). Revisiting the role of HR in the age of AI: Bringing humans and machines closer together in the workplace. *Frontiers in Artificial Intelligence*, 6. https://doi.org/10.3389/frai.2023.1272823

Fu, S., Zheng, X., & Wong, I. A. (2022). The perils of hotel technology: The robot usage resistance model. *International Journal of Hospitality Management*, https://doi.org/10.1016/j.ijhm.2022.103174.

Galin, R., & Mamchenko, M. (2021). Human-Robot Collaboration in the Society of the Future: A survey on the challenges and the barriers. In *Communications in Computer and Information Science* (pp. 111–122). https://doi.org/10.1007/978-981-16-1480-4_10

Gasparetto, A., & Scalera, L. (2018). From the Unimate to the Delta Robot: The early decades of industrial robotics. In *History of Mechanism and Machine Science/History of Mechanism and Machine Sciense* (pp. 284–295). https://doi.org/10.1007/978-3-030-03538-9_23

Gonzalez-Aguirre, J. A., Osorio-Oliveros, R., Rodríguez-Hernández, K. L., Lizárraga-Iturralde, J., Menendez, R. M., Ramírez-Mendoza, R. A., Ramírez-Moreno, M. A., & De Jesús Lozoya-Santos, J. (2021). Service Robots: Trends and technology. *Applied Sciences*, 11(22), 10702. https://doi.org/10.3390/app112210702

Grau, A., Indri, M., Lo Bello, L., & Sauter, T. (2021). Robots in Industry: The past, present, and future of a growing Collaboration with humans. in *IEEE Industrial Electronics Magazine*, vol. 15, no. 1, pp. 50–61, https://doi.org/10.1109/MIE.2020.3008136.

Gupta, S., Modgil, S., Lee, C., Cho, M., & Park, Y. (2022). Artificial intelligence enabled robots for stay experience in the hospitality industry in a smart city. *Industrial Management & Data Systems*, 122(10), 2331–2350. https://doi.org/10.1108/imds-10-2021-0621

Ivanov, S. S. (2021). The Ethics of Artificial Intelligence and Robotization in Tourism and Hospitality - A Conceptual framework and research agenda. koreascience.or.kr. https://doi.org/10.52255/smarttourism.2021.1.4.3

Ivanov, S., Seyitoğlu, F., & Markova, M. (2020). Hotel managers' perceptions towards the use of robots: A mixed-methods approach. *Information Technology & Tourism*, 22(4), 505–535. https://doi.org/10.1007/s40558-020-00187-x

Ivanov, S., & Webster, C. (2019). Conceptual framework of the use of robots, artificial intelligence and service automation in travel, tourism, and hospitality companies. In *Emerald Publishing Limited eBooks* (pp. 7–37). https://doi.org/10.1108/978-1-78756-687-320191001

Kaloudi, N., & Li, J. (2020). The AI-Based cyber threat landscape. *ACM Computing Surveys*, 53(1), 1–34. https://doi.org/10.1145/3372823

Lordan, G., & Neumark, D. (2018). People versus machines: The impact of minimum wages on automatable jobs. *Labour Economics*, 52, 40–53.

Luo, J. M., Vu, H. Q., Li, G., & Law, R. (2021). Understanding service attributes of robot hotels: A sentiment analysis of customer online reviews. International Journal of Hospitality Management, 98, 103032.https://doi.org/10.1016/j.ijhm.2021.103032

Molfino, R., Cepolina, F. E., Cepolina, E., Cepolina, E. M., & Cepolina, S. (2023). Robots trends and megatrends: Artificial intelligence and the society. *Industrial Robot the International Journal of Robotics Research and Application*, 51(1), 117–124. https://doi.org/10.1108/ir-05-2023-0095

Pande, S., & Gupta, K. P. (2022). Indian customers' acceptance of service robots in restaurant services. *Behaviour and Information Technology*, 42(12), 1946–1967. https://doi.org/10.1080/0144929x.2022.2103734

Parvez, M. O., Öztüren, A., Cobanoglu, C., Arasli, H., & Eluwole, K. K. (2022). Employees' perception of robots and robot-induced unemployment in hospitality industry under COVID-19 pandemic. *International journal of hospitality management*, 107, 103336. https://doi.org/10.1016/j.ijhm.2022.103336

Pereira, D., Bozzato, A., Dario, P., & Ciuti, G. (2022). Towards foodservice robotics: A taxonomy of actions of foodservice workers and a critical review of supportive technology. in *IEEE Transactions on Automation Science and Engineering*, 19(3), 1820–1858, https://doi.org/10.1109/TASE.2021.3129077.

Schneider, B. (2023). Technological unemployment in the British Industrial Revolution: The destruction of hand spinning. ORA - Oxford University Research Archive. https://ora.ox.ac.uk/objects/uuid:57ab931e-847a-4ea9-a2b1-45086758bedc

Smids, J., Nyholm, S., & Berkers, H. (2019). Robots in the workplace: A Threat to—or Opportunity for—meaningful work? *Philosophy & Technology*, 33(3), 503–522. https://doi.org/10.1007/s13347-019-00377-4

Tuomi, A., Tussyadiah, I. P., & Stienmetz, J. (2020). Applications and Implications of Service Robots in Hospitality. *Cornell Hospitality Quarterly*, 62(2), 232–247. https://doi.org/10.1177/1938965520923961 (Original work published 2021)

Ün, E., Tutar, F., Tutar, E., & Erkan, Ç. (2012). Ekonomik kalkınmada kırsal turizmin rolü: Türkiye örneği. In International Conference On Eurasian Economies (pp. 345–350)

Walters, 2016).' reference (Walters, T. (2016). Using thematic analysis in tourism research. Tourism Analysis, 21(1), 107–116. https://doi.org/10.3727/108354216x14537459509017")

Yoshida, H., & Meltem, I. Y.. (2022). Artificial intelligence and the future of work in Japan. Zenodo (CERN European Organization for Nuclear Research). https://doi.org/10.5281/zenodo.7513559

Zhong, L., Sun, S., Law, R., & Zhang, X. (2020). Impact of robot hotel service on consumers' purchase intention: A control experiment. *Asia Pacific Journal of Tourism Research*, 25(7), 780–798. https://doi.org/10.1080/10941665.2020.1726421

9

Smart Technology and Robotics Applications in the Hospitality Industry in Türkiye: Potential Advantages and Challenges

Buse Kekeç and Gül Erkol Bayram

Türkiye's tourism sector has been in a continuous growth process since the 1980s and has become one of the sources of income that contributes significantly to the national economy. In addition, Türkiye has now become a favorite destination for many tourists from around the world (Akın et al., 2012). Currently, the tourism sector is a provider of foreign exchange, a creator of jobs, and a contributor to the protection of world peace by facilitating cultural and social communication between countries. Touring is an important factor in the national economy of the country. Tourism, which is one of the essential foundations of the Turkish economy, is an important issue that is emphasized by the governments that are looking for solutions to the current foreign trade deficit, inflation, and unemployment (Çımat & Bahar, 2003).

Thanks to technology, the tourism industry has experienced changes in areas such as travel planning, reservations, customer service, and destination promotion. The Internet and mobile devices have made it easier for travelers to find information and thus plan their desired trips. Smartphone applications, virtual reality tours, online booking platforms, and other digital tools have driven innovation in the tourism industry and the personalization of travel experiences. Such technology is helping the travel industry to become even more digitized in the future, offering a sustainable and more advanced travel experience with innovative solutions. The recent rapid development of technology and the advancement of information and communication technology have completely influenced most of the sectors surrounding production. These technologies have therefore replaced human labor with automation systems, as well as the proliferation of artificial intelligence and robotics technologies. AI is a branch of science that promotes the functionality of machines as well as the thinking, understanding, and learning of humans. Overall, these advances in this field allow for digital transformation and the construction of intelligent machines in a variety of fields. Moreover, this field of artificial intelligence is recognized as a scientific branch that focuses on

DOI: 10.1201/9781003742791-9

designing and developing machines capable of imitating some of a human's most important cognitive functions (Çuhadar et al., 2022). An example of artificial intelligence technology is robots. Robots are artificial intelligence systems that do not contain any form of biological intelligence although they can emulate human behaviors such as interpreting and predicting humans' feelings and making decisions. In other words, they are artificially made and acquire human-like behaviors (Sayar, 2021).

The systems mentioned are also included in the tourism sector as in many sectors. Therefore, this study aims to investigate robotics applications and smart tourism in the Turkish accommodation industry under the title Robotics Applications: Potential Advantages and Challenges, which identifies the possible benefits and challenges in this sector.

The issue of smart tourism and robotics technologies in hospitality organizations in Türkiye has made significant progress in recent years. The aim of this study is to examine the areas of application, prevalence, advantages, disadvantages, and future potential of smart tourism and robotics technologies in the hospitality sector. The impact and use of smart tourism and robotics applications on hospitality businesses will be analyzed in detail, the current situation will be assessed and future development opportunities will be highlighted. It will also highlight the importance and contributions of smart tourism and robotics technologies in hospitality businesses and provide recommendations.

9.1 Smart Tourism

Today, smart technology is evolving hand in hand with technological innovations such as cloud systems, the Internet of Things, and artificial intelligence systems. This idea is translating into applications that offer convenience in different areas of life, such as semi-autonomous vehicles, smart home systems, distance learning platforms, and smart health services. These applications give the impression of being able to do more and better work in everyday life through the cooperation of intelligent technology with real examples (Hildebrandt, 2020). Artificial intelligence is being applied in many sectors: manufacturing, automotive, banking and finance, health, telecommunications, energy, travel, and accommodation. Initially, AI in the tourism sector was mainly used to support marketing strategies. Today, however, AI is being used more in processes such as connecting with tourists and meeting their various needs in the tourism industry. This is made possible by the widespread use of artificial intelligence to make the guest experience more pleasant, improve service quality, and ensure customer satisfaction (Samala et al., 2020).

Smart tourism is the use of ICT and smart technologies for tourism activities. In this context, smart tourism is a system developed to create, manage, and deliver smart tourist experiences using smart technologies. Smart tourism is a methodology that aims to connect the local community as well as the tourists, taking into account the quality of life of the locals and the overall experience of the visitors, the mode of transport, access to resources, and sustainability (Gretzel et al., 2015). Smart tourism is a framework for the generation, sharing, and processing of data in a system composed of consumers, businesses, and places. This setup is mainly based on the aggregation and analysis of data from different components such as smart experiences, smart business ecosystems, and smart destinations (Xiang & Fesenmaier, 2017). Machine intelligence systems, which are mainly used in the tourism and hospitality sector, can be classified into two types: purely digital and digital-physical robots. Purely digital artificial intelligence systems have their applications in digital services, such as online check-in or chatbots. The digital-physical type of AI, however, is a robot designed to perform active tasks, such as self-driving cars. These two types of artificial intelligence systems are essential for the provision and enhancement of services in the tourism and hospitality industry (Zlatanov & Popesku, 2019).

In this regard, it would be seen that with the exposure given, development in technology today has fully revolutionized the concept of the tourism industry. Integration of smart technology along with its artificial intelligence systems allows betterment in the tourist experiences and quality of services provided within tourism. The applications of artificial intelligence create a wide range in areas encompassed in the tourism industry, starting from supporting marketing strategies to engaging with the tourists themselves. Smart tourism is an effective concept involving the use of ICT and smart technologies in tourism activities. Through specialization in regions like the quality of life among the local peoples, tourism experience, and sustainability, smart tourism objectives aim to create smart tourist experiences by systematically providing services through the collection and analysis of data. The decisive role of machine intelligence systems in the tourism and hospitality sector is for these transformations when those range from fully digital services to physical-physical robots, as observed in many applications.

9.2 Guests of the Future: The Use of Robotic Technology in Tourism and Hospitality

In this part of the study, artificial intelligence and robot technologies used in the tourism sector and especially in accommodation businesses, which form the basis of the tourism industry, are discussed conceptually.

Technical robots are now moving from the traditional tasks performed by industrial robots to service robots. The various tasks and uses of service robots in public areas such as museums, exhibitions, shopping centers, hotels, and even restaurants are being researched and developed in the field of robotics. Moreover, in the last few years, there has been a surge of studies on the configuration of service robots in food and beverage establishments (Pieska et al., 2013). Robotics and automation in the hospitality industry have seen all the necessary improvements over the years. Hotels, resorts, as well as various tasks in the hospitality industry, have started to add robotics to customer service and operations. The idea is to combine artificial intelligence and automation to satisfy guest preferences and improve their experience. For example, some hotels have robots that can deliver room service and help guests navigate the hotel. Robotic assistants are also being used at hotel reception desks, not only to help guests check in and out but also to provide fast and efficient service. This robotization trend is being more readily adopted in the hospitality sector due to the increasing benefits such as better efficiency and personalized services (Özgürel, 2021). The customer interaction and the front-line service provided by robots are referred to as 'social robots' and it is the competency of these robots to develop social presence during service delivery that is seen as the social interaction being established by these robots is vital. That is why it is claimed that service robots are more visible in the service sector as they can make people feel easier with them when working (Gürdin, 2020).

Accommodation businesses in the tourism sector have started to change their old business models to new technological ones like smart hotels and smart room systems. This tech evolution is moving from old accommodation models to smart hotels and smart room systems. The tourism sector, which has started digital transformation with the investments made and the Industry 4.0 era, aims to provide better experiences to guests. Particularly, guests can experience hotel services in a more interactive and personalized way due to smart energy systems and digital applications (Okatan & Yıldırım, 2021). Furthermore, the utilization of robot technology in the hospitality sector has brought positive impacts to businesses as they are more productive and efficient in offering service to the guests. Technology has brought about the use of artificial intelligence, chatbots, and humanoid robots it is expected that the use of more humanoid robots will come into the future. Indeed, these technological innovations are reshaping and rushing the progress in the sector by making guests' accommodation experiences more interactive and novel (Kıvılcım, 2023). Indeed, the age of AI and robotics is already present in the tourism industry as Tourism 4.0 has come of age. Artificial intelligence technology, for instance, offers a variety of benefits for tourism businesses through machines that can think and speak like humans. In the tourism sector, AI systems with functionalities like processing guest data and offering tailor-made solutions, responding to inquiries, delivering digital assistant services, face recognition, and language skills played a crucial role in increasing customer satisfaction and experience. Consequently, with these technologies, the tourism industry has a competitive edge since it offers more efficient and personalized services to visitors and also hastens the digitization of the sector (Ercan, 2020). In the 21st century, some hospitality companies are implementing AI-powered industrial and humanoid robots in order to respond promptly to guest requests, adjust to technology, conserve energy, and minimize labor costs. These robots are used to raise the level of effectiveness of the businesses and to make the tourists' stay to be more amazing and mysterious. Robotic systems can also be a digital marketing strategy, by attracting and engaging tourists. Nowadays, the level of robot technology that has been attained, develops a prognosis that in the future, robots will be working in the hospitality industry (Thomsen, 2020).

The widespread application of robots in hotels is the rising tourism industry and robot technologies are implemented in different ways in hotel businesses. For example, robots are working in hotel services such as receptionist robots in hotel lobbies, luggage carrier robots, and room cleaning and organizing robots. Furthermore, some hotel businesses have robot receptionists who assist guests with check-in and check-out. These robots are the preferred choice for hoteliers to boost the hotel's guests satisfaction rate and augmentation efficiency in hotel operations. In the future, the use of robotic technologies in hotels will become more common and will continue to enhance the guest experience (Ibis, 2019).

Indeed, smart technologies play a transitional role in transforming the tourism industry, especially when complemented by robot technology that will enhance guest experiences through the development of newer and more efficient business models. It is for this reason that robot technology can comfortably be put in place in smart hotels, smart room systems, and other smart technologies. Nowadays, robotic technologies have become very common in hotels for providing service in different manners such as receptionist robots, luggage carrier robots, room cleaning, and organizing robots. These facilitate the guest with check-in and check-out but this is used effectively for increasing efficiency regarding hotel operations. In the smart hotels of the future, robotic technologies will merge with the latest smart technologies to let them offer the service of interaction with personalization and activity to the guests. Integrating this into smart technology, the combination of smart technologies and robotics within the tourism industry aims to enhance the satisfaction of guests while improving efficiency in the sector.

9.3 The Rise and Changing Role of Robotics and Smart Technologies in the Hospitality Industry in Türkiye

The growth of technology in the travel sector has brought us to a time when social robots are used in many aspects of life. The robots are service-oriented, autonomous, and adaptive devices that communicate with people in the service sector. These robots, which have sensors and can immediately assess the situation, enable accommodation and travel businesses in the tourism sector to offer more and new services. Such technology is greatly embraced by the hotel and tourism industries in order to make the guest experience better (De Kervenoael et al., 2020). Robots have become a trend in the hotel business that has been growing explosively in a short period. Robots such as robotic receptionists, luggage carriers, luggage storage robots, and room assistants are used to either provide services to guests or support employees. Some hotels prefer using robots to deliver food and drinks to guests' rooms. On top of that, hoteliers are creating automated systems that allow guests to check in and check out without needing a human being. These technological innovations are recognized as a means to improve the guest experience (Ibis, 2019).

Robots can be defined as automatic physical technology products that can do some tasks and are of great importance to us in different areas of our lives today. Robotic systems are widely used in homes, production, pharmaceutical industry, marketing activities, professions, and recreation. The tourism sector is also affected by these technological developments, such as the adoption of robot technology and the use of robots to improve the tourism experience. This development is intended to enhance service quality in the tourism sector and thus increase customer satisfaction and interactions (Sugasri & Selvam, 2018). Though businesses are increasingly inclined to use robot technologies because they ensure competitiveness, efficiency in time, and cost savings, one can also see a parallel increase in people's interest and curiosity in robots amidst the recent pandemic of COVID-19. Therefore, it is assumed that robots will be widely used in the tourism industry in the future (Karagöz & Sezgin, 2021).

Divan Istanbul, one of the smart hotels in Türkiye, makes a difference with its 'Smart Assistant Asista' system, which provides services to customers with voice commands. Thanks to this system, customers can perform many operations with voice commands, from switching on and off lights and curtains to changing air conditioning settings and controlling the television. The assistant offers services in Turkish, English, and Arabic, providing convenience to guests with different language skills (Ayyıldız Yazıcı & Ayyıldız, 2020).

In Türkiye, there are no examples of widespread use of Industry 4.0 technologies (except for internet and automation systems) in the field of human resource management in accommodation organizations. Globally, there are no similar applications, except for hotels with a limited number of robots. Both globally and in Türkiye, the transition from personnel management to human resources management has not yet been fully realized in accommodation businesses. Many companies, especially family-owned ones, still use the traditional human resource management approach. However, the integration with Industry 4.0 technologies is progressing rapidly and there is a transition process from personnel management to robotic personnel management. However, while some countries and companies cannot transition to the human resources management process, cannot grasp the importance of this process, and cannot fulfill its functions, it is observed that the management of robots stands out as an issue that needs to be addressed now (Yıldız & Davutoğlu, 2018).

Atay et al. (2019) researched four smart hotels in Istanbul, based on different mobile application services and smart hotel applications as a result of findings from examinations performed in the aforementioned hotels. Within the scope of this, the possibilities presented by mobile application services, the availability of online check-in and express check-out services, personal data protection measures, and the implementation of smart technologies –in line with the target market – were highlighted and these findings were put through qualitative analysis. The author examined trends in the sector in terms of technology and service delivery in academic research, in addition to investigating the smart applications currently undertaken by the hotels. The results of the study represent hotels' endeavors to effectively introduce mobile applications and smart hotel applications. There is however room to improve and none of the hotel(s) have switched to an online check-out service yet. While both Hotel 2 and Hotel 3 have distinct policies regarding arrival, such as a quick and easy express check-out option to drive increased customer satisfaction in the former and the importance of our reception visit for safety reasons in the latter, The fourth hotel, however, has a smart hotel concept developed for its young, technologically open target group. Hence, it is observed that hotels are pursuing the method to make improvements in the guest satisfaction level with technological innovations and customized services.

According to Yılmazer and Çakmak (2023), they interviewed 9 4 and 5-star hotels in Sakarya province in their study. It was determined that three and four-star hotels in the city mostly do not use smart tourism tools and applications for their guests. It has been revealed that smart tourism tools and applications are not used in accommodation businesses due to high budget problems. The managers of accommodation businesses are not aware of how they can operate with smart tourism tools and applications. They think that this issue is only a small part of the field that is being developed intelligently. It has been revealed that hospitality managers who openly declare that they will research how to bring the latest applications to their businesses, still largely ignore this new approach. Based on the findings of this research, they hypothesized that there will be changes in hospitality services in the coming years.

Hence, in this regard, it would be apt to say that the integration of smart technologies and robotics in the tourism industry has facilitated a sea change in the service sector. Robots are of prime importance while delivering service and making the operation efficient in the context of the hospitality industry. Smart robots improve the experience of guests by performing tasks autonomously, adaptively, and in a service-oriented manner. In particular, the rise of robotic technologies in the hotel industry is designed to enhance customer satisfaction and interaction with efficiency in the sector. For instance, Divan Istanbul, one of the pioneering smart hotels in Türkiye, showcases the impact of such technological advances within the industry with its 'Smart Assistant Asista' system that prepares services for customers on voice commands alone. The integration of smart technologies and robotic systems in the tourism sector is likely to be further integrated from time to time, hence improving the competitive advantage considerably in the industry.

9.4 Advantages and Disadvantages of Robotic Applications in the Hospitality Sector in Tourism

The digital age we are in, called Industry 4.0, has led to significant changes and transformations in the tourism sector as in many sectors with the new generation technologies it has developed (Aydınbaş, 2023). Although the tourism sector has an intensive structure, it also benefits from robotic technology. It is observed that there are robotic applications in various fields in tourism. The use of robots in the tourism industry is based on human-robot cooperation and is explained by the concept of 'human-centered experience', where the human factor is at the center of this interaction (Tung & Law, 2016).

As stated in the study by Sugasri and Selvam (2018), the use of robotic technology in tourism and accommodation businesses offers various cost advantages to the sector. Robots can work continuously 24/7 and can maintain their functionality with regular maintenance and repair work. This situation shows that human resources provide a higher efficiency compared to a 40-hour work week. For example, a receptionist may get bored of giving the same information to each guest over and over again or forget routine tasks. However, robots can fulfill the given tasks over and over again without complaining and remembering. This can provide significant savings in the human resources budgets of enterprises. In addition, robots improve service quality reduce worker fatigue, reduce costs, and increase productivity in enterprises. Employees in the tourism industry can work with higher efficiency thanks to robots, saving time and money for businesses. As stated by Ivanov and Webster (2017), applying robot technology in businesses has many benefits such as increasing productivity, reducing worker fatigue, and improving service quality.

The point emphasized in this study underlines the importance and benefits of robotic applications in the tourism sector. Robots have the potential to reduce the costs of businesses, increase productivity, and improve service quality. The continuous operability of robots means that human resources can be utilized more efficiently, while fatigue and errors caused by the repetitive nature of routine tasks can be avoided. In addition, thanks to their ability to adapt to seasonality and fluctuations in the tourism sector, the off-season shutdown of robots does not bring additional costs to businesses. In this way, the costs arising from businesses' legal obligations can also be significantly reduced. The study by Ivanov and Webster (2017) also supports important data on this issue and provides enlightening information on how robotics technology can transform the tourism sector.

Considering the disadvantages of the application in question, although AI applications have a high capacity, they are dependent on basic needs such as continuous power supply and internet connection. Meeting these needs not only increases costs but can also cause serious data or business losses in the event of unexpected outages or failures. In addition, the limited human-like experience and learning capabilities of AI applications also necessitate human supervision. These processes and requirements naturally increase costs (Çuhadar et al., 2022). The technical advancements notwithstanding, the human resources requirement in accommodation businesses is constantly on the rise. While robots and cyborgs can do many things that people do because they are programmed, making them faster, less error-free, and more reliable than humans, they cannot replace people because their rules are also made by humans and they are directed by humans just like the robots (Deringöl, 2010:30). Lack of data security is the biggest drawback of AI technologies, so it is also the biggest risk associated with the technology. Throughout the process, guests can be assured that their personal information is accurately recorded, which is an important factor that builds a trusting relationship between the customer and the company. In this context, designing and maintaining such a technology base will bring great financial weight to hospitality businesses (Demir, 2021)

Considering the rising importance and benefits of robotic applications in the field of tourism, a rational fact can be put forward that these technologies amplify operational efficiency and higher cost optimization. However, artificial intelligence applications have their basis in specific needs and limitations concerning human-like experiences. In this perspective, with greater use of robotics technologies in the tourism industry, businesses must ensure that such technologies retain the human touch and creativity.

9.5 Results

This study aims to examine the areas of application, prevalence, advantages, disadvantages, and future potential of smart tourism and robotics technologies in the hospitality sector. Technological innovations such as artificial intelligence and smart technologies are single-handedly revolutionizing the tourism industry and becoming the catalyst for remarkable change. Such technologies are the main point to make tourists happy by making the service better and even the satisfaction of customers is made possible. Smart tourism utilizes technology so that it has an effective methodology to manage and improve tourism activities. Machine intelligence systems are used as an indispensable tool that can be used to improve and enhance the quality of services in the tourism sector. As more technology-driven solutions are introduced, the ability of tourism companies to offer new experiences to customers has increased exponentially, therefore, the intertwined investments in this area provide many benefits for travelers as industry players have improved service delivery in the recent past. Within the scope of the study, it is seen that smart technologies are included in accommodation establishments, which are one of the stakeholders of the tourism sector in Türkiye, but robot technology has not developed. For this reason, some suggestions are offered for its development.

As robotic technologies can improve operational efficiency and simultaneously create an advantage in cost optimization, tourism businesses must strengthen their technology investments and closely follow up the sectoral developments. In addition, it is stated that the model of creating human-robot cooperation and inclusively integrating robots into business processes may show an increase in their efficiency. Training and application programs should be arranged for the staff and employees regarding robotic technologies, and effective use of the robots thus should be supported. A strategy to enhance the guest experience could be developing customer-oriented services and robots that interact directly with guests. Along with increasing the trend of robotic applications, it is pivotal to strengthen the security and data privacy policies and ensure protection and security regarding sensitive information. Finally, the development and utilization of robotic applications with the principles of sustainability and environmental awareness may contribute to the tourism sector. Based on the suggestions here, the tourism industry could enhance operational efficiency by increasing the guest experience, thus benefiting fully from the advantages brought by robotic technologies. When the findings obtained from the study are evaluated, it is concluded that accommodation establishments in Türkiye actively use smart tourism, especially in robotic applications.

Detailed studies can be conducted in this respect on customer satisfaction and expectations adopted in the tourism sector concerning the adoption of robotic technologies. Alternatively, ethical issues or human-machine interaction could also prove to be a very important subject of observation. Studies can be conducted on how robots influence service quality, changes in customer experiences, and the establishment of ethical standards. Besides, paying attention to education and innovation in the tourism industry may be an important step toward adapting this workforce to robotic technologies and increasing innovation potential in this sector. Social and environmental impact research of robotic applications can make a valuable contribution to the industry by taking up sustainability and ethical issues in the tourism sector. These studies will shed light on the future of the industry by showing the innovation opportunities and competitive potential of companies, considering the competitive environment and innovation. This different subject research will help to develop strategies for the sector by correctly analyzing the impacts of robotic applications within the tourism sector more holistically.

References

Akın, A., Şimşek, M. Y., & Akın, A. (2012). Turizm sektörünün ekonomideki yeri ve önemi. *Akademik Araştırmalar ve Çalışmalar Dergisi (AKAD), 4*(7), 63–81.

Atay, L., Yalçınkaya, P., & Bahar, F. (2019). İstanbul'daki akıllı otel uygulamalarının değerlendirilmesi. *Manas Sosyal Araştırmalar Dergisi, 8*(1), 667–678.

Aydınbaş, G. (2023). Akıllı Turizm (Turizm 4. 0) Teknolojileri Üzerine İktisadi Bir Yaklaşım: Türkiye Örneği. *Journal of Tourism Intelligence and Smartness, 6*(1), 26–44.

Ayyıldız Yazıcı, A., & Ayyıldız, T. (2020). Pazarlama Fırsatı Olarak Akıllı Turizm: Kuşadası Örneği, BMIJ, 8(1), 599–623. https://doi.org/10.15295/bmij.v8i1.1411

Çımat, A., & Bahar, O. (2003). Turizm Sektörünün Türkiye Ekonomisi İçindeki Yeri Ve Önemi Üzerine Bir Değerlendirme, Akdeniz İ.İ.B.F. *Dergisi. Sayı*, 6, ss.2–12.

Çuhadar, M., Demiray, G., Öztürk, M., & Alabacak, C. H. (2022). Konaklama İşletmelerinde Yapay Zekâ ve Robotik Teknolojilri: Bibliyometrik Bir Analiz (Artificial Intelligence and Robotic Technologies in Lodging Properties: A Bibliometric Analysis). *Journal of Tourism & Gastronomy Studies, 10*(2), 1550–1580.

De Kervenoael, R., Hasan, R., Schwob, A., & Goh, E. (2020). Leveraging human–robot interaction in hospitality services: Incorporating the role of perceived value, empathy, and social presence. Tourism Management, 78, 104042.

Demir, Ç. (2021). Konaklama İşletmelerinin İş Süreçlerinde Yapay Zekâ Teknolojileri ve Akıllı Otel Uygulamaları: Avantajlar ve Dezavantajlar (Artificial Intelligence Technologies and Smart Hotel Practiceses at Hospitality Organizations Business Processes: Advantages and Disadvantages). *Journal of Tourism & Gastronomy Studies, 9*(1), 203–219.

Deringöl, H. (2010). *Tarihsel Gelişimi İçinde İnsan Kaynakları Yönetimi Anlayışı, Amaçları ve Fonksiyonları Üzerine Çukurova Bölgesinde Faaliyet Gösteren İşletmelerde Bir Araştırma, Yayımlanmamış Yüksek Lisans Tezi, Çukurova Üniversitesi Sosyal Bilimler Enstitüsü.* Yayımlanmış Yüksek Lisans Tezi

Ercan, F. (2020). Turizm pazarlamasında yapay zekâ teknolojilerinin kullanımı ve uygulama örnekleri. *Ankara Hacı Bayram Veli Üniversitesi Turizm Fakültesi Dergisi*, 23(2), 394–410.

Gretzel, U., Sigala, M., Xiang, Z., & Koo, C. (2015). Smart tourism: Foundations and developments. *Elekcron Markets, 25*, 179–188.

Gürdin, B. (2020). Robonomi ve Müşteri Memnuniyeti: Hizmet Robotlarına İlişkin LiteratürTaraması. *Ekonomi Maliye İşletme Dergisi, 3*(1), 85–100.

Hildebrandt, M. (2020). Smart technologies. *Internet Policy Review, 9*(4), 1–16.

İbiş, S. (2019). Turizm endüstrisinde robotlaşma. *Türk Turizm Araştirmalari Dergisi*, 3(3), 403–420.

Ivanov, S., & Webster C., (2017). Adoptıon Of Robots, Artıfıcıal Intellıgence And Servıce Automatıon By Travel, Tourısm And Hospıtalıty Companıes A CostBenefıt Analysıs, International Scientific Conference "Contemporary tourism – traditions and innovations", 19–21 October 2017, Sofia University.

Karagöz, B., & Sezgin, M. (2021). Turizmde Robotlaşma Teknolojisinin Kullanımı. *Uluslararası Anadolu Sosyal Bilimler Dergisi, 5*(3), 946–959.

Kıvılcım, B. (2023). Geleceğin Konaklama Yerleri: Dijitalleşen Turizmde Yeni Konaklama Modelleri.

Okatan, D., & Yıldırım, Y. (2021). Endüstri 4.0 Teknolojilerinin Turizm Sektörüne Yansımaları: Literatür İncelemesi. *Journal of Tourism Intelligence and Smartness, 4*(2), 168–185.

Özgürel, G. (2021). Turizmde robotlaşma: Yiyecek-içecek sektöründe robot şefler ve robot garsonlar. *OPUS International Journal of Society Researches, 18*(Yönetim ve Organizasyon Özel Sayısı), 1849–1882.

Pieska, S., Luimula, M., Jauhiainen, J., & Spiz, V. (2013). Social service robots in wellness and restaurant applications. *Journal of Communication and Computer, 10*(1), 116–123.

Samala, N., Katkam, B. S., Bellamkonda, R. S., & Rodriguez, R. V. (2020). Impact of AI and robotics in the tourism sector: A critical insight. *Journal of Tourism Futures,* 1–15.

Sayar, B. (2021). *Yapay Zeka ve Robot Teknolojisinin Gazetecilik Pratikleri* Üzerindeki *Etkisi.Doktora Tezi.* İstanbul: Marmara Üniversitesi.

Sugasri, S., & Panneer Selvam, R. (2018). Recent technological trends in tourism and hospitality industry. *International Journal of Management, Technology and Engineering,* 8, (12), 883–889.

Thomsen, C. (2020). *The impact of hotel service robot appearance and service attributes on customer experience.* University of South Carolina.

Tung, V. W. S., & Law, R. (2017). The potential for tourism and hospitality experience research in human-robot interactions. *International Journal of Contemporary Hospitality Management,* 29(10), 2498–2513.

Xiang, Z., & Fesenmaier, D. R. (Ed.). (2017). Big data analytics, tourism design, and smart tourism. *Analytics in smart tourism design içinde* (s. 299–307). Cham: Springer.

Yıldız, E., & Davutoğlu, N. A. (2018)., December. Konaklama İşletmelerinde Personel ve İnsan Kaynakları Yönetiminden, Sanayi 4.0'lı Yönetime.... In SETSCI-Conference Proceedings (Vol. 3, pp. 1563–1569). *SETSCI-Conference Proceedings.* Istanbul, Türkiye.

Yılmazer, A., & Çakmak, D. (2023). Evaluation of smart tourism Tools and applications in hospitality businesses: A study in sakarya province, *Journal of Turkish Tourism Research,* 7(1), 161–178.

Zlatanov, S., & Popesku, J. (2019). Current applications of artificial ıntelligence in tourism and hospitality. *International Scientific conference on information technology and data related research* (s. 84–90). Singidunum University. Belgrade, Serbia.

Index

Note: **Bold** page numbers refer to tables and *italic* page numbers refer to figures.

For Product Safety Concerns and Information please contact our EU representative GPSR@taylorandfrancis.com Taylor & Francis Verlag GmbH, Kaufingerstraße 24, 80331 München, Germany